A Ye[...]

Pr[...]

'Funny, poignant and beautifully written' Lisa Jewell

'Genuinely funny and genuinely moving' Jane Fallon,
author of *Getting Rid of Matthew*

'I howled with laughter, tears of recognition at every bloody page.
My only problem with this book was choosing who to pass it
on to first' Jenny Colgan, author of *Amanda's Wedding*

'*Cold Comfort Farm* with booster seats. Funny, honest and moving'
Stephanie Calman, author of *Confessions of a Bad Mother*

ABOUT THE AUTHOR

Judith O'Reilly is a writer and journalist. Her first book, *Wife in the North*, was based on her blog of the same name and was a best-seller. Her second book, a novel, is living in a drawer. Her third book is this one. She is married with three children, and for one year she tried to be good.

A Year of Doing Good

One Woman, One New Year's Resolution,
365 Good Deeds

JUDITH O'REILLY

PENGUIN BOOKS

PENGUIN BOOKS

Published by the Penguin Group
Penguin Books Ltd, 80 Strand, London WC2R ORL, England
Penguin Group (USA) Inc., 375 Hudson Street, New York, New York 10014, USA
Penguin Group (Canada), 90 Eglinton Avenue East, Suite 700, Toronto, Ontario, Canada M4P 2Y3
(a division of Pearson Penguin Canada Inc.)
Penguin Ireland, 25 St Stephen's Green, Dublin 2, Ireland (a division of Penguin Books Ltd)
Penguin Group (Australia), 707 Collins Street, Melbourne, Victoria 3008, Australia
(a division of Pearson Australia Group Pty Ltd)
Penguin Books India Pvt Ltd, 11 Community Centre, Panchsheel Park, New Delhi – 110 017, India
Penguin Group (NZ), 67 Apollo Drive, Rosedale, Auckland 0632, New Zealand
(a division of Pearson New Zealand Ltd)
Penguin Books (South Africa) (Pty) Ltd, Block D, Rosebank Office Park,
181 Jan Smuts Avenue, Parktown North, Gauteng 2193, South Africa

Penguin Books Ltd, Registered Offices: 80 Strand, London WC2R ORL, England

www.penguin.com

First published 2013
001

Grateful acknowledgement is made to the Estate of Edgar A. Guest for
permission to reprint lines from his poem 'Miss Me But Let Me Go'

Set in 11/13 pt Bembo Book MT Std
Typeset by Jouve (UK), Milton Keynes
Printed in Great Britain by Clays Ltd, St Ives plc

A CIP catalogue record for this book is available from the British Library

ISBN: 978-0-670-92113-3

www.greenpenguin.co.uk

ALWAYS LEARNING   **PEARSON**

For my parents

Just begin . . .

Mother Teresa

Preface

Some years frame who you are for ever more. The year of expectation when I started my first job as a wide-eyed trainee journalist in Newcastle. The year of ambition when me and my shoulder pads moved to London. The year of desolation when I lost a child. The year of rapture when I gave birth to another son. The year of 'What the . . .?' when I moved out of the big city and up to the wilds of Northumberland. Then there was my year of doing good. When I can't remember my name or that shoes should match, I know I'll still remember these years, and that for a year at least, I tried to be good.

I didn't realize when I made the resolution that New Year what I was taking on. I'd made resolutions before, even if I can't exactly remember what they were, but the idea of doing one good deed a day morphed into something else again. I am no kind of moral philosopher – ethics make my head go squeak – but this year made me question what a good life is, how we give our lives meaning, and what it is to love. It also taught me that people don't always want the good you want to do, and that doing good – believe you me – is harder than it looks.

In a way, my year of doing good was an admission of my own failings. My parents are saints, and it is tough being the child of saints. People feel sorry for the children of murderers, because they think it must be hard worrying whether you've inherited a genetic predisposition to kill as well as those long-lobed ears; it is worse when you're brought up by those who are good. Really good. There is proof: the fact they looked after my gran, who lived with us till she was ninety-three; the fact my mum volunteered as a cleaner in a hospice on Saturdays, then as a classroom assistant in an inner-city school, then acted as chairman of governors at that school for years; the fact my dad visited the sick in hospital, drove busloads of the elderly to church, and that he and my mother put out poor boxes round the parish and over the years collected £20,000 for the hospice. My parents are modest, patient, and willing to do anything for anyone. Good people with good intentions living good lives. And what had I done all of my adult life? Earned a living. Married a man. Reared children. That was it, pretty much.

There was certainly no chance my children thought they were being brought up by a saint. Too much effing and blinding when they interrupted me when I was working. Too many empty wine bottles by the back door. Too much me and mine, and not enough time or space or energy for anyone else. Still, you are raised with certain ideals when you are brought up a Catholic:

- Only have sex when you're married.
- Have sex when you're married and have many, many children because of it.
- Treat with all the reverence it so richly deserves the Church's position on the equality of women and homosexuality.

My responses to these ideals are (in order of appearance):

- I don't think so.
- Are you kidding me?
- I do indeed treat it with the respect it deserves – that is to say, none.

But there are other ideals I do believe in: love, compassion for one's fellow man, charity and good deeds. Yet unless you count that sponsored swim for the hungry of Africa which I did when I was eleven, I had never done much about those things.

Good people left me breathless and wondering. How had they got that way? How good were they, anyway? How would it feel to be good? Then I hit middle age and suddenly I wanted to be a better person and to know that I was living a good life. Not that I was a bad person; don't get me wrong, I was all right. I did the odd thing: I helped out friends when it wasn't too inconvenient, I didn't litter and I never drowned a cat. But was I capable of more? Not Nobel Peace Prize more. Not OBE-for-services-to-one's-country more. But more than this? Surely I could do more. I could do something. Plus there were my children. My three beautiful children, whom I have cherished and fed and clothed, and in whom I have attempted to instill values and a sense of morality. I owed it to them to prove that kindness, respect and patience are virtues to be acquired. That they were not just the monopoly of Granny. If I were a better person, I could teach them, not just right from wrong, but compassion and generosity, and perhaps my sons and my daughter would grow to be better people than me – do far, far better things.

Across the world, civil wars rage, there is random death, brutal torture and appalling starvation, but not here. Here, there is plenty and there is opportunity, even with economic hard times. Perhaps especially with hard times comes the recognition that we have need of each other. Most of us are lucky, we have so much. Our children are lucky, they have so much too. My children have a drum set, computer games and a big-screen TV to play them on, they have bicycles and scooters, and a garden to run round in. They download songs and apps and complain when I drag them to the beach. My daughter has dancing lessons and rugby boots, my sons play football and watch their favourite team on Sky TV. They have everything and they want more. I have everything and want more. So much attention these days is focused on how well you parent – that God-awful question 'Are you a good mother?' But how can you answer that when you aren't even clear whether you are a good person or living a good life?

So, I decided: I would do one good deed a day for a year. It would be a start, and it couldn't be that hard – could it? As soon as I said it out loud, I worried about sticking to it, worried about the message it would send to the children if I couldn't keep it up.

'*Have a go and if you can't be bothered, give up, pet.*' And at the same time as worrying about giving up, I worried about not giving up, about how inconvenient it was all going to be if I did indeed stick to my resolution. Damned if you do, damned if you don't, when ironically enough, I don't even believe in damnation. Who goes to Hell? I do not believe any of us do. I do not look to an afterlife, or an eternity. I believe in the here and now, and if you believe in the here and now, logic dictates you want the here and now to be a good one, not just for yourself, but for others. I wanted to change myself and I wanted to change the world – one deed at a time.

Of course there were doubts. To live is to doubt. I doubted whether you could ever really become a better person, let alone mend society; perhaps you would just be the same ol' same ol' who did a few good things on the way. If I do not believe we are judged by an Almighty, if I do not believe our good deeds and bad are weighed on golden scales, then I am my own judge, and I am horribly tolerant. Could I up the stakes from doing no harm to doing some good, to living a good life? I didn't know. All I knew was that I was willing to find out.

Saturday, 1 January

Today was a three-hat day: a tangerine knitted beret, a black felt hat from Germany and a sheepskin Cossack number with earflaps. I'm short, so the inflated-head look wasn't doing me any favours, but the weather on the North Northumberland coast was bitter while inside the hats where I lived was cosy and warm. Frankly, the problem wasn't so much with how the hats looked, but that the Cossack one rendered me deaf, which was why I was bringing up the rear and walking alone. It also meant I had time to think. Every New Year I reflect on what is good and what is bad about the year that's passed, mark it out of ten, and make my resolutions for the year ahead. Reflection, consolidation, improvement – I have considered myself a work in progress my entire life.

What was good:

- My mother, who is in her eighties, had an operation on her spine and it helped relieve her pain. Hoorah.
- My three children are glorious.
- I have been writing a novel.

What was bad:

- My mother's health is still frail.
- My glorious children drive me demented.
- I am *still* writing a bloody novel, and everyone who reads it says it is pants.

Old year's score: nine out of ten (on the grounds that I am nothing if not an optimist).

I was so deaf and so busy mulling over my New Year's resolution that I only just heard the yelling. We were walking in a party of thirty out to the beach and the kids had abandoned the path almost as soon as we started out, and somehow, in a headlong dash through the grass, my friend's youngest son had managed to wedge the top half of his body one side of the fence that cut across the fields, his thigh between two wires in the second section, and his calf up to his foot in another section again. Every time Al put pressure on the cat's cradle to loosen it, the boy screamed blue murder. My husband Al is extremely good in crises. By contrast, I am useless in pretty much any emergency and prefer to panic immediately. I had already begun to wonder whether my teeth were sharp enough to gnaw off the poor lad's leg when, with a grunt of satisfaction, Al loosened the wires enough to extract him. The boy leaned against me, still shaky, and I made 'there, there' noises, bending over him to rub his thigh and knee to get the circulation going. He sniffed and, hunkering down, I dug around in my pocket for a small bar of milk chocolate; he took it gratefully, peeling and eating it tiny piece by tiny piece. It was the fact he ate my chocolate that decided me. In giving him my chocolate, I had my first good deed of the year.

Then, of course, I had to tell people. To keep a secret, you tell no one, but to keep a resolution, you tell everyone. I waited till we were back at Diane's farmhouse.

I cleared my throat, my back to the Aga – my bones still cold from the walk – and the others looked up at me from their empty soup bowls. The resolution I was about to make is not one I make every year, or indeed have ever made before, or am likely ever to make again. 'I'm going to do a good deed a day for the rest of the year.'

Across the room from me, my husband hid his face in his hands and groaned.

'Highly commendable,' said Diane. She is a mathematics teacher – sometimes you can tell. 'Tough ask, though.' There was a murmuring of agreement.

'What makes you feel you want to do that?' Diane's doctor

6

friend said in the tone she uses when she says to her patients, 'Tell me about these voices.'

Why? Because of how I was brought up, because I should, because I do nothing for anyone but me and mine. Doctors do good all the time. They heal – at the very least they listen. I am nothing. I am a journalist and sometime writer. I do not do anything for anyone. I am someone who bought antique-style metal letters at Christmas to spell out the words K.I.N.D.N.E.S.S, R.E.S.P.E.C.T and P.A.T.I.E.N.C.E, and when they fell off the wall – clattering and bouncing one after the other onto the ceramic hob – didn't stick them back up because I couldn't be A.R.S.E.D.

'Was rescuing that boy your good deed today then?' asked my husband. 'Because technically I rescued him.' I glared at him as he picked up a half-empty bottle of Sauvignon and gestured to Diane as to whether she wanted her glass topped up, and as he poured he grinned at me.

'My other New Year's resolution is to stay married,' I said. 'If at all possible.'

Good deed no. 1.

Sunday, 2 January

For reasons which defeat me, people think I am hospitable, when in truth I am the least sociable person I know. I blame being an only child. Even having a husband and three children crowds me sometimes. As for Christmas and New Year, we have had family staying throughout, and – thanks to bad planning on my part – we also have to factor two of the children's birthdays into the festive season. The next person to tell me I am the 'hostess with the mostest' or how much I love having people around me is liable to get a saucepan on their head. Exactly what response can you make to a guest who says, 'You just love all this entertaining, don't you?' You cannot say, 'You're so right. Is that the time?' and point to the door.

He was half right, though: I do quite like entertaining – if by 'entertaining' you mean chatting over a glass of wine about love, life and the universe with my favourite people. 'Entertaining' in middle age, however, is more likely to mean other people being entertained, courtesy of me shopping, cooking, serving and then clearing up after us all. Increasingly my fondness for those I entertain is on a sliding scale of how much washing-up they are prepared to do after we eat, because if I get varicose veins, I know exactly where I'll get them: at the kitchen sink. Not forgetting that when my parents are staying with us, as I am drying the last pan – round about ten o'clock at night – my dad usually steers my blind mother into the kitchen, saying, 'Your mother's feeling neglected. Make her a cup of tea and have a chat while I watch the football.'

Having said that, I'd rather make her a cup of tea than watch my dad do it. My dad has a permanent shake in his hands because of a car crash when he was young. His shake means that when you make him a cup of tea, you have to pour it short by a good inch otherwise he will shake it out of the cup. When he makes tea for my mum, he passes it to her and his hands are already shaking, and she is patting the air, reaching for it – bear in mind she can't see because she is blind – and I have to curl up on the sofa with a floral cushion in my mouth to stop me screaming. And God forbid you make any sort of comment about health and safety, because then the pair of them get all sniffy and start adding up just how many cups of tea they have made – and passed to each other – in their forty-odd years of marriage.

A simple thing like mealtimes during these times of celebration turns into one long sum: today's lunch equalled the five of us plus two (my elderly parents) plus six cousins plus one. Both of my husband's parents are dead, he has one brother and a niece who live in West Wales (which is almost as far away from us as you can get in the UK), one uncle, one aunty and a small smattering of cousins he never hears from. I have hundreds of cousins – two of whom have just moved across the world to be close to us, and five of whom are building a holiday cottage outside my back door. I blame Irish-Catholic DNA.

The 'plus one' round today's table was my beloved friend Daniel, who lost his wife four months ago. He was brave agreeing to come, and he arrived so sad – I could see it and it is not who he is at all, and I wanted to cry for him. He tried so hard over lunch, talking to everyone and making a fuss of my mum and dad, whom he has known for years, but he is lost. Getting through the first holiday season on your own takes some doing. When my first son was stillborn at term eleven years ago, that first Christmas we didn't see anyone or go anywhere. Aside from a walk through a bleak and wintry St James's Park, we stayed home in London curled up in a ball all wrapped around each other. We well know how commonplace death is, that it is part of who we are, and yet, grieving for a son, a wife, a father, it strikes you as outrageous, undeserved, a misfortune. You are the first and only person to feel this way, to feel so deep, to suffer. In that place in you where reason sits on a wooden chair in a bare room, the bulb swinging, you know that death has come before and death will come again, but reason is small and reason is lonely when death drops by.

Good deed no. 2: lunch with my friend who lost his wife. (Not enough. Nowhere near enough.)

Monday, 3 January

Everybody has left. Thank God. Really thank God. Much as I love them all – and I do love them all – thank you, God, that after the last birthday tomorrow, the festivities are done.

We celebrated our freedom with a yomp along the beach. The afternoon sky was immense and grey above us, white clouds heavy and crowding together for warmth. Ahead, black and white oystercatchers scurried across the sands, their tiny legs criss-crossing, urgent and hungry. Yelling at each other to wait, the children scrambled through the grassy dunes, while Al and I walked together, hand in hand. We have been together more than twenty years and used to hold hands all the time before the children. Why shouldn't grown-ups hold hands, one with the other – how else do you avoid getting lost? Mind you, my sense of direction is shocking. Nowadays we hardly ever hold hands. My hands are full of children or shopping; his hands full of phones or papers. Part of me is surprised we even remember how.

'Remind me what your New Year's resolutions were last year,' he said.

I dug around in the silt of my memory looking for treasure, finding only salty mud and corrugated worms. 'To get fit?' I offered.

He looked me up and down dubiously, and inside my puffa coat I sucked in my stomach so hard it slapped against my spine. My husband is one of those lean runners who have the same rangy body in their forties as they did in their twenties. I have someone else's entirely. A few years ago, heavies took mine away in the middle of the night, wrapped it in chains and threw it out of a low-flying plane into the sea; I've had to make do ever since.

'And did you get fit?' The bastard knew the answer.

'I went running.'

'Once. You went running once.'

Running is hard. All that effort. All those hills. Frankly, if I'm not working, I am with the kids and if I'm not with the kids, I'm working. But I can slot a good deed into my day without breaking a sweat. How hard can it be?

'Are you serious about this resolution?' My husband has been known to claim I complicate our lives. He can talk. As a journalist, he lives in a state of semi-permanent deadline: either he is working all hours at his desk at home or he is working all hours in London pulling together supplements for a national newspaper. He is driven – one of life's perfectionists; I, on the other hand, am one of life's amateurs. 'Does doing stuff for me and the kids count as a good deed, for instance?' He sounded momentarily hopeful.

I stopped walking to watch the dunes. We have a boy of nearly ten, a boy just turned eight and a five-year-old daughter with a smile like the first day of spring. Usually, you glimpse one or other child barrelling along the tops. I held my breath till first one and then the next and then the smallest appeared, running and leaping the gaps where the dunes fall away, their shouts of delight and fury carrying across the sands, over our heads and out across the grey-blue rolling sea. Reassured, I considered my husband's questions. I was serious. Did doing things for him and the kids count? Surely not. I am going to draw up some rules of engagement – like in war.

Good deed no. 3: rang Sophie, my best friend from school, who is sick with Lyme disease, to cheer her up.

Tuesday, 4 January

The lock has stopped working on the back door and a handy sort of mate came over to try and fix it. I didn't bother mentioning we are so neurotic that last night we decided Al should sleep on the sofa in the kitchen in case a paedophile tried to gain entry and abduct a child. At least that's how mad I thought we were. Actually, Al's even madder than that, because he confessed he slept with an axe within reach.

While my mate was fixing the lock he mentioned his sister is having her first baby, so out came two enormous boxes of baby toys I had cleared from the kids' rooms. A good-deed result. The only problem was that tonight when we got back from a day out, the boxes were still there on the kitchen table. This particular good deed may be on a slow burn. Whether he wants them or not, my mate is now morally obliged to take them. In any event, the question arises how much self-interest is permitted in a good deed? Frankly, I would fall at anyone's feet if they took away clart, debris or general baby clutter from this house. Question: is a good deed still a good deed if it benefits the giver as much as the receiver? (These good deeds are an ethical quagmire.)

Good deed no. 4.

The cottage where we live is a former farm labourer's cottage – one of a string, the others used as holiday homes. Built as one-storey, then there were two, the whinstone and sandstone walls are soft-buttered with pale mortar and steep-roofed in grey slate. Behind the cottages is nothing much – a massive breeze-block and iron barn where a farmer stores piles of golden wheat and plastic sacks of fertilizer like immense Chinese pork dumplings. But in front, quilted pastureland of green and golden silks falls away to the distant grey-blue sea, and despite the massive beech and sycamores that stand guardian alongside, there is openness, space and a sense of possibilities. The countryside isn't quiet, though – not this countryside anyway. Soft, brown garden birds sing and chirrup and whistle, and wings flap heavily as wood pigeons bustle through the trees avoiding the rooks' nests caught like knots of hair in their skinny wintry branches. And then there is the wind, sometimes so slight you scarcely notice it, sometimes pushy and loud and straight from the North Sea.

The problem with living in Northumberland and working from home, I am discovering, is that it's all big skies and sheep, and you don't see many people to do good deeds for. I was mulling over the fact I might have to go into the village and mug a pensioner so I could make him a cup of sweet tea when my friend Lily rang asking me to do her a favour and pick her son up from school because her four-year-old daughter had fallen over in the playground and she had to take her to Accident and Emergency. She seemed taken aback when I cheered.

The little girl was fine, though sporting an egg on her temple, and when Lily arrived she gave me a bouquet of roses with velvet petals the colour of a Caribbean sunset. The flowers were gorgeous but disconcerting. Question to self: can a good deed still be considered a good deed if you are rewarded so thoroughly for the same? The reward was not solicited, but the roses are very lovely and it is not even as if taking care of the boy was any great trouble.

I didn't realize I would have to think so hard about this good deed business.

Good deed no. 5.

Thursday, 6 January

We moved to Northumberland because my husband loved it. I came round to it, or it came round to me – who knows? When I moved from the East End of London, I left behind old friends who knew and forgave me for the fact I had moved away from them, but there was no one who loved me as deeply or as well in Northumberland. Who has friends when they move some place new? People who buy them off Amazon, that's who. I did that for a while – though the postman complained – but gradually, along the way, I acquired friends-in-the-North. It took me a while, though, to catch Lily.

Lily owns 149 pairs of shoes (I know because I made her count them) and 70 bags, many from Hermès, Mulberry, Prada, Gucci, Louis Vuitton and Fendi. She moved up to a smallholding in the wilds from a fancy gaff in Newcastle a couple of years after me, and she seemed just my type (although my handbag comes from M&S and I have no shoes to speak of). The problem was she was always busy, busy, busy, whirligigging around as if the pieces of the pale blue sky would fall down and flatten her if she stopped moving. It took me years of nagging to get her to stop long enough to realize she was my friend and there was no getting out of it, however hard she tried and however fast she ran in her paint-splattered trackies and her diamanté flip-flops.

Lily started life as a paediatric nurse and went on to a big job in IT with a six-figure salary (hence the bags and the shoes) and a favourite plane seat. Now she runs round in ever-decreasing circles juggling snippets of consultancy with managing the smallholding, a five-star holiday cottage business and her kids (which is an even bigger job but for a lot less money and absolutely no benefits). We have in common the knowledge that it is a thin line between a been-there-done-that career and a has-been-never-do-again life. It helps that once we both had proper careers – till she got made redundant and I got a bad case of family-first, career-second, which can frankly kill you stone-dead with regret if you let it. It helps too that her children and mine are the same age. She is late for everything – usually because she has tried to fit one more thing between the-very-last-thing-on-my-list and it-was-round-the-corner-so-it-seemed-a-crime-not-to.

The first time I invited her to my house for coffee with a few girls, she arrived early and promptly washed up my breakfast things and then ran upstairs to clean the bathroom. She was obviously brought up the same as me: you don't come for tea and leave a sink of dirty pots behind you. The only time up here I haven't done the same is when I was asked round for coffee by a very lovely, very posh mummy with lots of other posh mummies, and I had to physically sit on my hands to stop myself from washing up because there was no way on God's earth the idea of clearing the table was in anyone's mind other than mine.

Good deed no. 6: checked on a cousin recently bereaved.

Friday, 7 January

Distracted by a migraine that felt as if black rats were hanging from my eyeballs by their claws. It chewed up my entire morning, which I had to spend in bed with only my eyeball rats and drugs for company – beta blockers, paracetamol and codeine. It was so bad Al had to get the kids off to school while I wallowed upstairs groaning. Of course I now have almost a week of good-deedery behind me, so as a distraction, and to protect myself against charges of moral laxity, I drew up my Rules of Engagement:

- Some good deeds may require time, emotional investment and a great deal of energy, but modest – indeed

itsy-bitsy – good deeds are permissible. Life is in the detail. I am officially allowed to think small.

- Good deeds for extended family (including my aged parents) and my network of friends are as acceptable as good deeds for strangers, bearing in mind it is family and friends who dominate my life.
- Good deeds for the nuclear family of husband and children are not acceptable. I cannot count feeding my kids, putting them to bed or doing their washing as a good deed – even though many is the time such maternal duties are a considerable inconvenience.
- It is impossible to predict the consequences of a good deed. More important than the success or failure of a good deed is the intention behind it. The intention must be to provide benefit to someone other than myself or a general benefit to society.
- There is a chance that the good deeds will occasionally provide benefit to self (for example, thanks or roses or less clutter in one's own house). This is acceptable providing the main motivation behind the good deed is not to require said benefit.

Good deed no. 7: gave my expat cousins a CD of their favourite movie soundtrack, picked up while out shopping.

Saturday, 8 January

Good deed no. 8: picked up someone's change when it fell to the floor in the newsagent and returned it.

Sunday, 9 January

Had my expat cousins over for dinner. They grew up in Yorkshire but emigrated to Africa in 1975 when she was an air hostess and he was a policeman, to escape 'the rain, a Labour government and a terrible cricket team'. After thirty-five years in Africa, they decided that however brightly the sun shone over the rainbow nation, they didn't want to see out their days there, and a few months ago returned to Blighty. The year they left Britain, inflation was running at 24 per cent; *The Sweeney* premiered on ITV; sitcom stars Windsor Davies and Don Estelle were at number one with 'Whispering Grass'; Harold Wilson was Prime Minister; and the Conservatives elected Margaret Thatcher as their first woman party leader. Give or take another punishing economic crisis, they have come back to a different country: inflation isn't a problem, although everything else in the economy is; violent, no-holds-barred 1970s detectives are ridiculed, not glamorized; Don Estelle is dead – as is Harold Wilson; and they just made a biopic about the fact Lady Thatcher, who served as PM for eleven years, has dementia. I believe they are in shock. Luckily he still has the moustache he went out with.

She is sixty-three and he is sixty-eight, their parents are long dead, there are no brothers or sisters and they don't have children. What is 'home' after all? Not a flag, nor a cricket team, nor even your own history – home is who you love, so they have come home to us as their nearest and dearest. Both of them are wrapped in so many layers they are like birthday presents waiting to be opened come the day, and they have not been warm since they arrived. I cooked roast beef and trimmings – including very flat Yorkshire puddings – to remind them how bad British food can be.

Good deed no. 9.

Monday, 10 January

Finally went to the doctor about my migraines after my post-new-year stonker. I've decided to see a consultant, and needed a GP referral. The doctor said he would dig me out a name and told me my blood tests were all fine, which was a relief. At least I know

now that migraines aren't from a grapefruit-sized tumour, which is what I was beginning to think, and which would have been a shame because I have always liked grapefruits.

After the doctor, as my good deed, we went to see the little old lady who used to live in this house and who moved down to the village after her husband died. She lives in a neat little yellow-brick bungalow on a well-tended little estate with handkerchief lawns and palings around the very tidy gardens and, to my utter horror, it turned out that we had completely forgotten her New Year's Day drinks. Every year she has open house with bottles aligned on the cabinet, and her family sit round in her living room and people wash in and out of the house and drink whisky at ten o'clock in the morning. This year, I had so many people washing in and out of my own house, her invitation completely went out of my head. While we were there, her neighbour came in, as she does every morning and every afternoon. The neighbour is about to go to Australia, where she heads every year, and was full of stories about pythons trying to eat her brother's cockatoo and my personal favourite: a whirligig dustball blowing into the house which turned out to be a spider mother (festooned with spider babies) who got stomped on and all the spider babies fled to the four corners of the room. It quite put me off my golden crunch biscuit.

Al is heading for London tomorrow and is not due back till very late on Thursday night. This removes tomorrow's fallback position of a blow-job which he kindly offered to let me give him (at no extra cost) in the event of running out of other good deeds to do. I have told him I can always cheer up the postman.

Good deed no. 10.

Tuesday, 11 January

Good deed no. 11: let the electricians into a neighbouring holiday cottage.

About noon there was a barking and a tremendous commotion, and when I went outside, the access road outside the cottage and my garden were a heaving muddy mass of panting, stiff-tailed hounds searching out a scent. Blow my horn, the hunt was upon us. From atop his horse, the whipper-in was shooing the hounds back out, and as I went to shut the farm gate the hunters in their black jackets all waved cheerily and thanked me with exquisite courtesy as they trotted on and the doggy tail-end Charlies leaped and scrambled over the ivy-clad stone wall, back to the pack.

I had no sooner gone back inside to my desk than there was more hallooing and clipping-clopping, and when I went back out into the winter sun, Ally and the Lovely Claire were up on their enormous shiny horses waiting for me by the shut-up gate. Ally and I met through the school, while Claire is the partner of the farmer who owns the land around our cottage and the barn full of wheat and Chinese dumplings behind it. They are both deeply glamorous and looked like something from a 'County Belle' photo-shoot captioned, 'How tight to wear your jodhpurs this season' – unlike me, who wasn't to know the county set would invade my garden and was caught out in a murky sloppy joe with a serious case of bed-head. We held an impromptu coffee morning, but instead of coffee I served up plastic beakers of Pinot Grigio, and as soon as she'd drained dry her plastic beaker Ally announced that she was giving up alcohol for the month of April and would I like to join her.

Giving up alcohol strikes me as a terrible idea, but in the spirit of good-deedery, I said: a. for the record, I had no idea why she thought I might be suitable for such an experiment; and b. if the friend she is doing it with dropped out on her, I would take her place.

I absolutely didn't mean it. Surely doing good deeds means I get to drink twice as much as normal?

As a thank you for the refreshments, once she had emptied her

Mr Incredible beaker, Claire suggested I get up on her horse and she would lead me up and down the access road. The Lovely Claire is the only person I know who trills over large and small pleasures – sometimes I imagine her perched on a branch of a tree clad in jewel colours and an ostrich-feathered headdress and tail, trilling out her joy that dawn has come again. She has one of those naturally sunny dispositions – plus, she is beautiful, statuesque and blonde. Perhaps it is easier to have a sunny disposition if you are downright gorgeous? I am five feet two inches – if I was only that bit taller, I might be less cranky myself. Although I am immensely fond of her, I normally refuse to stand anywhere near her, on the grounds she makes me look bad.

At well over six feet tall, she needs a horse of seventeen and a half hands (which doesn't mean much unless you know about horses, but the term 'monster' would genuinely cover it). It is her life's ambition to make me love horses. It is my life's ambition not to. Once I had mounted the damn thing – that is to say, stood on a garden bench, put my left foot in the stirrup, stood up in it and then thrown my right leg further than I thought possible – it struck me that I was far closer to the sky than I wanted to be. Regarding me thoughtfully as I sat there trembling, Ally advised a twelve- to thirteen-hand pony would be fine for me and that I might feel safer on something smaller. I am guessing she put it on the record in case I went online once they left, googled 'monster' and bought one on eBay. In any event, aside from sitting on an engaged missile heading for a Taliban stronghold, it is difficult to see how I would have felt less safe. On the grounds she knows everyone in Northumberland, I asked Claire as she led me up and down the access road whether she could persuade someone in the local radio station to take the little old lady's seventeen-year-old grandson for work experience. She is going to ask a presenter mate of hers and get back to me.

By the time we finished, and Claire had managed to get me off the horse again, which involves letting go of everything and trusting the ground will eventually meet your feet (skydiving would have got me there quicker), the hunt had long gone. I doubt the girls managed to find it again, but they didn't seem to care. I heard them clipping-clopping down the lane as I went back to my desk. Clip-clop-trill. Clip-clop-trill.

Good deed no. 12: asked a favour for someone else.

Thursday, 13 January

I'm working for six weeks on company write-ups about how well employers such as debt collectors treat their staff. I've done it before and the project always leaves me convinced I should run out and get an extremely well-paid nine-to-five job in IT and spend my day getting my feet massaged, checking on my work–life balance and dreaming of the Saga cruises I will go on courtesy of my enormous pension. Since I have spent the last two years writing a novel which I fully expect no one will ever read and which will earn me less than nothing, such jobs leave me sweaty with envy.

I did not lift my head till 5.30 p.m., and in the interests of good neighbourliness I stumbled through the darkness along the terrace with my five-year-old daughter to one of the other cottages. Because they are not occupied all the time, they occasionally get an upwardly mobile mouse or two who scurry in from the inhospitable fields around. The last time Dr Will and his wife were up, they left a trap behind the sofa. His wife is vegetarian and his nineteen-year-old daughter Jess is vegan, and if they see a dead mouse they will keel over with regret and self-hate. I was half hoping I could check on the trap, find it empty and still count it as my good deed, but unfortunately there was a furry little critter-corpse slumped over the luscious but poisoned sultanas, his tiny legs stretched out and stiff as winter twigs. Yuk . . . I mean, yuk. My daughter, who wants to be a 'singing' vet and has nerves of steel, held the black plastic bin-bag out while I shovelled in the mouse, and together we set another trap with chocolate. Vegetarian or not, they are doing the next one themselves.

That should have been my good deed for the day right there and then, but I was slumped on the sofa in front of a roaring log fire reading a thriller, darkness all around, when there was a rapping at the window. My first thought was the mouse was back; my second, that it was a psychopath come to slaughter me; my third was where's an axe when you need one? It turns out living in the country with no full-time neighbours, your husband working in London for weeks at a time, and reading blood-spattered crime novels is a bad combination.

Palpitating, I headed to the French doors and outside was the little old lady's grandson and his mam. Karl is a broad-shouldered teenage hulk with straw-blond hair. He quit school because he was being bullied – despite the fact he looks like a Viking and is the size of a four-bedroomed house, though size of course matters little in these cases. He got low after he dropped out of a construction course at college, and the local vicar hooked him up with the community radio station. Now he has decided he wants to work in radio.

Our friends' kids have middle-class parents who know how to work the system; they get work experience in glamorous places which helps with their confidence and self-esteem, their university applications and their careers. When Karl drove his gran over to mine at Christmas for a cup of tea, I made an airy offer about helping him with his CV, not particularly thinking he would take it up, although I did remember to ask the Lovely Claire to see if she could get him some work experience locally. All credit to the lad, after we spoke he went to Connexions (a scheme that helps sixteen-to nineteen-year-olds get work), and they told him where to look on the computer for a CV template. He tried to call it up at home on the Internet but everything was in Arabic, so tonight he told his mother he wanted to come up and talk to me about what to do next.

I set my computer up on the kitchen table and drafted a long list of things for him to do, including reading about what is happening in radio and figuring out what podcasting is. The community radio where he is hosting a weekly programme has links with a couple of local radio stations, so I told him to ask the woman who manages things there to get him set up with some work experience. I also had a brief look at courses, and I will check out what he can do bearing in mind he dropped out of school. I also copied over the Connexions CV template (in English), emailed it to him and told him to draft something and then bring it back to me and we would make it sing.

Truth be told, I am frightened. I have told a seventeen-year-old without a lot of self-confidence that it is OK to want something and to try for something that is really hard to get. What happens if he starts wanting it really badly and I can't help him get it? Wanting can eat up your soul. Good deeds should have good intentions – though it is possible to imagine a deed which has a good consequence but is poorly motivated. It is easier, though, to imagine a well-intentioned good deed which ends badly all round. I hate that expression 'No good deed goes unpunished'. It is a misery and an excuse for apathy and neglect. I also very much hope it is not true, otherwise I am all undone and heading into a perfect storm of troubles. Is it possible that my good deeds could have a real effect? That they wouldn't just be something self-contained and momentary, something worth little more than a brief 'thanks' – soon to be forgotten? Marvellous if I do a deed like that, ring out the bells. Horror upon horror if the effect it has isn't good.

Good deed no. 13: told a seventeen-year-old it is OK to have dreams.

Friday, 14 January

Despite my somewhat patchy faith, my eight-year-old is down to do his first Holy Communion. The reasons for this are:

- Having it any other way would be a matter of sadness to my parents.
- I grew up being taught about Catholic martyrs, so I feel an obligation to cascade the faith down the generations.

Plus:

- I want to believe in God – it is just that I am very bad at it.

Bearing in mind there's instruction at the weekend and strict rules on attendance, my son will have to miss football and rugby. There was hell when I told him, a situation which was not helped by my Protestant husband pontificating about football being more important than religion, which meant I had to tell him that football *was* his bloody religion. I ended up storming out of the kitchen, slamming the door behind me and going to bed without speaking to him.

Luckily, I came up with a plan. Bribery. I should have thought of it earlier. Straight after I dropped the kids at school, I hared up the road to Currys in Berwick. Nice though it would be if my eight-year-old son preferred to do as his mother told him and do his Holy Communion rather than what his father wants, that is to say score goals and make tries, it is not going to happen.

This year, I refused to let the boys ask Father Christmas for an iPod touch on the grounds they were far too young and the iPod touches were far too expensive. This morning I bought him one, in return for which he has to turn up to his Communion classes with good grace. It is, after all, a mother's prerogative to make up the rules as she goes along. I spent every last penny I had in my account. An iPod I can buy; scruples, however, are a luxury we mothers cannot always afford. The official line is as follows: you are doing your first Holy Communion for Granny (Granny being a devout Catholic), so Mummy (who is a bad Catholic) wants to say thank you for making Granny happy. It wouldn't get him – and it certainly wouldn't get me – through any pearly gates, but strangely enough protests over missing football dropped off immediately. Can an action which is bad if you look at it one way still be good if you look at it another? Now there is a question.

Good deed no. 14: made my mother happy. (If I were a nicer person, I wouldn't count making my own mother happy as a good deed – but I'm not.)

I have been worried about Lily for a while. She adopted Ellie almost three years ago when she was two (the kid having been taken into care when she was one), and Lily's life hasn't been her own since. Ellie looks like a fairy, with soft ginger ringlets and big hazel-green eyes like champion marbles; she is also damaged beyond belief. She asks the same question over and over again – 'Can I? Can I? Can I?', like a woodpecker breaking through your skull to get to the good stuff. If you look at someone else, if you talk to someone else, if you do something that doesn't involve her – that is when she thinks you don't see her any more, don't love her any more, that's when she thinks she doesn't exist any more, and that is when the problems start. Lily loves her, but her neediness is burning Lily out.

We've shared the run to dancing classes since the girls started. Lily takes Ellie and my daughter to ballet on a Wednesday night, and I take both girls to tap and modern dance on a Saturday morning. I am putting my money where my mouth is. I am going to keep Ellie for lunch and for a couple of hours after dancing on a Saturday. That way Lily can draw breath and spend some time with her husband and son, and away from Ellie. The only problem is who gives respite to the respite-givers?

Ellie maintains my daughter is her best friend. If my daughter has a toy in her hand, Ellie wants it, and if she doesn't get it she 'tells' or says, 'You're not my friend any more,' and then my daughter cries. She sits in the car as I zip up the dual carriageway to dancing and asks, 'What happens if I open the car door?' and in the rear-view mirror her big hazel-green eyes are bigger and greener than ever. The other day, I was still parking the car in the churchyard opposite the dancing school (despite the sign that says it is for churchgoers only) when she actually managed to open the door and start climbing out. Ellie is adorable, and Ellie melts my brain.

Today, however, the kid was as good as gold over lunch. The only problem this time was taking her home afterwards. Lily had dashed to the shops and her husband was somewhere in the fields, so I was forced to plod through the fields with two small girls in jazzy leotards and pink frothy tutus, all of us sinking into shin-deep mud, with Ellie shrieking hysterically that the horse would bite us if he was hungry. Lily rehomed a rescue pony and also has one rescue cat and two dogs (one of them a rescue dog), two rescue geese, two rescue ducks, twenty-eight sheep (three of them orphaned lambs farmers didn't want), five pigs (two of whom are rescue pigs), two chicken-reared ducks, one incubated duck, seven turkeys, half a dozen chickens, and a rooster called Lucky Lazarus who was born on Good Friday, died on Easter Sunday and whom she brought back to life. She names them all – not just the rooster. I have two guinea pigs called Nibble and Dark Dude, and I resent them both. I once asked her why she seems compelled to rescue both animals and people, and she described herself as 'a sucker for a hard-luck story'. She went on: 'I don't like to think anyone or anything is not going to have a decent life.'

And I said: 'OK.'

She said: 'And I was raised that way by my mam – you don't walk by someone who is suffering when there is something you could do to help.'

And I said: 'OK.'

She said: 'And when my dad left us, I was six. I remember how that abandonment felt then – and since.'

And there wasn't anything I could say.

Good deed no. 15.

Sunday, 16 January

Good deed no. 16: rang a grown-up friend in Bristol to see if she would go out for a run with another friend's daughter (new to the city and having difficulties settling in).

Monday, 17 January

My brother-in-law Rob is a natural scientist with a first from Cambridge and a Ph.D. from Oxford. He is incredibly tall and incredibly clever. Occasionally, when we are driving, we pass a telegraph pole and the children will say, 'Is Uncle Rob taller than that pole?' and I say, 'Yes.' When I was telling him about my resolution, he told me about 'reciprocal altruism' in the animal kingdom.

Between 1978 and 1983, Gerald S. Wilkinson (now a professor of biology at the University of Maryland and a leading expert in animal behaviour and genetics) found that vampire bats (which feed on blood at night) sometimes regurgitated blood for those who had not fed – mostly if there was a genetic relationship, but sometimes among bats who were unrelated but who 'tended to be frequent roostmates'. Wilkinson claimed that individuals who shared gained 'an immediate advantage in terms of increasing their own survival and sometimes the survival of their relatives' because bats die if they fail to feed for two nights in a row. So bats will do a good deed – providing they know the other bat involved and because there's something in it for them. (I know people like that.) There are even indications that there may be competition among bats to feed the hungry, possibly because that too increases the bat's own chances of survival. Later, I rang and asked Wilkinson whether animals were as altruistic as people, but he has his own line in the sand and said that they weren't. Wilkinson maintains that he knows of no persuasive altruistic behaviour among animals that goes as far as choosing to give their life for another animal (unless they are related). 'That,' he says, 'is uniquely human.'

Good deed no. 17: chased up Lovely Claire for Karl's work experience.

Tuesday, 18 January

Good deed no. 18: picked up litter on the beach.

Wednesday, 19 January

Good deed no. 19: sorted out four school pinafores and a couple of teeny-tiny jumpers that used to be my daughter's, and breezed into school with them for the mum who has a daughter even smaller than mine. (Ah, if all good deeds could be so easy.)

Thursday, 20 January

I may be imagining it, but there's a chance my handy sort of mate is beginning to avoid me. Last week I dug out baby books for him, and today when I handed over a couple of baby-music CDs for him to give to his sister, I sensed a lot less enthusiasm. Eventually, he confessed he still has the toys in his car. Seriously? Who is doing who the good deeds around here, I want to know?

Good deed no. 20.

Friday, 21 January

The early bird catches the worm and gives it to another bird; that is to say, I made a nice early start on my good deeds today. There's a woman at school who walks with a crutch – courtesy of someone driving over her foot a couple of years ago, shattering the bones in it, which has got to hurt. It makes me wince even thinking about it, but she is always incredibly jolly, with a little blond boy and a teeny tot of a fairy-girl. I helped her once before when she was struggling with a car seat, and this morning – fortunately for me – she dropped her handbag, so I picked it up and held the little tot's hand as she clambered up the steps of the school entrance. And when I got into school, the mum to whom I'd given the school uniforms had left me a gift bag with a bottle of wine and a box of Ferrero Rocher chocolates. It amazes me how often you get thanked for doing a good deed.

As I got ready this morning, there was an interview with Bryn Parry, the co-founder of Help for Heroes, the charity that helps soldiers wounded in Britain's current conflicts. Their very first event earned more than £5m for stricken soldiers, and over four years they raised £100m. Puts me carrying someone's handbag into perspective. Do I need to make some money for charity? Raising money for charity is generally as dull as hearing about other people's triathlon training or how they minimize their carbon footprints. Who gives a toss? Not me. God forbid I have to sit in a bath of baked beans. Or shave my head. I am not abseiling down anything – I did that once off Bamburgh Castle ramparts and it was terrifying. I could go on a run but for the fact I can't run. Perhaps I could go on a leisurely stroll, stopping off at a café for a nice cup of coffee? But there always seems to have to be a degree of suffering involved, and if I have to suffer, I whinge – a lot.

Good deed no. 21.

Saturday, 22 January

Took the girls to dance again and we met up with Al and the boys for hot chocolate in Barter Books, which is the world's best second-hand bookshop in my opinion. It used to be a railway station, which could be why so many men with beards haunt it. A model railway track runs overhead, and lines of Gerard Manley Hopkins and Tennyson on wooden boards connect the columns of books. The original Victorian station is everywhere around – the pitched roofs, the ticket offices, the enormous clocks – but these days books instead of trains carry people away. My favourite place is an old waiting room with a glass-panelled door, which reflects shelves of books; a blazing coalfire burns in the darkness there, and a huge wrought-iron lamp hangs from the ceiling inscribed with fabled destinations – Shangri-La, Toytown, Camelot – and the words 'et in Arcadia ego' (or 'I, too, am in Paradise').

The only problem in this Arcadia was that I'd left my debit card at home and Al's card has stopped working because we'd smashed through his overdraft, which left us with a £10 note to our name and loose coppers. The kids had to share a hot chocolate, while Al and I shared a coffee and bubbling, mustardy cheese on toast.

Middle-class penury, definition 1: sharing a cappuccino in a second-hand bookshop.

Housework in the afternoon, and then bought two escapist novels for bereaved cuz Merry on Amazon as my good deed.

Middle-class penury, definition 2: buying books on Amazon, even though you know you are broke, on the grounds that online shopping doesn't involve real money.

We are official members of the 'squeezed middle'. The Saab we drive is temporarily buggered; we are running a solitary clapped-out Volvo we call the Ratmobile due to the fact rats have eaten big holes in the back seat (real rats, not my eyeball rats), having come up through the wheel arch. We don't eat out in fancy restaurants, don't buy clothes and don't go on holidays, so who spends all the bloody money? My head hurts from sums – and my head hurts enough already. I have to repeat numbers endlessly before I absorb them; there are some calculations that make my entire brain shut down and smoke come out of my rat-infested eyeballs.

Merry, for whom I bought the books, is one of my favourite cousins. She once went on holiday with us when we were on the cusp of adolescence, and for seven whole days in the summer of 1973 we were the best of friends. Of course we grew up and didn't speak for the next twenty years on the grounds our mothers did our talking for us, and I doubtless knew more of her business and she doubtless knew more of mine than was entirely wise, but that's family for you.

She is contemplative, infinitely patient, softly spoken and gentle. I am amazed we share the same genes, since I prefer a strategy of 'do-first-think-how-later', am hideously impatient and regularly shout 'Bollocks' at all-comers. Tragically, her partner died last year at forty-six. So there she is – my age with a soulmate already in the ground, and there aren't many sticking plasters big enough to make that better. At Christmas, her three children went to an ex-husband and she went to bed for the day. When I checked on her after New Year, she had managed to stay up and watch Jools Holland – friend to lonely souls everywhere – and drink a bottle of red wine, which has to be a healthier option than taking to your bed for the day. (Well, maybe not the wine part, but I would have been tempted to boil it up in a copper pan, slice an orange, drop in fat slices and skinny, fragile cinnamon sticks, take a hot bath, a few spicy mouthfuls and open up a vein.) In the event, when I called her to offer comfort, I did as much talking if not more about headaches and exhaustion as she did about heartbreak and desolation.

Question: is the truth of good deeds that very often they are as good for the doer as they are for the done-to? And if they are, does that matter – providing good is done for someone other than the good-deed doer? Perhaps I should be a psychotherapist, like my best gay boyfriend. The problem is it takes seven years, which is a long time. Also, you have to go for therapy sessions yourself four times a week and I would run out of things to say. (Actually, that's a lie: I wouldn't run out of things at all.) Perhaps I could save time and just call myself a counsellor? I am genuinely good at listening and I already have several cardigans.

I am sending Merry books because my advice as an amateur, cardigan-wearing counsellor to the grieving is that in the event of bereavement – and I speak from personal experience – filling up your headspace with books and DVDs and good conversation is as effective a survival strategy as any. Grief is a desert to be crossed. Grief is a marathon to be run or walked or crawled. You can cross that desert. You can run that distance. Killing time any which way till you reach the other side is a mercy you owe yourself.

Good deed no. 22.

Sunday, 23 January

Good deed no. 23: stood by somebody else's child, who had gone on ahead of his parents in a car park, till his dad arrived.

Monday, 24 January

Good deed no. 24: invited someone who wanted to talk for a cup of tea.

Good deed no. 25: dug out a couple of contacts for a stranger who wants to write a book.

Wednesday, 26 January

My ten-year-old left his PE kit at home so rang me, which was disconcerting because the last time I checked he didn't have a mobile phone. He begged me to bring the kit in, which I reluctantly agreed to do. The problem was that I was so busy crawling to the garage excruciatingly slowly in case I ran out of petrol, I completely forgot, and went to a friend's for a coffee instead.

It may have meant forgetting the PE kit, but coffee with Kathryn was my good deed because I managed to drag Diane along with me. Kathryn lives in a centuries-old stone-built farmhouse, perched up a height, which can see straight through to the Cheviot Hills away in the distance. Often, I drive straight by the tight turning to the farm, and I have to watch hard for an ironwork windvane which marks the bend, and which, if looks are anything to go by, must screech like a banshee when the north wind pushes it around and around.

Kathryn has four sheepdogs with pleading brown eyes and a twelve-year-old daughter with autism. A warm and very pretty woman twenty years younger than her husband, she often has her hair dyed; occasionally it is a joyful chestnut, today it is a glorious aubergine. I brought Diane along because, ever one to solve a complex problem, she has come to the heart-wrenching conclusion that her own three-year-old girl is also autistic. Her daughter is a doll but was slow to walk, has delayed speech, won't come out of her cot, insists on routine and doesn't engage as you might expect her to. I have watched this child grow up, watched her grow prettier – her silky, soft brown hair cut in a French bob; I have listened for words that don't come, sat by her as she sorted the food on her plate – here potato, here meat, here peas, sniper alleys between – no pea allowed to stray into this no-man's-land, punishment immediate. I have watched her and wondered.

Diane used to play hockey and lacrosse. I have never asked whether she captained the teams, but I'd put money on the fact she did. She rode competitively and, whether it was the sport or the falls or just 'one of those things', she damaged her spine. Since I first met her, she has had two major operations on her back and keeps an X-ray of her sometime-pinned-and-caged spinal column in the downstairs loo like a nineteenth-century adventurer keeping a stuffed grizzly bear that took out his eye on that fateful hunting trip in the woods. I am always surprised she doesn't lock up and sink straight to the seabed when she swims. She happens to be frighteningly posh, which is perhaps why she is so good with pain – well-bred phlegm. She is showing similar equanimity about the daughter. If I believed my breathtaking girl to be autistic, I would ball up my fists and beat the knuckles bloody on the plastered kitchen walls. That, however, is not what you do when you have grit, the right stuff, and when you do not have a choice.

Instead, Diane considers how the child will 'come across' at school, which she is due to start in September. She isn't worried, she explains carefully, her hand sliding down to scruffle one of the dogs behind the ears, who squirms ecstatically; the key is an official diagnosis and getting the right support at school. Kathryn nods, been-there-done-that, and there is a hairy, panting flurry of collie dogs as she moves first one then another from between her and the cupboards to get out the chocolate biscuits. (She always has chocolate biscuits in – it is one of her best qualities.) Diane will fight for her daughter with exquisite manners and determination as steely as the rods that were once in her spine. But I worry that she herself will need more support than she expects, than she believes is necessary, than she believes her due. In the living room, the two remarkable mothers talk. The special little girl lies on the wool carpet and plays with leggy Barbies and plastic-fantastic horses with flowing manes. Utterly ordinary me lies alongside her – and plays too.

Quid pro quo, as we left, Kathryn gave me a dozen brown and fresh farm eggs from the hens that strut and peck the grassy bank outside the farmhouse. As she hands me the cardboard tray, the eggs whole and perfect, for a moment I think that they are warm.

Good deed no. 26.

Thursday, 27 January

Good deed no. 27: looked round a house the expat cousins are thinking of moving into.

Friday, 28 January

I checked up on Merry again. How tiresome are my loved ones starting to find my constant check-ups? Do they feel as if they are under surveillance? Bereaved? Sick? Depressed? Stand by your sickbeds – the good-deed doer will be calling any second. Pretend you're out.

Good deed no. 28.

Saturday, 29 January

Good deed no. 29: had a child for the afternoon, to let her poorly mum rest.

Sunday, 30 January

This evening, Mum rang to say my uncle died. He was eighty-five and ill with cancer and died at 3 a.m. in hospital. She says my dad's heartbroken.

What can you say to bring any kind of peace when a husband dies after fifty-two years of marriage? You want to make it better and you can't, but you try anyway. I feel so sorry for my dad, sorrier yet for his sister – my darling Irish aunt. How terrible to get into your eighties and lose the person you love. How do you remember what it is to be on your own if you have been with someone else for more than fifty years? How do you remember that they aren't there any more? That they haven't just stepped out to the kitchen to make you both a cup of tea? Or that they aren't in their allotment and won't be back for lunch with some freshly dug new potatoes?

When I rang, she told me how on his last day their youngest daughter washed him, cleaned his teeth and shaved him, as she had shaved him every day on his sickbed, and he asked whether she had made him look beautiful. For forty years, a father tells a daughter that she's beautiful, and in the telling he makes it so. Hearing him, believing him, she walks through life lightly – her feet bare, her smile open – she meets the dawn and stretches, greets other men who'll love her too, with the sure and certain knowledge that she is lovely. She knows it's so – her father told her years ago and yesterday and every time he looks her way. And at the end, when no daughter, however loving, can stop her father leaving, she does the thing she can: she shaves this dying man, she holds his hand, and nods in answer to his question. Her gift to him. His gift to her. She makes him beautiful.

Good deed no. 30: consoled the bereaved (not true – tried to console the bereaved).

Monday, 31 January

Good deed no. 31: wrote a letter to someone who's ill.

THE HELPER

I am trying to set my kids a good example, having been set the best of examples by my own parents. I may fail. Epically, as my son would say. Still, epic fail or not, I'll know I tried. What happens, though, if you don't learn about charity and generosity from those who should teach it to you as a child? What then? Do you grow up hard and loveless? Or do you teach yourself what goodness is?

Jean taught herself. Standing four feet eight and a half inches in her tiny stocking feet, 61-year-old Jean makes you want to pop her in your pocket and take her with you wherever you go, like a lucky charm. After twenty-seven years of working with the terminally ill and those with mental health issues, she retired as a community support worker because of acute osteoporosis and osteoarthritis. Since then, two days a week for a decade, the pupils at my kids' school have taken it in turns to sit next to Jean as she hears them read. 'That's marvellous,' she says as they stumble through the words. 'Superb,' she tells them as they turn the final page. Encouraging children when she was only ever discouraged. Boosting their self-esteem when hers was covered over with ash and beatings. Her arm around these children, when her own mother would never hold her.

Jean grew up in poverty in Ashton-under-Lyne with an alcoholic father who served in the merchant navy during the war, was unemployed thereafter and whose mood depended on the 2.30 at Chepstow. 'I used to protect the kids. I can remember standing with my three brothers behind me' – she stretches out her arms as she talks, as if to bar a doorway – 'and saying, "Don't hit them, hit me," and he did. That's how it was. That's what life was like, but he was still my dad and I loved my dad – worshipped him. Three weeks before he died of lung cancer – he was only forty-six – he apologized for all he'd done, and I did forgive him – and my mum – because you have to.' Jean says that life was hard in the 1950s. 'Nobody had anything after the war. It was all make do and mend and it was all big families. I was around six and I remember my mother saying to my dad, "We can't send her to school – she's too many bruises." You'd get a good hiding and that was one of those things. It wasn't any different for the girl up the road, but it was a horrible childhood – hard and cruel. I've got more bad memories than good.'

However tough life was for that 'girl up the road', there was certainly no sanctuary to be found for Jean in her mother's arms. Jean's mother worked shifts in a cigarette factory and as a piecework machinist making handbags at home. 'A grafter', Jean describes her as. 'Grafter': a word of respect – a compliment. But compliments didn't flow the other way. 'I can't remember a word of encouragement – none whatsoever. The only thing I can remember from my mother is her saying, "Go into the other room – you make me feel sick."' The woman had spent her war in the Land Army, had five children in five years, ten years fallow and then two more children. She had an alcoholic husband and worked all hours. But there are all kinds of poverty in this world – did she work so many hours, was she so spent, that there was never a moment for a fond word or a loving gesture? 'I can't remember my mum or my dad ever giving us cuddles,' says Jean. 'I tell my children I love them every day, but there was none of that when I was growing up. That wasn't just my upbringing, that was the 1950s for you, but she was a hard woman. Mind you, she had to be.' As she speaks, I wonder that tiny Jean was strong enough to keep growing on the inside to the size of a giant. Years after, a woman can still feel a father's fists fall on her young girl's body, however heartfelt his 'Sorry'. You can't recover from the thousand tiny hurts where there should have been a hundred-thousand-million mother's kisses. But you can hold your own children tighter, cover them in the kisses you never had, and say, 'I love you, love you, love you, child, love you all the more for never knowing this myself.'

When Jean fell pregnant at sixteen she was sent to a Church of England home for unmarried mothers and their babies in Blackburn, the girls taken together for antenatal classes but not given pain relief in hospital during the birth of their babies and talked down to by nurses. 'Inside you were all in the same boat – in a lot of ways it was better than home. Outside, though, they segregated you. You felt awful, you had to walk down the street with your head down, you felt shame – I still do sometimes.' Her newborn son should have been put up for adoption; instead – ever the protector of the vulnerable – Jean fought for him. 'I prayed on my hands and knees to my dad to keep him, because you were in that home to give the child away. I thought, I just can't, and finally my dad said, "If you bring this baby home, you're not to ask me or your mum for anything because we won't help," and by gum they stuck to their word.' Jean cleaned houses with her baby in tow while bringing up her two youngest siblings, now one and three – siblings who when they left school came to live with her and her husband.

I am looking at Jean and thinking, 'Why are you here doing good? Why aren't you mean and angry after the start you had in life? When your health broke in your forties, why didn't you say, "I've done enough," rather than, "What can I do now?" Why don't you take rather than give?' I ask her whether it helps her to do good and she says, 'I've seen it – I've been there, but you have got to have hope, you have to know that things will get better. I am who I am because of what I have gone through and I can never see me not caring, not doing what I do.' In nature, where there should be bitter herbs and rank weeds, occasionally a tangle of wild roses bloom: scented, startling pink and beautiful.

Tuesday, 1 February

Yesterday the eight-year-old was off sick and today it was my daughter's turn. She drifted around all day in a one-piece, fake-fur, pink leopard-skin pyjama suit complete with ears, saying, 'I'm sick. You have to do whatever I want when I'm sick, and I am really sick.' The logic of a five-year-old; I may try it.

This good-deed thing is getting serious, though, and I'm not sure I like it. I decided I couldn't in all conscience continue to ring up one of my nearest and dearest to talk through their particular crisis or I risked a totally groundless accusation of emotional stalking. In *The Screwtape Letters*, C. S. Lewis writes that 'a sensible human' once said, ' "She's the sort of woman who lives for others – you can always tell the others by their hunted expression." ' So instead of hunting down my 'others' I decided I needed to find an alternative source of good-deedery. Tonight I signed up to raise £500 for charity within the year – more specifically for a local cause – and committed £10 a month from my own money to kick it off. I have a JustGiving website page and everything. Annually HospiceCare North Northumberland needs to raise around £255,000 of its £300,000 running costs from its own fund-raising. That is a lot of money. The JustGiving page advises you to contact everyone on your email contacts list and to put it up on your Facebook page and the like. Not sure about that. I can't see acquaintances giving much dosh, and the people I'm closest to will think I am David Cameron's Big Society crack-whore. I'll keep it low profile.

Good deed no. 32.

Wednesday, 2 February

Good deed no. 33: drove round to give Diane a pot of hyacinths.

Thursday, 3 February

Lily's boy has been off sick for the past couple of days and she is shattered. Two nights on the sofa in his room will do that to you. (I didn't ask whether she kept an axe handy.) It wasn't him, though, but Ellie she talked about when I called to check how things were. The child's starting point is 'I'; the first words out of her mouth every morning are not 'Love you, Mum' or 'Did you have a nice sleep?' but 'I want . . .', 'I need . . .' 'Her whole wiring is for survival,' Lily said. She is overwhelmed.

Lily first asked for help in August, but there has been no sighting of the cavalry. Weekends are the worst. Without the routine of school, Ellie's on a downward spiral. Tension in the family has been so explosive that they went to the beach at the weekend despite the fact it was bitter and blowing a gale, and they sent Ellie off into the dunes with her brother. She didn't want to leave her mother, but Lily was desperate for a moment's peace and her husband insisted. Sobbing, the kid climbed up into the dunes. But as Lily walked towards the sea, the child panicked that she was being abandoned and, hysterical, stepped out over the edge of the dunes to get to her, falling two metres and crashing onto the sands – which, had they been walking on a different beach, could so easily have been rocks. Lily ran to comfort her and the shaken girl clung to her.

'When she was back on her feet, I stared out at the sea,' Lily said, 'she was just sobbing inconsolably the whole time. I let out this roar of desperation and my husband said, "I'll take her," but I told him, "No, she needs me," although I knew I couldn't cope with her. She broke her heart all the way there and all the way back, her lips were blue and she was blotchy and had snot in her hair and all over her face, and I've been left thinking that I'm way out of my depth.'

Lily took her to the GP. Lily cried, and as she cried, Ellie slipped off her knee to fetch her a tissue and stroked her mother's face. 'I'll make it better, Mammy,' she told her. The GP is referring Ellie to the mental health team.

Ellie patently adores this mother – would climb into her and stay there if she could. Unborn. Reborn. I just listened; sometimes that is all the good you can do. But how do you keep giving and giving like that? Because once you make a commitment to adopt, there is no going back. It is not like my good deed for a day; this is for life. God knows I regret getting the guinea pigs, so I already know there's no way my heart is big enough to adopt a child – Lily's heart is, though. She would do anything for anyone, whatever the price she herself pays. Every time I've known someone need something, Lily is there for them with cash, practical help or an arm around them. Often she glitters when she walks. I think it's what she wears, but it might just be her.

Good deed no. 34.

Friday, 4 February

THE CAMPAIGNER

Today's good deed came to me. Kate, another mother at school, sent a round-robin email asking people to send on a letter to their MEPs to lobby for mandatory cameras and sensors in HGVs.

They have a blind spot, which means that cyclists are getting killed. Kate's sister Eilidh was thirty and had recently got the job of her dreams as a TV producer. I never met her, but I know that she snowboarded and skied and was the sort of person who took a big bite out of life whenever she got the chance. Then, two years ago, cycling to work in London, she was in front and to the right of a fully loaded 32-tonne tipper lorry approaching a pedestrian crossing when the lorry hit her, dragging her underneath its wheels. Pinned underneath a double wheel which had crushed her pelvis, but fully conscious, Eilidh quietly asked passers-by, 'Please help me, please help me.' Two hours later she was pronounced dead by surgeons at the Royal London Hospital. It is the second anniversary of her death tomorrow.

Kate has dealt with her grief – in part at least – by campaigning for HGVs to be made safer for cyclists, in the sure and certain knowledge it won't mend her broken sister, because there is nothing in this wide world that can bring that little sister back. Regardless, Kate and her mother Heather have shuttled back and forth to London, to Parliament, to Strasbourg, arguing and pleading and protesting. A blind spot was found on the driver's right-hand side where the lorry struck Eilidh – the driver himself said he never saw her – if only there had been a camera, a sensor, if only, if only, if only. So why do good when bad happens? 'People have said to me, "Why do it, when it won't bring her back?"' Kate says. 'But I don't want it happening to other people. Imagine if it were to happen again, maybe to someone I know, and I had done nothing. That would make me culpable – it would be a sin of omission.'

Against the railings in Notting Hill where the crash happened, there is a permanent memorial: a ghostbike painted white with wheels but no tyres, draped all about with roses and plastic-wrapped love. But Kate wants a better memorial: she wants an end to avoidable deaths, she wants other families to avoid the heartbreak and horror her own has gone through, she wants lives lived which might otherwise be lost. No amount of campaigning can change the past; it can, however, change the future. And who says hope cannot grow, unfurling leaves of green, in a soil of desolation? Who says when the worst of times come, the best in us won't stand tall?

'I will keep going till it's safer,' Kate says, 'because if I don't do it, no one else will.' Sending a letter isn't much, but I will do it. Why do you have to fight for something so obvious? If there were a way to make something safer, to save lives, why wouldn't you take it? Look here at a sister's tears, the grainy photo of a laughing, beautiful girl with platinum-blonde hair, the mangled wreck of a bicycle, its wheels spinning. Why wouldn't you feel the grief, the absence, why wouldn't you think – as a politician, or a civil servant, or the director of a haulage company – 'Not on my watch. No more. Let's change the way we do this.'

Good deed no. 35.

Saturday, 5 February

I've had it in mind for a while to dig up a bunch of snowdrops for the little old lady who used to live in this house and who moved down to the village soon after her husband died. He was a keen gardener and made it his business to spread snowdrops around the garden, so that at this time of year, snowdrops with their tiny drooping white bells fill the lawn and the glade between the back wall and the sheep pasture. We loved him, and I always think of him when the snowdrops come. I am sure she thinks of him all the time. Together, my daughter and I found a trowel and we extracted a small bunch of snowdrops, their heads white and shy, hanging down as if they were admiring their new, leaf-green shoes.

We drove carefully through the rain with the pot on the floor of the passenger seat, reaching down every now and then to steady it. When we got there, the little old lady was preparing dinner. I've dropped in before when she is cooking dinner, and black smoke will be curling from out beneath the kitchen door, but she would not dream of telling you. She sits there patiently while you drink a cup of tea, and when you've gone, eats ash. We didn't go in; instead we put them by her front door on the porch, out of the cold north wind, and I told her how I think of him at this time of year when the snowdrops come.

Good deed no. 36: said, 'I remember.'

Sunday, 6 February

Went to Mass today, and strangely enough, it had a lot to do with good deeds.

> 'And if thou draw out thy soul to the hungry, and satisfy the afflicted soul; then shall thy light rise in obscurity, and thy darkness be as the noonday . . .'
>
> (Isaiah 58:10)

That's who I want to be: a light in the darkness.

I'm ashamed to say I got into a total state getting ready to go down to London tomorrow for my uncle's funeral. The expats have offered to babysit. Bearing in mind they don't have kids of their own, this is astonishingly brave – or foolish, depending on your perspective. Their thinking is we did them a good turn by welcoming them home, and in turn they will do what they can to help us out. After a night with the kids, they might have a sudden change of heart on that one.

They are sleeping in our bedroom so they can hear the kids if they wake up. But our room was in a state, and the bathroom was in a state, and the kitchen was in a state, and it all seemed endless. Diane, with a farmer husband and three children, keeps her house immaculate. She once moved out to get building work done and when she moved back in, I said, 'It looks great. When are you moving your stuff back in?' and she said, 'We have moved back in.' My house is full of junk. Full to the brim. Even if I throw it out, it sneaks back in at night with the sole intention of making my house look like shite.

The worst thing is that, as a result of my rising hysteria, my husband got all manly and decisive (which is never good), and announced that we are going to leave at lunchtime rather than straight after the school drop-off because we have too much to do and will otherwise be up all night doing it.

This is fatal. This means we won't leave till midnight.

I almost gave up on the good deeds. I was deciding that I might have to wimp out on making the world a better place due to 'personal circumstances', when I discovered a box of baby socks for a friend's baby that I had failed to get round to giving her. I pulled them out, dusted them off and hey presto – a good deed. All together now, 'One day at a time, sweet Jesus, that's all I'm asking of you . . .'

Good deed no. 37.

Monday, 7 February

Managed to leave home at 2 p.m. – but only because I insisted. This is roughly four hours later than I wanted to leave, and four hours earlier than my husband wanted. My husband hates extended periods away from us, and after the funeral he has to stay down in London on deadline for one of his projects. He'll be away for three weeks, which is a long time by anyone's reckoning. All weekend he drifted around looking miserable. 'I love my job, but I don't want to leave you all,' he grumbled, as if I could rub it better and say, 'Don't go then, darlink.' Unfortunately, I can't.

I cannot think the last time I went anywhere by train, but I love it – even with the prospect of a funeral at the other end. Hours on my own are rare, the chance of a gin and tonic, uninterrupted reading, or a DVD on the laptop. But Al had pleaded for me to drive down with him and all his work in the Saab rather than go by train, so I agreed. Even with the late start, it wasn't too bad. We did some talking about the children, about how to pay the bills, I admired his profile. We spent time being married.

Good deed no. 38: travelled to a funeral.

Tuesday, 8 February

In the church, my dad was bent over praying; his hands, which are large and red and scarred from his work as a grocer, were shaking even though one of them kept tight hold of the other. I was OK with the coffin and the photo of my uncle smiling and sitting in his allotment, but then my aunt came in, her grown-up children and their sombre-faced children filing into the front pew, and that was it. My beloved aunt's head was hanging and she reminded me of a solitary snowdrop and I started crying and I couldn't even look at them for fear I would get worse.

It was a very personal service, and I particularly liked the reflection by Edgar A. Guest:

> Miss me a little but not for long
> And not with your head bowed low.
> Remember the love that we once shared,
> Miss me, but let me go.

It finished up:

> When you are lonely and sick at heart
> Go to the friends we know,
> And bury your sorrows in doing good deeds.
> Miss me, but let me go.

Good deeds as a way out of grief . . .

I cannot even flatter myself that I brought comfort. Out of the church, in the cold sunshine, as the undertakers slid the coffin into the hearse, amid the milling mourners I hugged my widow-weeded aunt – but where were the words of comfort? Where the honeyed wisdom to mend a hurt? Fresh out. Instead, I held her in silence, unable to speak, let alone to say what she might need to hear. She was so small and thin and temporary, and the word 'widow' so final and immense.

It was a very Irish affair. The crowd of people around the grave were all of a certain age and height, and they all seemed to have that short, straight Irish nose and full cheeks. A Celtic Windrush, a diaspora generation, and afterwards over lunch, as I sat with them, my dad and his friends talked about coming over from the green farms and the villages to the hustling, bustling London of the 1950s, the cranes along the Thames, bombsites and building sites, red buses in a black and white city. An emigrant generation falling between the cracks in the floorboards. Soon, no one will remember how it was to be Irish, living in damp English lodgings with sandwiches of luncheon meat, asking freckled, rosy-cheeked girls from home to jive on a Saturday night.

I was talking to the family about trying to do my good deeds, and a bearded Irishman made the point that, according to the catechism they used to teach the children, burying the dead was a Catholic corporal work of mercy; so I nodded wisely as if I well knew a great deal about corporal works of mercy when in fact I knew nothing.

Now that I've looked into it, it turns out there are corporal and spiritual works of mercy. Spiritual works include advising, consoling, comforting, forgiving, and bearing wrongs patiently. I am far too quick to advise (as are many in my family; only occasionally do you get to finish explaining the problem before the solution is presented to you), addicted to consoling (those of a morbid disposition often are) and comforting (large breasts help). I have nothing to forgive (I lie: I have a list, a long list, and when I remember where I put it there will be trouble) and I am utterly useless at bearing wrongs patiently (they just make me really mad).

Corporal works of mercy include feeding the hungry, sheltering the homeless, clothing the naked, visiting the sick and imprisoned, giving alms to the poor and, as was said, burying the dead. So burying the dead was indeed my good deed for the day. It might be argued I have given alms with the monthly charity commitment, but I haven't done any of the other stuff. Nada. Unless you count giving a stranger a Mars Bar on the train on the way home as feeding the hungry. He had wanted a Mars and the trolley lady didn't have any and as luck would have it, I happened to have one in my handbag, so then he said he would buy me a Twix. It could have been the start of a beautiful friendship if only I was single and we didn't both look like we had eaten a few too many Mars Bars to begin with.

Good deed no. 39.

Wednesday, 9 February

My ten-year-old was off sick as per the children's rota to stop me working. Did very little all day aside from take children to school, pick up children from school, buy a chicken from the butcher's, tell a sick child he will feel better soon, tell a sick child TV will not of itself make him better, tell a sick child that no, he can't go play football for his team when he didn't go to school during the day. I'd really love to count looking after sick children as a good deed, but it's in the job description. Maternal compassion is wearing so thin you could sieve marmalade through it.

Instead then, I rang an aunty; elderly relatives dying all around you always necessitates a quick headcount, so I thought I'd check on the welfare of my oldest aunt. Aunty Effie and my mother are sisters. Once upon a time, like in a fairy tale, I had handsome uncles and all sorts of magic aunts: the tragic aunt who died too soon when scaffolding fell; the aunt who always let me wear her garnet rings; another (wildly Catholic, this one) who warned against reading of Borgia lust and murder 'at my age' (I was twelve) – or at all, she meant; and the aunt who fed me custard creams and orange squash in slidey velour seats, guarding us from matinee perverts with a hatpin . . . the list goes on.

Alcohol was never served in my house as a child when the aunties and the uncles came; 'old times' took the place of booze and 'Remember when . . .' was the only sharpener they ever needed. When Aunty Effie visited, she brought white bags with twisted paper ears full of stripy liquorice chews with crunchy shells, and I'd lie in my mother's bed, under pink candlewick, and chew with a black tongue in sweet lockjaw agony, while I listened to the chime of thin china cup against thin china saucer and the howling laughter of grown-ups in the paradise of downstairs. The other thing she brought was a tiny dog; my all-time favourite was Tinkerbell, a chihuahua runt fed milk-and-rusk slop with a tiny teaspoon. These days, Aunty Effie is in excruciating pain because she needs a hip replacement, still misses her husband eight years after his death, and her new chihuahua just bit her. I have told Al that I am definitely dying first.

Good deed no. 40.

Thursday, 10 February

Looked out some old clothes to take into the Sue Ryder shop in the village, which is having a shout-out for donations. You wouldn't think a small fishing village would support a charity shop, but somehow it does. I took various jeans and a nice black lace top, a green corduroy military jacket and a new blue-and-white striped cotton dress that made me look like an overstuffed mattress when I got it home and which consequently still had the label 'king-sized' attached. I filled in a gift aid form and was given a card so the proceeds of my donations can be tracked and the tax claimed back on them. Having your own charity shop card encourages the thought that you might go back. When I wrote down my address, the woman behind the counter informed me she knew me and then said accusingly, 'But you look different.' That would be the two stone I've put on over the last couple of years. 'You've grown your hair,' she said, not quickly enough. When the two volunteers went into the back, probably to look through the bag, I suddenly thought, 'Now they'll know the size I wear my trousers,' and in my rush to leave the shop, walked slap-bang into a clothes rail. You don't really want strangers knowing how big your bottom is, do you?

The bigger problem is that the children, shock horror, are beginning to ask what my good deed was today. Oh my God. I mean it. Oh my God. That means I can't stop. Ever. Or at least not this year. As a mother, I want to teach them resolve, I want to teach them to stick at stuff until they are through the other side, I want to teach them how to live good lives and think of other people. In theory I want to do that. Bangs head on desk.

Good deed no. 41.

Friday, 11 February

It is the expat's sixty-ninth birthday today, so I took the highly unusual step of making a birthday cake as my good deed. Despite having three children, I never make birthday cakes because I usually pull the ingredients out of my larder, cross my arms, stand back, look at them, think 'Nah' and put them away again.

Good deeds requiring a bit more effort on my part, I resisted the siren call of the supermarket's chocolate caterpillar cakes with their beaming smiles and Smartie spots, and made from scratch an 'Ultimate' Chocolate Cake. My first problem, having whipped the damn thing up, was the discovery that I didn't have any matching cake tins, so I had to break and enter a neighbour's holiday cottage. Fortunately, I have not yet set up the local Neighbourhood Watch. The second problem was the cakes wouldn't cook. I kept pulling them out to check and they got more and more burnt on top but were still sloppy as a salty sea in the middle. Finally, I gave up and donned my padded gauntlets. I pulled them out, shucked them from their stolen tins and chopped away the charcoal frills with a serrated bread knife. Shiny, dark chocolate ganache now fills the dip where the cake rose and fell, and the uneven surface is covered in ruby raspberries and emerald-green and gold wax candles in the shape of tiny champagne bottles. Luscious, decadent and frowsy, but I suspect in the middle it is raw. I'm back to the chocolate caterpillars next time.

Good deed no. 42.

Saturday, 12 February

I am mortified.

I dropped my eldest son at football on the wide open green space above the market town, and my daughter at dancing, and took the eight-year-old along to his Communion class. Fortunately the church is opposite the dance school. Shabby Catholic that I am, I resent the fact it is not just the children who have the Communion class, but that mums and dads do too. This morning's class was supposed to be about baptism, and I can't even say what there was in it that set me off; maybe it was all the discussion about the importance of baptism and what it meant in terms of welcoming a child into a community.

When my son was stillborn we wanted him baptized but the hospital priest wouldn't do it; he did perform a naming ceremony, but refused an official baptism. You could get cross about that sort of thing, but you have to let it go or it sweeps you away to live in Angry-town where the mad people squat outside huts of corrugated metal and throw stinky poos at passers-by. There I was, hiding on my hard wooden chair at the back of the church, when of course the nice woman organizing the sessions asked me to move to the front row as she had a sore throat and didn't want to shout. The session started, the tears began to fall and I was lost. No tissue, no hanky, no place to hide. I lasted as long as I could – even blowing my nose on my best purple scarf, which, now I think of it, I should take off – but finally I had to walk past everybody and out the church.

It wasn't even one of those subtle weeps, but an all-out,

piggy-nosed, puce-faced, pink-eyed, hysterical crying jag. Then, right at the church door, if I didn't walk into another mother arriving late with two of her children. She ended up having to get me tissues from her car. She disappeared back into the church for my coat as I stood shivering in the cold by my own car, and finally the session finished and my eight-year-old came out along with the other children, followed by the nice catechist, who started walking towards me. I'm rooting around in my handbag, desperate for some make-up to hide what's been happening from her – from everyone – when she puts a hand on my arm. I look up at her, and I don't really want to because I know how ugly I must look, how mad I must seem. I think, 'Please don't be nice. Please don't say "How terrible" and "Not to worry" and "These things happen."' But she doesn't say any of those things. Instead, she says how she had lost a son at thirteen, that he'd gone out to Scouts and never came back and that tomorrow would have been his twenty-first birthday, and as she speaks I think, 'I'm not the only one.'

After, when everyone had drifted off, the oaken church doors shut and locked, and there was quiet in the churchyard but for the blackbirds' song, my son held out a warm toffee ball. The children were given a sweet after the Communion class and he'd chosen a golden toffee penny. He had taken off the crinkly wrapping, rolling the toffee round and round in sticky fingers to make it a keep-for-later caramel treasure till he saw me wipe away my tears and suddenly it was mine.

Good deed no. 43: picked up litter on Bamburgh beach.

Sunday, 13 February

En route to Mass we drove into the local market town, bumping over the cobbles to the florist's, which unusually was open, preparing for Valentine's Day. I picked up a small galvanized tin bucket of lucid-blue hyacinths for the catechist and a card. There are moments you brace yourself for in the aftermath of a child's death:

the anniversary itself, when you see a friend's child you know would be his exact same age, the day he should have started school with shiny face and shinier shoes, the birthday when he'd have stepped proudly into double figures. I already know that this year, when he would have been twelve, will be bad because I remember being a whip-smart, precocious, plaited twelve. And eighteen and twenty-one with keys he won't turn and doors he won't open. There are other moments, though, that catch you raw and unawares. A football match where the cold wind whistles down the touchline, a fond dad calls out your son's name and his son answers. Those moments, years after, when a world stops turning and you fall off, spinning, your arms and legs spread wide, your eyes closed, one thought: 'How I do miss you.'

The catechist told me her son's friends remembered him and that she'd been to the grave yesterday and there was a sunflower and a rose already there.

Good deed no. 44: said, 'I understand because I've been there' – after all, she did the same for me.

Monday, 14 February

Better fettle today, helped by my daughter's Valentine letter, which she gave me over breakfast before clambering onto my knee to open it for me.

I Jud (To Judith – apparently she didn't write 'Mummy' because that would have given the game away. Cunning for a five-year-old, huh?)

I love so much (I love you so much)
theut (that)
I cud dust (I could burst.)
fum (from)

And a back-to-front question mark.

Good deed no. 45: picked up litter along the lane.

Tuesday, 15 February

An email popped up yesterday from Karl, the teenage radio-wannabe, and I imagined him sitting in his teenage boy's bedroom lined with posters of wagons, spot cream and Old Spice aftershave on the shelf and an old toy farm under the bunk beds where he and his twin brother still sleep, his broad shoulders hunched, huge fingers carefully pecking at the keyboard, enquiring ever so politely about his missing work experience. So I have pinged off an email to London radio presenter and political pundit Iain Dale asking for a favour. This willingness to help the young that aren't our own must be biological – most of us don't burn goodwill begging a favour for ourselves, put someone out, testing their patience, risking rejection – yet we are willing enough to ask on behalf of a child or a young person, to cajole, to plead, to persuade. How else does the species survive? Result. When I asked Iain whether there was a chance Karl could spend a day with him at LBC, I said it would be like *Billy Elliot* but on radio with a really big lad who couldn't dance and Iain as Julie Walters. And thank God he loves Julie Walters. He's agreed – hurrah. And although I know him through his blog and he knows me through mine, I have never even met him so that's a pretty starry thing for him to do. He says Karl can spend the day in the Global Radio News Centre, which supplies lots of different stations, and be there for his programme going out. I am very excited.

In point of fact, I have been noticing a bit of a buzz lately when I have done my good deed, and I have discovered why. It turns out that good deeds may have health benefits. (I wonder how they are with migraines?) According to research by Allan Luks (then with the Institute for the Advancement of Health in the US) which was published in *The Healing Power of Doing Good* in 1991, weekly helpers who had personal contact with those they helped were 'ten times more likely to say they were in good health compared to once a year volunteers'. Luks (who surveyed 3,296 people) reported that 95 per cent of these regular volunteers also described 'a feel-good sensation that gave them a personal lift, reducing stress'. It came in two stages: an initial physical rush (with helpers reporting various sensations such as warmth, energy and euphoria), which Luks termed the 'helper's high'; followed by a second longer period of emotional well-being involving 'increased self-worth, calm and relaxation'. It is claimed that helping triggers a drop in stress-related chemicals and a release of endorphins (which are the brain's neurotransmitters – or messenger chemicals – killing pain and acting as the body's natural high).

Further research by Jorge Moll and colleagues (published in the *Proceedings of the National Academy of Sciences* in 2006) indicated that when a person makes a donation, the brain is engaged in the same way as when he receives money. Magnetic resonance imaging was used to show that making a donation engages a particular pathway in the brain that depends on a neurotransmitter called dopamine (the release of which signals reward or pleasure to the brain).

According to this research, if I do good deeds, I am going to feel good. That should save on the wine bill.

Good deed no. 46.

THE ADVOCATE

I haven't got a very scientific brain – at school I gave it up pretty much as soon as I could. The only things I have retained from school science lessons is how mercury looks in a dish – jostling and spreading and silvery-rolling – and that the chemistry lab always smelled of blackcurrant. One man who knows more than most about the state of scientific research into giving behaviour is Dr Stephen G. Post, co-author of *Why Good Things Happen to Good People* and a professor in the department of preventative medicine at Stony Brook University in New York. In an academic review of more than fifty scientific and medical investigations into the experience of individuals 'who act sincerely for the benefit of others', Post reports benefits in terms of happiness, health and longevity across the various studies. His review states that 'when we help others, we help ourselves', and suggests healthcare professionals should consider recommending such activities to patients.

I am interested that unwittingly I may have been boosting my immune system, sleeping more soundly and enhancing my self-esteem while adding years to my life. I ring him. Post sounds affable and mellow and clever, like a man who has sussed how to live and live well, but he warns me against putting 'the cart before the horse'. People do good to help others and not because they can be certain of happiness or health. 'Benefits are really a by-product or a side effect of sincere helping,' he says. Like a true American, he quotes the essayist and philosopher Ralph Waldo Emerson, who said, 'No man can sincerely try to help another without helping himself' – emphasizing 'sincerely'. 'Motivation matters. If people were being helpful for their own interests, that would be unsustainable, but what happens is that when people get involved in helping others, they discover a new self – it is transforming.'

I wonder how a scientist becomes so interested in the idea of doing good to one's fellow man, and Post describes a long personal interest in moral philosophy and comparative religions. But he argues that science adds another dimension to the conversation about goodness. 'Especially because there are real sceptics out there who have been raised on some very cynical, ungrounded assumptions about human nature.' He mentions Freud and Sartre. 'Science gives people some certainty about their own good nature if they need it, and some people really do need it.' I wonder whether I need reassurance about the basic decency of my fellow man, and decide I don't. I wonder whether my motivation to undertake a year of doing good is a response to cynicism – it's not. But I do like the fact science appears to indicate that good deeds are a good thing for the good-deed doer. Yes sirree, I do.

Wednesday, 16 February

Good deed no. 47: made the workmen fixing a leak along the road a nice cup of tea.

Picked up a packet of Lifeboat Tea this morning. I have bought Royal Air Force Tea before – loose tea from the Rare Tea Company described as 'tea for heroes' and 'calming in times of national peril, fortifying when courage is required', which is pretty hard to resist (particularly when 10 per cent of the £5 price goes to the RAF Association Wings Appeal).

Today I thought I would try a spot of ethical shopping with Lifeboat Tea – 7p (out of the £2.49 price) going to the RNLI for equipment and training. According to their website, 'by drinking Lifeboat Tea you too can save lives'. The tea was apparently created after the Fastnet race of 1979 when freak weather conditions blew up during the offshore yachting race, 15 people died and 140 had to be rescued by lifeboats, military and commercial vessels, aircraft and helicopters; and it has since raised £100,000 for the charity's funds. On the front of the packet is a picture of lifeboat men in an inflatable boat riding choppy waves and on the back a picture of a chap called Mark Criddle, RNLI coxswain at Torbay Lifeboat Station in Devon, telling how he received a silver medal for gallantry in 2008 for rescuing the crew of a merchant ship listing and powerless in force 9 winds and rough seas. The packet says, 'It took Mark and his volunteer crew over 50 attempts to bring the eight men across to the lifeboat.' He did his bit and I did mine; I drank a cup of tea and didn't drown in it.

Good deed no. 48.

Have finally got Karl's draft CV and told him I need more details because it is so thin, and I need something more to work with. Academically, the lad appears to have three C-grade passes at GCSE and a City and Guilds, Level 2. I don't even know whether to put D, E and F grades in. Heart sinks.

Good deed no. 49: liaised with Karl's family over a date for the work experience and chivvied him up on his CV.

Saturday, 19 February

Good deed no. 50: bought pork pies and quiches for a pooled supper and attended fund-raising Valentine Family Disco in aid of the kids' first school and village hall.

Sunday, 20 February

Caught train to London for half-term week. Al is working all week, but at least this way we see him for breakfasts. We are staying in the house of friends who are away on holiday.

Good deed no. 51: donated £10 to my JustGiving charity page for the local hospice (including Gift Aid, I now have a grand total of £25.54. This might take a while).

Monday, 21 February

Before Al disappeared off to work this morning, we took the kids to breakfast at Carluccio's in Canary Wharf. The children were as good as gold, but even so the sharp-jawed guys in sharp dark suits at the table next to us moved away to better talk about markets and yen, which I tried not to take personally. We ordered pains au chocolat for everybody, cappuccinos for us and hot chocolates for the children, which they plunged headlong into in a race to see who could rot their teeth first.

'Do you realize my good deeds probably mean I'll live for ever?' I said to Al.

He looked at me, then down at my plate. 'Are you trying to make yourself feel better about that pain au chocolat? Because I'll eat it for you if you want.'

I adopted a pious expression. I have been reading books. I have been reading scientific papers. This means I know things. 'Research has proved that good deeds add years to your life.'

My husband glanced at the clock on the wall as if he thought he might catch it in the very act of measuring his brief span and measuring it briefer yet. 'I don't see how good deeds could make you live longer,' he said, and sat back in his chair, 'maybe it just feels that way.'

Because I know I am right – that good deeds will indeed lengthen my mortal coil – I ignore him, wave at the waiter and order another basket of bread with an extra pain au chocolat.

When I got home again, I looked it up. In an article published in the *Journal of Health Psychology*, Doug Oman, currently an associate adjunct professor of public health in the School of Public Health in the University of California at Berkeley, found as long ago as 1999 that older people who volunteer for two or more organizations have a 44 per cent lower mortality rate – compared with a 30 per cent reduction in mortality associated with exercising four times a week. According to Oman, volunteering 'has the potential to add not only quality but also length to the lives of older individuals worldwide'. Hey, hey, hey – moving my arms around my body in a victory dance. Ah'm going to live for ever.

Good deed no. 52: bought a £2 raffle ticket (the prize a mini break) for Macmillan Cancer at Canary Wharf.

Tuesday, 22 February

Good deed no. 53: liaised between Iain Dale and Karl and his mother re dates on work experience.

Wednesday, 23 February

Good deed no. 54: mentored a media student who is worried about essay writing and study skills, offering to put her in touch with study skills expert. (I have a Dickensian connection to this kid. My natural father died of lung cancer when I was a baby. This first father had a half-sister. This kid is the half-sister's great-granddaughter. As it happens, I went to grammar school with her mother. At fifteen, the mother dropped out with a teenage pregnancy. Thirty years later she makes contact about the daughter. Such is life.)

Thursday, 24 February

Good deed no. 55: donated £1 at the till of an organic shop to Whole Planet Foundation, which provides micro-credit loans to impoverished women.

Friday, 25 February

One of the reasons we came down to London this week was my friend's fiftieth birthday dinner. We ate Beef Wellington, and Orange Bavarois – which is like eating air made of citrus and cream – and we all seemed very grown-up sitting around a dinner table discussing what proportion of income you should give to charity if indeed you have any money to give.

My grand total so far this year is £25, which is ridiculous compared to one of the guys at the dinner who gives 'around the three and a half per cent mark'. According to the *Sunday Times* Giving List, which runs alongside the Rich List, to make it into the ranks of the UK's top thirty philanthropists (ranked on the proportion of wealth they give away), you would indeed have to donate at least 3.2 per cent of your wealth to make the cut. You would have to go some to beat the top giver in 2010, though: Chris Cooper-Hohn, a hedge fund manager who has ploughed over £1.1bn into a charitable foundation.

It surprises me how the expectation or obligation on us to give can cut across cultures: rich men's foundations; collecting tins by tills; and the ancient Jewish core tradition of tzedakah – a religious obligation to perform charity (regardless of your own financial standing) and which a twelfth-century scholar Maimonides fleshed out and categorized, from the least honourable when donations are given in a spirit of resentment, to the most honourable when someone gives an interest-free loan to a person in need, forms a partnership with him, or gives him a grant or job so that the person no longer has to rely on others. But why do we give at all? What makes us want to share that which is ours with others? *Toward a Meaningful Life*, a book by Rabbi Simon Jacobson based on the teachings of the Rebbe Menachem Mendel Schneerson (the world-famous Jewish spiritual leader), reminds us that the key to understanding charity is appreciating that it is a gift not just to the receiver, but to the giver as well: 'The need to be charitable is one of the most fundamental human needs; just as we need food and protection and love, we need to share what has been given to us.'

Good deed no. 56: made a £1 donation to the Dream Team bucket lady in M&S. (Dream Team grants the dreams and wishes of sick, disabled and terminally ill children.)

Saturday, 26 February

We took the children along to see *The Wizard of Oz* at the Palladium. My daughter sat on the edge of my knee gazing up at the technicolour stage as if she had never seen anything so true and wonderful in her entire life. Even the middle-aged chap sitting next to us turned to me in the interval and commented how absorbed she was, and when Dorothy threw the bucket of water over the Wicked Witch of the West and melted her, my munchkin girl lifted up her arms and cheered. The show even had a message for me in it. Having been revealed as a fraud, the Wizard of Oz is rewarding the friends as best he might, and to the Tin Man he says: 'Back where I come from, there are men who do nothing all day but good deeds. They are called phil . . . er . . . phil . . . er . . . [trying to say 'philanthropists'] yes . . . er . . . good-deed doers.' He tells the Tin Man that their hearts are no bigger than his, but they have one thing the Tin Man doesn't – a testimonial. So 'in consideration of your kindness', he announces, 'I take pleasure at this time in presenting you with a small token of our esteem and affection. And remember, my sentimental friend, that a heart is not judged by how much you love, but by how much you are loved by others.' And he gives him a clock. Perhaps after my year of good deeds, I could have a clock too.

Good deed no. 57: gave £1 to a bucket collector for an Indian charity.

Sunday, 27 February

Travelling is difficult in terms of good deeds, unless you are driving, when I suppose you could keep letting other cars in ahead of you, although I imagine eventually that would lead to road rage and you would have to kill someone.

We stopped at Peterborough services for lunch and I positively leaped on a man with yet another bucket collecting for the Ronald McDonald house charities and gave him £1. (The charities support families with children in hospitals.) 'Mazel tov,' I said. He looked pleased but slightly taken aback at my keenness to donate, and rewarded me with a plastic-wrapped air freshener in the shape of a small swinging house. The air freshener was health and safety gone mad. The size of a folded-up tissue, it had a total of eighteen instructions and warnings written on the back. Who knew air fresheners could be so dangerous? My personal favourites were 'Hang freely so that product does not interfere with or obscure the driver's clear view of the road or control of the vehicle' and 'If swallowed seek medical attention immediately'.

I was tempted to swallow it round about the time the Saab's big end went and the engine ground to a complete bloody halt. My big end went years ago and I am just about reconciled to that, providing I never look at my rear view in a full-length mirror, but I was not reconciled to the Saab deteriorating in the same way, even if it has done 156,000 miles.

We had to wait the best part of an hour and a half to be 'recovered'; the car was then attached to a tow-truck and we spent three and a quarter hours in the back of the van banging along before we arrived in Northumberland at around 9.45 p.m. The only good thing about the experience was our rescuer, who was a Sikh called Dave. As soon as I clambered out of the darkness by the side of the road and up into the truck, I asked him whether he would like to overnight with us, bearing in mind the time he would otherwise get home, and he looked touched but said he would take a break and he would be fine. Courtesy of Dave (or Hardave), I now know more about Sikhism than I had thought possible, including the fact Sikhs wear the five ks: kesh (uncut hair), a kangha (a small comb), a kara (a steel or iron bangle around their wrist), kachha (cotton breeches) and a kirpan (a sword worn in a sheath). I know so much, I am virtually a Sikh myself. Then of course there is the turban. Long hair is combed, tied in a topknot then covered, which acts as a sign of disciplined holiness, as does the comb worn under the turban; the bangle is a reminder of infinity and God; the breeches represent sexual restraint; while the sword represents the call to uphold justice and protect the weak. Dave's dad used to starch his turban for him when he was younger, so that once the starched cloth had been wrapped around his head and the ends tucked in, it effectively 'set' and Dave could lift it on and off more easily. Now he's a grown-up, he told me proudly he can do it himself in a couple of minutes. Unfortunately, Dave wasn't wearing his turban in the van, only a woolly hat.

It is strange, though, how I keep running into the idea of good deeds being important in life: Dave volunteered the information that concern for others is central to Sikhism and that Sikhs believe good deeds are integral to a good life. Not that Dave made it easy to do him a good turn – he wouldn't even let me give him supper or a cup of tea when we got home. But as the rear lights of his tow-truck disappeared back into the darkness, I thought how he was indeed living a good life: finding the lost, rescuing the needy, bringing them home. Do those who believe in the critical importance of doing good for their fellow man carry that belief through to the choice of their job? I find that uplifting, that those in jobs that heal us or teach us or rescue us aren't just taking the pay cheque at the end of the month, but that every day they walk the walk with or without a turban and a sword at their side.

Good deed no. 58.

Monday, 28 February

Everywhere I look there are good deeds in faith systems. Not just in Christianity, not just in Sikhism, but in Buddhism, Islam and in Judaism. In Judaism, strictly speaking, a 'mitzvah' is a commandment and there are 613 mitzvot set out in the Torah (the first five books of the Hebrew Bible) – some of which are positive and some of which are negative. Loosely, however, a mitzvah is also a good deed. A deed which might be charity to the poor, or inviting a hungry person to your home, going to a funeral or visiting the sick. My mitzvah of today is that I have checked on my neighbour's leaking toilet, mopped it out, and I'm about to ring her to tell her she needs a plumber. Maybe I am not a Sikh, maybe I'm a Jew. In any event, someone should tell these religions what they have in common: it would save us all a lot of trouble.

Sikhism is not only big on good deeds, it is also big on karma. I know about karma not least because according to SikhiWiki (a Sikh version of Wikipedia), 'One's actions in this life will have a direct influence on the type of life now and in your next existence.' Surely then, after sixty-odd good deeds (and that is sixty-odd mitzvot if G–d turns out to be Jewish, and if I do too), I could catch a bleeding break, because what do I do this afternoon when picking up the children from school in the Ratmobile? Drive over an old 'Flood' road sign bent and hidden in the rutted mud as I do a U-turn in the entrance of a field. I tried hard to pretend it wasn't happening, but there was a distinct dragging and a scraping of metal as I edged back up the country lane to the school. When I clambered out of the car, I could see the bumper and two-thirds of rear moulding hanging off the back. I am not impressed by karma.

Good deed no. 59.

Tuesday, 1 March

Good deed no. 60: arranged for my Leeds University friend to advise the media student on study skills, ringing the student and giving her the academic's number and instructions to call.

THE EVOLUTIONARY PSYCHOLOGIST

So why does anyone do a good deed? Because it's not just me out here. Admittedly, we are under pressure from our culture and from religious conviction. Scientific research indicates health and happiness benefits may be triggered by helping others, too. But the plot thickens, because there may also be an evolutionary pressure on us to do good. Evolution can be looked at in terms of genes, individuals and groups, and for many biologists, doing good for others is about successful reproduction, and not so much about the glow of satisfaction we might get from having done the right thing. In *The Selfish Gene*, Richard Dawkins argues there is a pay-off at the level of the gene for apparently altruistic behaviour. In other words, an act of self-sacrifice by one organism is worth it if the benefit is greater to the other organisms carrying the same gene (dying to save ten close relatives would do it). Kinship, then, explains a lot – as can reciprocity, where you can expect a favour in your turn, and there is plenty of evidence of such animal altruism – not just the vampire bats but among birds and monkeys and social insects. Of course, I am more interested in my fellow man than any ant, and humans behave altruistically to their kin and to those who help them, but I already know they do more. Why?

Robin Dunbar, professor of evolutionary psychology at Oxford University, says altruism is one element in something academics refer to as 'prosociality', or cooperative behaviour and attitudes – the idea of behaving generously towards other people at some cost to yourself, which enhances the cohesion of social groups. And the argument is that this generous behaviour has evolved – sound of drum roll – because of the benefit there is to humankind in the maintenance of that social cohesion. As Dunbar said, 'It might be one of the reasons primates are such a successful group of animals in evolutionary terms. It has given us an evolutionary edge.' In order to survive predators, to survive at all, to successfully reproduce, we work best together.

It is interesting to think an evolutionary compulsion to do good might run through humankind so that humankind itself benefits. I tell Dunbar that from my experience, leaving the species to one side for a minute, there regularly appears to be an immediate return to the good-deed doer herself – the 'helper's high', a sense of satisfaction, the feeling that one is necessary, or simply being thanked. He mentions oxytocin, a neurohormone which makes you more trusting of others and more generous towards them. 'If everybody behaved selfishly, we wouldn't be able to maintain the kind of societies that humans do, and that would have had a major impact on our evolutionary history. In order to have those kinds of societies, people have to behave courteously and in the interests of the other person. For that to happen, you have to have motivations which pat you on the back. There has to be reward or you wouldn't do it.' So the rewards too may all be part of some evolutionary pattern. Theoretically then, we are wired (and culturally encouraged) to feel satisfaction when we do good which persuades us to do good again, and we are wired (and culturally encouraged) to express gratitude when good is done to us thereby persuading the good-deed doer to do it all over again. Clever, huh?

Not everybody does do it of course, Dunbar warns. There are 'free-riders' who benefit from others being willing to sacrifice their own interests – benefiting twice over by not having to make a sacrifice themselves while at the same time profiting from the sacrifice of others. And their return can be enormous, but with too many free-riders, society collapses. I don't want to be a free-rider. I prefer the idea that with my twopenn'orth of good deeds, I might help the whole of humanity slog on a while longer, maintaining the social contract, successfully propagating mine and others' genes, doing what needs to be done.

Wednesday, 2 March

When I remember all the times my children have embarrassed me, farting in crowded cafés, or the time one of them banged his head on the pavement repeatedly because I wouldn't let him buy a bag of crisps, I blush scarlet. Then there is today, when I sent my daughter to school in a baggy pair of her brother's stripy grey Y-fronts, complete with a little hole for a boy's willy to peep through while he piddles. I had no choice – behind my back she had outgrown all of her pants, and every time I tried to put her into a pair she squeaked, 'Too tight, Mummy' in protest. She did complain that the elastic on the Y-fronts was loose and they were falling down, but I bundled her into stripy woolly tights, assuring her the tights would hold the Y-fronts up. In my defence, I don't make a habit of putting her in boy-knickers. Just today. I knew she didn't have gym, so I figured it was safe enough. I had forgotten ballet.

Lily took her to ballet along with Ellie, which meant Lily had to supervise changing them. Just in case she was considering tactfully not noticing the boy-knickers, my daughter pointed them out with a helpful 'Look what Mummy made me wear', which would be why when Lily brought her home, she handed me ten pairs of brand-new girly knick-knacks in pastel shades with sparkly hearts in plastic envelopes with poppers. According to my daughter, the Y-fronts fell down '577 times, Mummy' at school. Lily slipped out to a supermarket during the ballet class to buy the little-girl pants. 'It's swimming tomorrow,' Lily reminded me, patently thinking I would have sent my daughter back out tomorrow in another pair – or possibly the same pair – of her brother's pants, leaving her open to public ridicule in the changing room. I really wasn't. Bloody-do-bloody-gooders.

Good deed no. 61: gave someone who was lost the directions to a neighbour's house.

Thursday, 3 March

Breathtakingly good idea when I was driving back from M&S in Berwick, having gone shopping for a nice tea for the children: encouraging people to give to charity in their own homes by installing their own little charity bucket, that is to say an empty jam jar that they fill with loose change. We can campaign under the banners 'Join the Jam Jar Army' and 'Ditch the Change' or 'Let's Change' or 'A Jam Jar for Change'. If you collect more than £3 you could be a Blackberry in the Army, over £5 a Strawberry, over £7.50 a Raspberry, and over £10 you could be Lemon Curd (although, personally speaking, I find lemon curd sickly). The first collection would be for the hospice, but perhaps I could roll it out nationally and, if you keep collecting, maybe after ten jam jars you could be a 'Star in the Jam Jar Army' and you could get a real pot of jam with a gold star on top. There is a chance I am on to something, although I admit there is also a chance I am losing the plot.

Good deed no. 62: took Lily's children after school while she worked.

Friday, 4 March

I want my money back on the alleged health benefits of good deeds. I had to go down to Newcastle for a meeting with a consultant about what to do regarding the migraines. The hospital is only small but I still managed to get lost, so I stopped by a desk and opened my mouth to ask directions, and the woman behind it said to me, 'Cosmetic?' Seriously? On my way in, I had passed a poster for their cosmetic surgery and weight loss centre. I resisted saying, 'Do I look like I need cosmetic surgery?' on the basis she might have said, 'You certainly do. Next turning on the left, madam.'

She wasn't to know that the last time I met with the consultant he mentioned Botox as a treatment option. At the time, part of me thought, 'You have to be kidding,' while the rest of me panted, 'When? When?' I went off the idea big time today as he talked me through what it involved when you have it for migraine. Injections in the forehead – fair dos; but you also have injections around the skull, down the neck and in the shoulders – eeeeeeurgh. Plus it is around five times the dosage you have for a cosmetic procedure. Plus he had only done it three times before because it has only just been licensed. 'I'm happy with the pills,' I said.

My chance to do my good deed came at the multi-storey car park. A bunch of glossy, sweet-smelling Geordie girlies were stalled in front of the ticket machine. They were probably in their late teens (unless they were Botoxed of course, in which case they were in their fifties and I just made a big mistake). The machine wouldn't take the driver's ten-pound note and they only had three pounds in change when they needed five. They stood there chirruping at each other about what to do and how this shouldn't happen, in the way you do when you are young and puzzled that life isn't turning out the way it should. So I gave them £2. They thanked me very politely, and as they moved off through the swing doors and into the car park they were still chirruping about what a nice woman I was. By rights, I should have left these foolish virgins standing, advising them to be better prepared for what might come their way, to think laterally, seize the initiative and go get some change, which would have been an infinitely more valuable life lesson for them all. Now they will turn out to be passive believers who think things will turn out dandy if you wear enough mascara and keep hoping for the best.

Good deed no. 63.

Diane has two degrees: one from Newcastle University and one from Cambridge. I once said to her, 'If I had to use just one word to describe you, I'd say "intelligent". What word would you use for me?' and she said, 'Quirky.' Quirky? Not clever, not funny, not good in bed – admittedly she wouldn't know the last one, but she might hazard a guess. I'm not even sure you can build a friendship on quirk. I am pretty sure quirk is like quicksand – you think you are OK right up to the moment it slurps you down and smothers you; maybe, being quirky, it would tell you a joke before you died. My favourite joke of the moment:

What did Batman say to Robin before they got in the Batmobile?

'Get in the Batmobile, Robin.'

Diane is very organized, highly mathematical, pathologically sociable and a United Reform Church Elder. She is also a card-carrying Conservative, recently telling me, 'Obviously I don't believe in anything you believe in, but I do believe you have a right to your beliefs' – pause – 'however ridiculous they are.' In her spare moments she judges dressage and is my polar opposite, because I don't believe anyone has the right to be a Tory.

I officially launched the Jam Jar Army at her farmhouse tonight, sitting in her immaculate kitchen at a ridiculously long table in front of her immaculate Aga. How does she manage to cook for a dinner party and not have a pan dirty on the side when the remains of yesterday's breakfast are still sitting on mine? Over pheasant stew and green peas, I pitched my idea to the guy sitting next to me and Diane.

'I take it this is one of your good deeds?' Diane asked, and I could see her mentally filing the Jam Jar Army under 'Fresh evidence of quirk'. They may think me bonkers, but they are my friends and I have my first recruits. Huzzah. Neither of them would even take the jam jar I had brought along, which had seventy pence in it, to start them off. Perhaps recycling is the way to go. That way I wouldn't have to collect thousands of jam jars, plus it is environmentally friendly. I could get some graphics worked out and then recruits could print out a label for their own jam jar. Diane was looking at me expectantly. I shook my head, and inside it, thousands of glass jars rolled about clinking and empty. A china bowl of Eton mess sat in front of me that I hadn't noticed arrive, the cracked meringue white and glacial, the whipped cream a luscious yellow, berries syrupy-black in the candlelight.

'I was asking how you're deciding which good deed to do. I love helping people, but I wouldn't go out of my way to do a good deed a day just because I felt I should.'

'Why would you do it then?' I asked, spooning up a dizzying pile of meringue shards and fresh cream.

'It would always be because I was interested in the person and in their situation,' Diane answered me, as if such reasoning were self-evident, and I made a mental note written in ink the colour of hope that Diane would find me 'interesting' enough to help me out in the event of acute and urgent need. Perhaps I could still be dull (though quirky) but my problem a particularly interesting one. Would that qualify?

'Some people,' she went on, 'like my friend who lost her husband, and my friend who was badly hurt when she fell from her horse, get first call on my time because I feel there's a need. I know there are others where there's need but it is less need, so I don't bother, not least because they have their own support network around them.'

Somehow it does not surprise me that Diane is as systematic about the good she does as she is about every other element of her life, that she assesses need, and factors in relationship and duty. She probably has an equation for it somewhere.

Do we all prioritize the good we do? We will do good for strangers, give to feed a hungry child we will never see, or a homeless man in need of a hot meal. But if those closer to our own back door need help, will we still do good for strangers regardless? Or is it indeed more sensible to do good to those in our own circles, our own communities, first? We have only so much time, only so much patience, after all; then again, there are those who stand outside any circle, outside any community. Idly, I envisage a points system the next time someone comes knocking at my door:

Bereaved: 10 points
Life-threatening illness: 10 points
Poorly: 8 points
Bit of a sniffle: nul points
Disadvantaged by circumstance: 6 points
Lonely: 4 points
Lonely because of unsavoury personal habits: nul points
Nothing wrong at all but would benefit from a kind word:
    1 point

I am not convinced I am capable of such fine discrimination. I consider how close I have come in the last couple of months to giving up, how inadequate I feel offering consolation to the grieving, how little difference I am making in the scheme of things, how hard I am finding it. The last thing I need is a decision-making process to tell me who would best benefit from my good deeds – not least because the answer might be no one.

Good deed no. 64.

Sunday, 6 March

We have had a weekend dominated by religion as my eight-year-old studied for his first confession, or reconciliation as they call it now. (It is of course vital to be forgiven for all those terrible childhood sins before the First Communion.) I wonder why there is this emphasis on which rules you have broken. So, from the very start, you admit your humility, acknowledge the rightful order of things and are forgiven? Shouldn't there be just that one rule 'Love thy neighbour . . .'? The church is vast and Victorian and there was a lot of parental bottom shuffling along the hard wooden pews and yawning behind our irreverent hands as we all waited for the children to go up to the altar in turn to sit with the priest. A few of the parents went up as well – including me. I haven't confessed a sin for years, so I took the opportunity while it was there. Thank God you don't have to run through them out loud these days.

At a certain point, the priest addressed us from the steps of the altar, advising the parents that we shouldn't ever lose patience with our children. Never to do it. The priest is telling us this. The very nice, very childless, no-clue-what-it-is-like-at-all priest. Occasionally, he mentions nieces and nephews over in Ireland, but fundamentally – no idea at all. And I thought, 'Right you are, Father. Never again. As you say. Good man.'

Good deed no. 65: let a granny in ahead of me for confession.

Monday, 7 March

Good deed no. 66: looked after another child so his mum and dad could work.

Tuesday, 8 March

Good deed no. 67: emailed an old friend who works on local TV to see if she can help get Karl in.

Wednesday, 9 March

They must have been talking about Lent at school, because the children announced over plates of steaming pancakes covered in syrup and lemon juice that they are giving up chocolate and crisps. Al promptly came over all freakishly pious and said he would give up crisps and chips. Suddenly the whole family was looking at me as I stood at the stove with my spatula in one hand and a frying pan in the other, my own pancake shrivelling and blackening in horror, when my eldest pronounced that 'Mummy had better give up coffee.' Taken aback, I couldn't immediately think of a reason not to – particularly as I'm supposed to be giving it up anyway to help with the migraine – so I've given up coffee for Lent. Reluctantly.

Good deed no. 68: washed my neighbour's bath mat, which she had left out on the line when she last came up.

Thursday, 10 March

Had my first coffee of Lent – I never did like giving up a good thing. Surely the good deeds should be enough to take me through Lent. Why should Lent be about the negative and not the positive? Though frankly, being good all the time is proving bloody irritating, or perhaps that's the caffeine speaking.

Al went back to London and the expat asked for a lift from the garage because he had taken his car in to be looked at. I had planned on going straight from school to Berwick to get food for tea and hopefully to see a girlfriend for a coffee, which I had to cancel. While we were in the car, he asked if he could borrow the car for the day because he needed to do some shopping and pick up his wife from her job, and of course he would pick up the kids from school and could I do without it? I agreed through gritted teeth, because it was a perfectly reasonable request and it was ridiculous to say I wanted the option of climbing in my car and going down to the village Co-op to buy tea and I'd needed to go to the bank, and I'd already changed my plans for the morning. Grrrr. He would without hesitation do the same for us, indeed he took the boys to football last night, but I am surfeiting on the requirement to be good rather than my normal mean selfish self. Enough already.

Good deed no. 69.

Friday, 11 March

Good deed no. 70: took the expat man back to the garage to pick up the car.

This afternoon was Lily's daughter's fifth birthday party in the local soft-play area. Lily had invited the entire school because she hates the idea of anyone feeling left out, so despite the fact I hate with a vengeance all children's birthday parties, even my own children's (perhaps especially my own children's), as my good deed I helped to stuff party bags with all sorts of Disney pencils and blue whale rubbers and fun-sized sweeties and keyring torches that work once and never again. I also mopped down some child who'd banged her head on the slide. She was all hot and sweaty in a gingham flannel blouse with big glassy tears running down her flushed cheeks, so she sat on my knee and I poured blackcurrant juice into a pink plastic cup and wiped away the tears, and together we decided if she took off her vest she could perhaps manage one more go on the slide. What solitary thing in this entire world is more useful than comforting a child?

Good deed no. 71.

Sunday, 13 March

Good deed no. 72: rang my friend Kirsty, who had a knee replaced this week, to check on her recovery.

Monday, 14 March

Have bought up the domain names for the Jam Jar Army because if you do not have a domain name, you do not exist. They cost over £100 – trying to get this charity initiative off the ground is actually costing me money. I'd have been better writing a cheque for £100 and giving it to charity – it would certainly be less bother.

Good deed no. 73: email exchange with an old friend as I continue trying to get Karl work experience with the local Beeb (she's warning it doesn't look good).

Tuesday, 15 March

More than twenty years ago, Kirsty and I were journalists together on the North-East morning paper the *Journal*. Briefly she and Al were flatmates, and she is godmother to my eldest boy. She has to be one of the bravest people I know. Although she is only in her mid-forties, she has lupus, which in her case means she needs to walk with a stick and has already had one hip replacement, she is due another, and last week she had her knee replaced. We drove up to see her in Edinburgh, though I resisted looking at the scar and the staples up and down her leg on the grounds of acute squeamishness. I have never heard her complain about anything, about any operation or medication or crimp to life. Indeed, she smiles more than most and laughs easily. If that was me, if I had suffered like she suffers, if they stood close enough, I'd hit people with my stick.

Good deed no. 74.

Wednesday, 16 March

I checked my emails only late last night because of the trip to visit Kirsty in Edinburgh, and when I did, I found one from Karl telling me he didn't think he could go down to London for next week's work experience with LBC after all because of 'his work'. (At least he didn't say 'career', because this is a part-time gig in the fish and chippie, which hasn't opened for the season yet.) I had that urge I keep getting, to beat my own head against my desk repeatedly. Instead, I drew a few deep breaths and rang him to explain that no, he couldn't put it off for a month till it was more convenient, it was now or never, and that the lads who owned the chip shop would understand, and had he changed his mind about wanting a job in radio? (No, he hadn't.) Then I talked to his mam, and she said they would come up this afternoon.

When they arrived, his mam said Karl had got very nervous

about the work experience and was shy. There was a man at my kitchen table – tall and blond and powerfully built – who could push down a tree, wrestle a bear, join the Army. But his mother sees a boy who isn't ready to eat up the world with a wooden spoon just yet. I speak softly. I say, 'It'll be fine' – because it will be fine. Together, we draw up another list for him of how to behave at the radio station and we practise shaking hands – my hand tiny in his – and I tell him to smile and buy kippers and bring them down to London as gifts. We also talk about whether he could go to college, and the need to write letters to the local stations, and to take advice from all and sundry in the business and work for free. I have no idea how to get him a start in radio.

Good deed no. 75.

Thursday, 17 March

Around seven o'clock in the evening, my eldest announced he had a cake sale on for Comic Relief and needed cakes or biscuits and they 'had to be made and not bought'. Where is that commandment written down? How are they even smart enough to realize that particular short cut is available, moreover that the likelihood is we are taking it? I resisted telling the kitchen dictator from the 1950s that more notice might have been good; instead, I started rooting around the fridge for ingredients. The eggs were only three days out of date and didn't smell, and there was just about enough butter to do the job if I wasn't too bothered by accurate measurements, so as my good deed I managed thirteen completely flat lemon-flavoured buns and a packet of chocolate chip cookies; and despite the fact my eldest isn't keen on lemon cake and the cookies broke the rules, he had the good grace to tell me the thirteenth taster bun was yummy, so I didn't mind too much.

Good deed no. 76.

Comic Relief makes it remarkably easy to do a good deed. All I had to do was go along to school for the children's talent show and keep sticking my hand in my pocket. It was worth it: my little girl was ridiculously cute dressed as a ladybird in a frothy red and black-spotted tulle skirt and red and black silk wings, clutching a microphone and telling jokes in a hushed and tiny voice, all of which she started with 'I say, I say, I say . . .' My favourite was:

I say, I say, I say, how do you make a sausage roll?
I don't know, how do you make a sausage roll?
Push it.

Although I'm counting going along to the talent show as my good deed, in reality my good deed was probably listening to the ladybird practise the joke thirty-seven times last night as she stood on the kitchen table. My daughter is frighteningly quick. The other day I lay with her before she went to sleep and she started sing-songing, 'You-love-me-the-best. You-love-me-the-best.' I am scrupulously fair in my dealings with the kids, and because they are so different that is easier than it might otherwise be, so I said, 'That's not how motherhood is, darling,' and she said, 'Well, that's how it is in childhood.' I am already dreading her adolescence.

Good deed no. 77.

My best friend from school, Sophie, invited me to go with her to a spa near where she lives in the Midlands. Sophie, who has cropped blonde hair, green cat's eyes and is generally horribly fit and trim, is still recovering from the Lyme disease she got paint-balling in Sweden. As part of her recovery, she has been coming here to use the gym. Lyme disease is horrible. No one could figure out what was wrong with her at first – not even the consultant who scanned her brain. I diagnosed it from googling her symptoms and comparing the bull's-eye rash on her arm (which came from a tick bite) with particularly gory images from the Net. I should have been a doctor.

My mother cherished her sisters in the way that I cherish my friends. At night when I can't sleep, sometimes I turn them over in my head, admiring their lustre, kindnesses, comforts, thinking on their confidences. The older I get, the more I believe true friendship is an orchid of rare beauty that grows in the darkest and most unlikely of places. We have no right to it, no claims on it; it does not bloom because we tell it to. Friendship is a flower we cannot own and scarcely deserve, but which we search for, lonely through the swamps, and when we discover it, pluck it and pin it to our grateful heart. Sophie and I have been friends for more than thirty years and I don't think we look any different from how we were at school, aside from the fact she played squash at university, chose not to ruin her body in childbirth, has a hard-muscled personal trainer, runs half-marathons and goes on walking holidays. Admittedly body-wise, that's all beginning to tell and it's not a story I like hearing.

Hoar Cross Hall is based in some red-brick Gothic pile, splattered with photographs of soap actresses. *Coronation Street*'s Janice Battersby has stayed here, and a pretty black girl who used to work in the street's knicker factory. There is a picture of Julie Goodyear, who was Bet the barmaid, and a particular favourite is Deirdre Barlow pictured with her husband, both in white towelling robes. I have felt an affinity with Deirdre Barlow ever since I was crossing the road and a white van man leaned out of his window and yelled 'Oy, Deirdre!', possibly because I was wearing glasses, but it might have been because he sensed I trailed a wake of grief, marital shenanigans and domestic chaos wherever I went.

Tragically, no one famous is here this weekend, although Sophie tugged at my sleeve at one point when Stephen Joynes, the owner of the spa, walked through the restaurant. He wrote a book, which he leaves in the bedrooms, about his journey from chip van to the owner of a stately-home-cum-spa. In it he advises, 'Justify the faith others have in you,' which should be a fridge magnet – I'd buy one. When we were here before, Sophie kept dragging me outside on yomps through the woodland, which entirely defeats the object of a spa in my opinion. Since she is not yet at full capacity, she reluctantly mooches into a lounge full of women in white towelling robes and shiny faces for peppermint tea.

'I'll help you with this Jam Jar Army thing,' she says, wrinkling her nose at the peppermint tea, and I almost inhale carrot cake and lemon frosting into my lungs in excitement.

I do not think I have ever done anything without Sophie supporting me. Supporting my Jam Jar Army effort is particularly good because she is a very successful businesswoman with her own car-cleaning products company (with sales of around £20m), while I cannot add up. I might very well need her if we have to persuade a bank to help us with the collecting and counting the jam jar money.

'You can handle presentations to the City,' I tell her. 'Are you willing to dress up as a talking strawberry?' and it is her turn to inhale lemon frosting.

Good deed no. 78: gave away my spa voucher for a glass of champagne when I really wanted it.

Sunday, 20 March

Sophie's favourite place in the spa was the gym; mine was a slumber room with massage chairs which knead you from your calves up to your skull. That's the theory. I went in and sat on one and they have little displays with arrows so you can raise and lower the footrest, and raise and lower the seat back. Bliss. Unfortunately, I don't think I can have been doing it right, because I turned it on, raised the legs, lowered the back, started the massage and it worked for ten seconds before the legs slowly lowered themselves back down, which made reaching for the display difficult. I just about managed, raised the legs again, lowered the back again and started the massaging. It was great for another ten seconds, before the legs went slooooooowly back down. Undeterred, because I am that kind of gal, I raised the seat back and raised the legs again and started the massage and down went the bloody legs. I was determined to relax even if it killed me, so I did this about half a dozen times in this completely quiet room before the other guests began staring. Eventually, I stood up and slunk out, trying hard to look as if I hadn't really wanted a massage anyway.

Later, Sophie told me she was prompted to do a good deed because of my resolution. She was travelling through Charles de Gaulle airport on business and noticed a Canadian woman panting with distress and on the point of tears. She said she would have walked by her normally in the way that British people do when confronted by emotion, but instead, she stopped and lent her a phone to ring the people who were meeting her, and then escorted her right through to the other end of the airport where her worried friends were waiting on yellow lines. The woman kissed her on the cheek and waved at her madly as they drove off.

Good deed no. 79: gave £1 to Marie Curie (I know – pathetic. I thought about dragging a homeless person off the streets and insisting they go to the spa instead of me – but I didn't think about it for long).

Monday, 21 March

Good deed no. 80: fed the hungry (palmed all-day breakfast sandwich off on a student. I am pretty sure he didn't want it, he just had very good manners).

Tuesday, 22 March

I want a bank willing to take in the jars of coins, count them and deposit them with the charity's account. I emailed Barclays back after they sent me a brush-off message which included the warning there would be a charge for counting the money if the hospice didn't already bank with them. I very politely highlighted the fact that most people think bankers are tossers (I didn't use the word 'tosser', I said banks and bankers were 'unfortunately at an all-time nadir re reputation') and perhaps they might like to be tied to a 'major charitable initiative'? If we had a bank involved, we could go national. We will see what they say.

I also contacted a jam manufacturer to ask them to put us on their labels – that way, people have a ready-made, labelled jam jar all ready to fill with money as soon as they eat their jam. Win-win for the jam manufacturer. They get to be a good guy, people eat their jam and the jar sits on their kitchen counter as a reminder to buy more jam. There is an outside chance the people on the other end of these missives think I'm mad.

Am I mad?

While I was watching Comic Relief, which made a grand total of more than £74m, I was thinking about the fact I was trying to do something similar but with an empty jam jar and even if I get 1,000 people to do it and they raise around £3 each in their jam jar, that is still only £3,000.

Good deed no. 81: lent £100 to a broke friend.

Wednesday, 23 March

Good deed no. 82: lent £20 to another mother who came out without her purse at the supermarket. I should set up my own bank and open a branch up a hill. They could call it Brokebank Mountain.

Thursday, 24 March

After I did the school drop-off, I met with Tom, a young graphic designer who has agreed to help with the Jam Jar Army. His graphic design company Chunky Orange is down a little alleyway off the main street in the local market town in rooms which have the feel of the upstairs offices of a bank. The windows were too high to see out of, but the office was light and spacious and the desks enormous. I was tempted to ask him if he'd ever shagged on his desk, it was so big, but bearing in mind I hadn't met him before and he might have got the wrong idea, I resisted. I have, however, dangled the prospect of heaven in front of him on the grounds that raising money for charity is the 'right thing to do', and he says he thinks it sounds like a wacky idea.

We were exactly like Mad Men only we had instant coffee instead of Martinis and Greggs raspberry jam doughnuts instead of more Martinis. Tom is a one-man band, apart from a junior and a chap he brings in occasionally to do PR stuff, so part of me feels bad asking him to do something for free. However, it is a creative project which would be interesting to work on – particularly if we put together a trailer. Tom is suggesting a little jam jar man with arms and legs (I definitely had money on the talking, walking strawberry). We played around with a few ideas and whittled it down to Geordie the jam jar being like a family pet, miserable if he's empty but perky, perky, perky if you fill him up with coins. I really need these graphics in place. That way, when I approach the banks and jam manufacturers, I'll come across as much less of an eccentric – or perhaps I will just come across as an eccentric with a website.

Good deed no. 83: took two fire logs into my neighbour Stephanie's house so she can light a fire as soon as she arrives with her aged mother.

Friday, 25 March

I have been writing about Bob Geldof for the *Sunday Times* Rich List, which has involved researching all the Band Aid and Live Aid stuff. Geldof saw reports about starving Africans on the BBC, and decided to use his fame and contacts to do something about it. So there's me and a jam jar and there is Bob Geldof and Live Aid. Perhaps I could persuade the jam jar to sing. He could put out a single at Christmas. Perhaps I could get Geldof to bring out a single with the jam jar.

This evening I started sewing my charity elephant. I picked up the pattern and the cut-out pieces of cloth yesterday after I popped into the hospice to discuss my jam jar brainwave. I met Angela, one of the fund-raisers there, and she didn't laugh at me, which is always good. She did, however, say the hospice sent out 1,000 little cardboard collection boxes last year and had a 2 per cent return. Two per cent – that is a return of twenty boxes. They aren't doing it again because it wasn't cost-effective. Angela was making me a cup of tea while she broke the news. Bearing in mind I was in a hospice, which is like being in a church, I refrained from shouting 'Bugger' very loudly. What happens if I get a 2 per cent return on the jam jars? If I got 1,000 out in the first phase a 2 per cent return with an average of £5 a jar would be £100.

While I was at the hospice, Angela gave me an elephant to sew. The material is cotton with a peachy-pink candy stripe down it and scattered wisteria. A volunteer called Susan Taylor along with forty other volunteers raised £2,000 with these toy elephants, all made with different scraps of cloth and put up for 'adoption' when finished. You are supposed to do a master class in elephant sewing, but I thought, 'I don't need a course to make an elephant. I can sew an elephant no problemo.' Except I put it together tonight and when I'd finished my eight-year-old son casually remarked, 'You've sewed it inside out, Mummy' and I had. Which might be why my husband offered me a paltry £5 for it, despite the fact it took me hours. Hours of my life I won't get back.

Good deed no. 84.

Saturday, 26 March

This morning, I did my most self-righteous good deed to date: I rang the police. I was taking my little girl to dancing first thing when a woman flagged me down so I didn't hit a little red car which was reversing out of a stone wall, or what used to be a stone wall. I parked, leaving my daughter in the back, and walked up.

There were two women huddled together by their car, which was parked up on the other side of the road, as a stunned-looking man walked round the red car and peeled all the lower half of it away. The younger woman said to me in hushed tones that the bloke had been hanging upside down in the car when they'd come across the accident. At this point, the bloke gets back into the car and acts as if he is going to drive away, no harm, no foul – give or take a wrecked car and an enormous hole in somebody else's wall.

The driver's door was entirely caved in and there was no glass left in it. I bent down to talk to him and said in my most reasonable, caring and considerate voice that I didn't think he was in any fit state to drive away. He didn't speak, he just shook his head. I said I thought he was in shock and suggested he get out of the car and have a cup of sweet tea in a nearby cottage, but he shook his head again. I asked him his name and there was a long pause while he tried to remember, then he said he would drive the car to the garage up the A1. I kid you not – I wasn't entirely sure the car wouldn't collapse like a Keystone Cops car if he started the engine. I told him that it wasn't a good idea for him to drive on the A1, but he said he knew a friend in the next village and he'd drive to him and then on to the garage the back way.

He wouldn't call the local mechanic to recover him and when I asked his friend's name, there was another long pause while he struggled to remember that too. He made as if to go again and I said I really didn't think it was a good idea because he was definitely in shock and what about other cars coming in the opposite direction? If he'd had a window in his car door, I suspect he would have wound it up at this point. As it was, he ignored me and drove off so I borrowed a mobile from another driver who'd stopped and rang the police.

Afterwards I wasn't sure if I'd done the right thing because I didn't want to get the driver into trouble, but I know people in that village too. He was in no condition to drive, his car certainly wasn't roadworthy, and what happens if you just let someone drive off and then they drive straight into another car full of children? Priggery? Active citizenry? It's a narrow line.

Good deed no. 85.

Good deed no. 86: stood back and let a customer go in front of us in a café, despite acute and desperate need for coffee.

Monday, 28 March

Barclays have sent another email re the Jam Jar Army telling me thanks but no thanks. The 'community adviser' told me she had 'referred your email to quite a number of people in the team and also the business'. She carried on: 'I am therefore unable to advise anything further. I do hope that you have success when contacting the charities direct as they may deal with this situation regularly and be able to offer advice through their own experiences. Good luck with all your fund-raising.' Yeah, right.

Good deed no. 87: arranged to have a child for tea when his mum is in hospital next week for an operation.

Tuesday, 29 March

The expat woman has flown back to South Africa for a couple of days to tie up a few loose ends, so I invited the expat man round for a dinner of steak and salad and French fries. I'm worried about him being lonely. This is the first time since I was a kid that I've had relatives living close by, and I feel a sense of responsibility. They would both shriek like shiny blue parakeets in a hot and tangled jungle if they heard me say it, because for thirty-five years they lived joyous, entirely independent, contained lives on the far side of the world, distant from any kith or kin but each other. It is true, though. It has been interesting watching the children's relationship with them develop. It strikes me that if you are willing to love a child, the child will love you back: the best sort of bargain.

Good deed no. 88.

Wednesday, 30 March

Good deed no. 89: lent expat man a bottle of milk.

Thursday, 31 March

Incredibly windy day – the noise through the leafless trees to the side of the cottage is like an aircraft landing. The banks that hem the hawthorn hedgerows are decked gold with daffodils and the fields are filling up with tiny skippety lambs, but it is so cold and so windy that it doesn't feel like spring at all.

En route home from school yesterday we passed a copse of sycamore and ash, and my eight-year-old son insisted on stopping to watch the ambling, gambolling lambs.

'They're incredibly cute when they're little and not cute at all when they grow up,' he mused.

I said: 'The same goes for people, kiddo.'

I do love it when the lambs arrive, but you have to distance yourself from the reality of their certain fate – mind you, that's also true of people. I was considering rustling a lamb as a good deed, but then it would grow up into a sheep and what do I do with a sheep? It's not like it would pay its way – not unless I pimped it out to those with strange tastes. I could perhaps send it to tap-dancing lessons with my daughter, film it and turn it into a YouTube sensation. Would it be a good deed anyway if I steal someone's lamb? Perhaps I could buy one and set it free in the wild. Are there sheep sanctuaries in the same way as there are donkey sanctuaries? Perhaps it is like those sci-fi movies you watch occasionally – somewhere beyond the pastureland there is rumoured to be a place of safety for sheep, where they can live without fear of the slaughterman, they just have to make a run for it when they reach a certain age.

Later, I googled sheep sanctuaries and sure enough there is an American one with pictures of sheep at sunset pootling through sun-dappled woodland. It even quotes Gandhi: 'To my mind, the life of a lamb is no less precious than that of a human being. I should be unwilling to take the life of a lamb for the sake of the human body.'

Still, I'd never get a lamb through customs.

Good deed no. 90: sent fantastic scriptwriting book called Save the Cat *to media student who half wants to be a scriptwriter.*

Friday, 1 April

There are many glorious things about living in Northumberland and one of them has to be the weekly newspaper, the *Northumberland Gazette*. Last week it started a campaign against dogs pooing everywhere with a lovely picture of a squishy poo. This week it has not one but two full-colour pictures of dog poo on the front page. Presumably there is some poor photographer out night and day looking for the fattest, chunkiest poos they can find. It's a good job the *Gazette* doesn't have scratch and sniff. The story also quotes some poor public-spirited citizen wandering the mean streets with plastic bags and rubber gloves picking up the bagged poo. Should I join her as a good deed? Let me think about that for thirty seconds . . . No.

Mother's Day service in church this evening. We parked up along the narrow lane with the car almost in the hedge and half walked, half ran through the lychgate and up the trodden-down earth path through the graveyard. We were late – we are always late for some reason to do with the fact we cannot ever be on time, so we had to sit at the back, which made it utterly impossible to hear a word any of the children were saying. The prayer of penitence was apposite – though downbeat. 'You call us to do good. We seek our own good. Christ have mercy.' I really don't want to end up getting religion big-time because of my goody two-shoes experiment. I've got just enough, like salt in cabbage water – if I can liken my life to cabbage water without wanting to kill myself.

My younger son had written a limerick and a poem. According to the limerick I'm a 'great mummy who laughs like a bunny', which is nice though not entirely flattering, while the poem has me as a 'love spreader, me hugger, great mum, house cleaner and children lover'. Not sure about the house cleaner bit either, but it will have impressed the other mothers. My little girl had painted a picture of me with enormous ears, eyes like a black furry spider and a down-turned mouth. One of the teachers said sweetly it looked just like me, and I scowled at her with my mean spider eyes and my down-turned mouth. I'd really like to put the picture up, but I look so damned miserable in it. Overleaf, my little girl had written:

My muymmy lucks reft me (My mummy looks after me)
anb my mummys cisis me (and my mummy kisses me)
Sigh.

Technically, I did two good deeds. I picked up litter again en route to the service when we were waiting at a level crossing – not dog poo, though, I have my standards. Some louts had picnicked, carefully bagged up their sandwich wrappers, tinnies and the like in a plastic bag, tidily knotted it and promptly lobbed it right by the crossing into a bush. If you are going to throw rubbish away in the countryside, why bag it first? Why not go the whole hog and scatter it merrily, whistling an Olde Englishe folk tune. The children are getting used to me screeching to a halt, climbing out of the car and picking up litter out of hedges. At least they didn't complain this time. A bigger good deed, though, was after the Mother's Day service.

We were rewarded for our attention with tea and an iced bis-cuit, and since we were at the back in prime position next to the steaming urn, my husband went off sharpish to get me a cup of tea and then handed it across to me over the oak pews. My husband is a very good hunter-gatherer. Despite the fact I was parched, I gave the tea to another mother. Over her head, my husband raised his eyebrow and shook his head as if to say, 'I got that for you, you dope.' I am not convinced he is all that keen on my good deeds. He thinks our life is complicated enough, what with my extended family, and insistence on friends and emotional connectedness, let alone the good deeds. Men like to keep things simple: 'I man. You woman. These children. We eat now. We sleep now. We do coochy-coochy now. Me just check on football score.'

Anyway, that cup of tea definitely rates as a good deed because I really didn't want to give it up. Plus it was in church so it should be double points. I only hope God was watching and it absolved me from the sin of sliding the iced biscuits the kids brought over for us into my handbag. It's bad enough having to eat your own children's iced biscuits, but my heart sinks when we're expected to eat biscuits iced, and I suspect licked, by other people's children.

Good deed no. 91.

Saturday, 2 April

My mother has managed to wreck her back again. She is eighty-two. Last July, she had a major back operation and had two shunts put in her spine to separate the vertebrae and help her with the pain. What does she do a few days ago? Move a television with my dad. A television. At eighty-two, this lady with macular degeneration who can't hear and has chronic rheumatoid arthritis, osteoarthritis and osteoporosis is shifting TVs around the garage. The sheer stupidity of it infuriates me. But you can't say that when they are eighty-two and come on the phone weeping, having done themselves a severe mischief; you have to say, 'Oh dear, oh dear,' when what you want to say is, 'Are you completely mental?' As a consequence of the removals escapade, she had to have an X-ray yesterday and we've all had to drive down to Yorkshire to see what state she's in and cheer her up.

Good deed no. 92.

Sunday, 3 April

Rang Karl to find out how his work experience went with LBC, having sent him an email trying to find out but to no avail. He was out, but his mam described him as blank with fear that morning as they walked through London to the radio station. When he came out for lunch, though, his face was lit up, and by the end Karl was buzzing with the day, told her it had been 'fantastic' and was full of the fact the guys there had toured him round, and talked to him, and put him in the newsroom for all the Global Radio stations that operate out of the building. Iain Dale had been on holiday but they had looked after him brilliantly even so. Karl's mam also said – and bearing in mind this is a lad who the week before had lost his nerve about going down at all – that later, walking down a busy Oxford Street, suddenly he was way ahead of her, unconcerned by the crowds, by the strange city, he had grown in confidence and was walking tall. This is what the old can do for the young: extend a hand in invitation, make a few minutes for a conversation, give them courage.

Good deed no. 93: wrote a press release for a local nursery after a brilliant Ofsted inspection report, despite getting home at 10.30 p.m. from a weekend visiting my sick mother and having to put three shattered, grumpy children to bed first.

Monday, 4 April

I was mulling over whether I have changed at all since starting my good-deedery, whether I'm generally more courteous, let people in front of me in queues, give more to charity; indeed, whether I am more thoughtful and an all-round better human bean. Then I had one of those days where I decided what I really needed was a sign to hang on the door that reads, 'Fuck Off – I'm busy'.

So far, today:

- The expat man rang three times – the first time at eight o'clock in the morning wanting to print something out because he hasn't got a printer installed yet. I said no.

Then:

- He turned up unexpectedly with the South African money he wants changing into sterling.

Then:

- He turned up again with his wife for a cup of coffee.
- A mate of mine turned up.
- The chap who used to cut our grass turned up at the back of the house.
- Then he turned up at the front of the house. (Occasionally he likes to come and potter round the place with a dog, but he informed me the dog he has been walking died. Usually I would have made him a cup of tea, but I couldn't this time because I was up to my neck with the expats.)

Also today:

- The son of a former elderly neighbour we used to live next to in London rang to tell us his mother had died. She had cancer and, it turned out, asbestos poisoning. Her husband worked in demolition and there's a chance she breathed in the dust when she washed his work clothes. She was a tiny little thing and so kind, I'd bring the children in to her and she'd always give them chocolate biscuits, which meant every time we passed her door the boys would drag me over to knock on it for their Kit Kat fix.

Later:

- I rang my mother to check on her.
- She rang me back to complain that some oik had pinched her big plant pot from the front of the house and left an empty tinnie in its place. While she was talking to me, she suddenly realized it would have fingerprints on it so she starts calling to my dad to go out to the bin and bring the tinnie back in and bag it up so they can give it to the police. She watches far too much *CSI*. She also wanted me to chase up her X-ray results, so:
- I rang the doctor for her.
- Then I rang the hospital, trying and failing to get her results.

As I'm walking out to get the kids from school:

- My Irish aunt whose husband has just died rang wanting a phone number from me, I had a brief talk to her but it wasn't long enough, so:
- I rang her back in the evening.

Finally:

- A friend rang whose pregnant daughter is sick in hospital with a suspected pulmonary embolism (which of course stirs up all the dead baby stuff for me).

Technically, I failed to let someone print something out, failed to give someone a cup of tea and failed to put my mother's mind at rest. Then again I did my share of listening. Is listening enough? Sometimes, it's all you've got.

Good deed no. 94.

Tuesday, 5 April

Is it still a good deed if you have no choice in the doing of it?

I had my good deed all set for today because the expat man wanted to borrow the car again while his is in for a service. Then I was at the Co-op and the lady was ringing my things through – a grand total of £83.64 – and she asked whether I had my 'divi card' and I didn't. Usually we run through a rigmarole of pretending I will put the points on my card at a future date. Really I just use the card as a passport in the local Co-op shops – 'I may not talk like you, but look, I have a dividend card.' Instead of getting to pretend this time, though, the assistant cut to the chase and called out to the queue of fellow shoppers, 'Anyone got their Co-op card?' and a grey-haired lady smacked hers up in the air and zip-zip-ta-ever-so she got my points and I never even got a say in it. Maybe I encountered the assistant at a particularly seize-the-day moment, because she told me she is sixty on Sunday. 'You wonder what you've done with your life,' she said mournfully. 'In your case, given away my divi points,' I felt like saying.

Good deed no. 95.

Wednesday, 6 April

Went round to Diane's for coffee, and I had hardly sat down when she started up about her little one refusing to use her bed at night, sleeping on the floor rather than using the bed. Diane is like me: she expects her children to do as they are told, and it is coming as a shock to her that autism doesn't play by the house rules. She looked tired and she never looks tired, never allows herself to look tired. The little one had gone into a blue funk last night and ended up curled up by the childproof gate they have at her bedroom door. An official diagnosis is a slow process, but Diane said the good news was that an educational psychologist is coming into school alongside a speech therapist – still, she was pale with violet shadows under those brown eyes.

The doctor rang about my mother's results. Courtesy of the osteoporosis, she has fractured a vertebra. At least that's their explanation for the pain. It was incredibly kind of her to ring. She explained that with osteoporosis, my mother might have fractured it sneezing – let alone moving a television. But she said it should mend within three months, and if not, they can inject bone cement in there. That has to hurt.

Good deed no. 96: swept out mouse traps for neighbours.

Thursday, 7 April

Originally I was going to count having a little boy over to tea while his mother was in hospital as my good deed; instead, I am counting the fact that I sent my own flowers to the school for another mother whose birthday I knew it was. Earlier this morning, I bumped into her and her friend at the supermarket. It was excellent timing. In one of those dinky trolleys, I had a bottle of what looked like champagne in it with the gold foil-wrapped cork (which made me look like I had fun), a couple of broadsheets (which made me look intelligent), rocket and steak (which made me look like I had money), a bottle of San Pellegrino sparkling water (which made me look like I had too much money) and some lush, fat and scented, mauve and shell-pink stocks (because I'm worth it). It was one of those shops you have never, ever done when you meet someone you know. Usually, when you meet someone and they glance into your impossibly full trolley, what they see is the basic range (because you're broke), toilet roll (you're human, for God's sake), sanitary towels and tampons (likewise), white bread, cheese and onion crisps and HP sauce (because that's your sandwich of the moment), lady razors (because you're hairy) and too much alcohol (because you need it).

Having finished admiring my trolley, she mentioned she was in town for her birthday. If I'd thought of it I would have given her the flowers then and there, but the idea didn't come to me till I got home. I am worried that the flowers won't last: her youngest son was going to bring them home on the school bus (which probably means she will end up with a fistful of warm and grubby blossom and a bunch of green fishbones. It still counts).

Good deed no. 97.

I was about to sit down and write a job reference for someone as my good deed when the chap who used to cut the grass for us appeared, having lost his dog. Technically, it's his sister-in-law's rather than his dog, and she has only had it two weeks. They got it from a dog shelter, and he was taking it for a walk when it slipped its leash and vamoosed. I strapped my youngest son into the car and we went out looking.

Every two minutes, my youngest son pointed at a tree and shouted 'Dog!' very loudly in my ear. We kept stopping and climbing out and peering over five-barred gates into the fields and along the hawthorn hedges, yelling 'Lola!' very loudly, thereby infuriating all the sheep, who bleated furiously at us. I got as excited as my son when some animal appeared out of a ditch and started loping along the road ahead of us, but it turned out to be a hare. We were looking for a Great Dane crossed with a Rhodesian Ridgeback, so admittedly thinking the hare was the dog was a bit of a stretch, but I'm not very good with animals. We had no luck whatsoever, but as we arrived back home, Lola's owner drew up at our house to thank us for our efforts, an enormous, smug, panting dog sitting upright on the back seat of her car.

'You were gone ages,' my husband said, putting his arm around me as Lola's car pulled away.

Tired suddenly, I leaned into him. 'Shaggy dog stories take time.'

'Shame you weren't the ones to find her, though,' he said, and squeezed my shoulder in consolation that my good deed wasn't as good as it might have been.

Lola gazed at us through the rear window of the retreating car.

'That dog is only slightly smaller than me,' I said. 'She might have eaten me.' I waved, but Lola didn't wave back.

Good deed no. 98.

Saturday, 9 April

Went across to Diane's farmhouse for dinner. It is without question my turn to return the favour, and I am so not doing it. I am doing good deeds, which is my get-out-of-jail-free card for dinner parties for the rest of the year.

Before we sat down at the table, we tripped out to the lambing sheds to feed the lambs who had been orphaned or who are triplets and do not get enough to eat. Hay bales wall the barn, and deep hay carpets the floor of the pens as the lambs bounce and bleat and mooch about together, the lucky ones with their mothers, the unlucky with their posse. A black-faced boy lamb called Titty kept knocking the feed bottle away from the less assertive lamb I was feeding, desperate to suckle at the rubberized tit in his slurping, burping eagerness for more warm milk. I have eaten a lot of lamb since I moved to Northumberland. Every now and then, I stop eating it. Usually after I have been over to Diane's lambing sheds and watched my daughter bottle-feed woolly, warm-nosed, skinny-ribbed orphans.

Thank God tonight we were having venison and beef casserole (the beef butchered from Diane's cows) with prunes. I have never felt guilty about eating a prune. Perhaps I would if I worked more with the elderly. I am, however, aware of the fact I am becoming obsessed by this good deeding. Shoot me, it is eating up my life. The doctors who had been there at New Year when I announced my resolution were round again, and conversation turned to people's motivations for the deeds they do.

'I singularly failed to give up coffee over Lent . . .' I admitted as Diane offered coffees round once we had finished our hot chocolate puddings with their dark and liquid hearts, and I took my mug.

'One day she managed,' my husband chimed in from the end of the table. I ignored him.

'. . . but I am slogging on with the good deeds and the kids actually seem interested, and they were one of the reasons I started doing it.'

Diane set the cheese plate off on its travels round the table and the pungent smell of Stilton slapped me across one side of the face and then the other, yelling 'Eat me!' I don't eat cheese at dinner. It gives me bad dreams – dreams that I'm eating cheese at dinner.

'I've worked out what it is to have a moral life,' she said, 'because I've got children. Because of them, I am much more genuinely good in my thoughts and in my actions than I would otherwise be. I know I need to be an exemplar because having the right values will help them in their adult life.'

Leaving aside whatever constraints evolution puts on our behaviour for a moment, is anyone motivated purely by the desire to help others or is there always something else involved: an example to the children, money, the desire for salvation, the feel-good buzz that comes with giving? In the scheme of things, my own good deeds may not add up to a peck of virtue, but I want to believe in the right choices, in self-sacrifice and goodness. In mar-tyred virgin saints kissed and made better, in angels who enfold you in arms and radiance and snowy feathers, and in Santa Claus, a lightning bolt in one scarlet-mittened hand, a refreshing Coca-Cola in the other.

Amid a certain amount of eye-rolling, Diane has said I can buy a lamb from her to save from the broth-pot. Perhaps she'll let me have Titty? With a name like that, he is due a bit of luck.

Good deed no. 99: wrote a job reference for someone.

Sunday, 10 April

My 100th good deed. Glorious sunny day. Still no sign of karma. Car smells of chicken poop, having been driven through a slurry slick on the narrow country roads. I can't decide which I hate most – chickens or farmers.

Good deed no. 100: picked up litter on beach.

THE BELIEVER

Perhaps I could take a short cut to being a better person if I just believed harder in the whole God thing – like Cryssie's mother, Andrea. Cryssie is sixteen and has congenital myotonic dystrophy, a disease whereby her muscles waste, leaving her with difficulties walking and moving, problems in speaking or indeed moving any of her facial muscles as well as moderate learning difficulties.

So here I am with all my weaknesses and myriad moral failings. Here I am, this flawed person living a comfortable life in a nice house with a nice husband and nice kids, having it easy enough to indulge in the luxury of a spot of self-improvement but who doesn't fancy Pilates. A good deed a day. What is the best that can happen? Three hundred and sixty-five good deeds, and maybe, if I am lucky, I am a slightly better person at the end of it. Unlikely, but possible. So I collect my good deeds and, like any collector, I am acquiring the odd favourite, ones I take out and buff with a lint-free cloth, bringing them to a high coppery burnish and myself to a righteous climax. But over the Sea of Moral Reality are those who don't number their good deeds, because they are too busy living a 'good' life. The life of a carer. That of a mother. That of Cryssie's mother.

Andrea has the same haircut as Cryssie, cropped. Mothers quite often have the same haircut as their teenage daughters – sometimes I wonder if they are trying to make their daughter more like them, or if they are wanting to be more like their daughter. Andrea, however, takes devotion to a whole new level – devotion to her disabled kids and devotion to God. Her 'Praise the Lord' honesty about her Christian convictions always leaves me dazed; there is more certain faith in her sneeze than there is in the whole of me. She and her artist husband have three kids – each with their own needs, two of them with massive physical disabilities. Then again, reason dictates that if faith is what drives you, you cannot sit back and do nothing with your life.

I asked her whether she and her husband regarded what they do for Cryssie and her equally disabled brother (whom they adopted as babies) as 'good', whether it was part of their own striving to be good people. She shook her head: 'It is part of our attempt to live out our belief that we were created to love one another, created to be channels of love. How can you be that if you keep your love in and if you don't share that with those people around you?' There is a note of puzzlement in her voice that anyone would make a choice against love, against sharing what they have. I picture her garden, the richness of the soil into which her husband digs, planting fragile seedlings, growing row upon row upon row of green stuff, enough to feed a world, and I think how narrow and few some love, how little they grow in their own backyard.

Andrea, an energetic, skinny-as-a-lath PE teacher, expected to spend her life as a successful head of a secondary school; instead, she found herself abandoning her own career. 'There are areas of life where there is immense need to step out in faith. We didn't set out to adopt anybody, but we believe we were called to adopt these children specifically, and we have done it with glad hearts because it is a way of making what we believe a reality.'

There is a chapter in *The Oxford Handbook of Philosophical Theology* called 'Moral Perfection', written by Laura Garcia, an adjunct associate professor of philosophy at Boston College (this is the stuff you read when you start down a path paved with good deeds – it is killing me). She describes an eleventh-century monk called St Anselm who 'claimed to have discovered a proof of God's existence based simply on the definition of God as a being than which none greater can be conceived'. From this comes the idea of God as morally perfect, and of course, if God is morally perfect and you are a fan, the chances are you will try to reflect that moral perfection in your own life. Maybe that is why in this God-lite world, we accept our own imperfections these days with such an easy, tolerant heart: *I'm not perfect. Who's perfect? Nobody's perfect.* Some people try damn hard, though.

I asked Andrea whether she believed she was attempting to replicate divine goodness in her own good life, but something in her squirms at the word 'good', refusing to own it.

'I believe that God is Love. The person of Jesus is God personified, and there is no doubt whatsoever in my mind that Jesus lived a life of redemptive love. We seek to follow that – not because it makes us good, but because beliefs are empty if you don't live by them.'

Andrea would have an excuse to do nothing for anybody but her own family, because what she does for her own family on one hectic single day is more than most people have to do in a year. She is, however, a school governor, she helps run a support group, she finds furniture for the needy, support for the vulnerable. I wonder if she would be willing to define even this extra-familial life of hers as 'good', but she doesn't – the message is still one of love and blessings.

'I had a wonderful start in life with a father and a grandma who were all about love – hard school, not gooey marshmallow love, but unconditional all the same. I always knew I had this love in my life and I feel blessed because of that. I want to give what was given to me, to bless others as I was blessed – that is what motivates me to do what I do. The judgement that really matters is the Lord's, at the end of the day. I would like him to say to me, "Well done, my good and faithful servant."'

I ask her whether she thinks if I do my good deeds I can become a better person. There is a nano-second of hesitation. 'I believe your motivation is to be a blessing to those you are around, to be good news to those you are around,' she said, and it is my turn to squirm.

Monday, 11 April

Andrea dropped by for coffee, and while we were chatting on about the good deeds she got a distinct gleam in her eye. In September, Cryssie starts at a special school about forty-five minutes away.

Because of the distances involved and the fact she can't travel back and forth for the best part of two hours a day or she risks getting sick, she'll go into school on Monday, Wednesday and Friday rather than attend the full week. Consequently, her parents have been thinking about what to do the rest of the week. They are effectively designing a bespoke curriculum with the afternoons spent swimming with her and her brother who has the same condition; the mornings, however, are more of a problem.

According to her mother, Cryssie reads all the time and wants to be a writer, so her mother is going to talk to her about whether she wants to take a writing class with me and we can try to pull together a few short stories. Very daunted. To say the least. To teach her anything, I need to see the child, I mean fully see the child, and not get distracted by the disability, and I am easily distracted.

Good deed no. 101: advised a new food blogger, who is trying to promote her B&B, on blogging: establish blog roll, read, comment, think about video blogging.

Tuesday, 12 April

My eldest son's middle school is going to join the Jam Jar Army at some point next term, which is great. That's about eighty to ninety children. Say fifty of them do it, that is fifty jam jars out there – at £3 each, that is £150. Excellent.

Good deed no. 102: bought a neighbour's child an ice cream.

Wednesday, 13 April

I had my first squeal of delight from a good deed this morning. I had sorted out a couple of bagfuls of clothes the boys had grown out of for a neighbour's little boy, and then I realized I could palm some old toys off on him as well. I dug out a couple of big puzzles you build on the floor and a beautiful wooden castle my boys never look at, and a big bag of plastic tools – hence the squeal. Apparently the little one loves tools. What I should really have done with all the money we've spent on cars and knights and Scalextric over the last decade is invest it in a pension plan. All they really needed was a regular supply of cardboard boxes for rockets and ships, blankets and a kitchen table for dens, and a football. If I had realized that earlier, I could indeed have spent my retirement cruising the Aegean. As it is, courtesy of my freelance career and my glaring lack of pension, I am hoping at least one of my grown-up children has a house with a garage because I will probably have to live in it.

Good deed no. 103.

Thursday, 14 April

Last time I was in London, I found it hard to do good deeds and had to resort to giving money to charity on a daily basis. Admittedly, I was being followed around by three small people, and children do distract from good intentions. In London for work, this time was easier. Walking along the Strand, I came across two Japanese girls taking it in turn to take pictures of each other across from the immense Victorian edifice of Charing Cross Station. The perfect opportunity. Initially, the girl with the camera looked confused as I attempted to take the camera from her (there is an outside chance she believed I was a mugger), but once she caught on, she and her pal were very grateful. They didn't squeal like my friend's boy when I gave him toy carpentry tools, but when I finished snapping, they did put their hands together and bow, so I bowed, and they bowed again. We could be there yet but I had a bus to catch.

God has obviously got a sense of humour, though. Bastard. Here I am trying to do a good deed a day, costing me time and energy and money I don't have, with benefit to parties other than myself (which is my rough rule of thumb), and what does God decide to do? Call my bluff. I was walking along Camden High Street on my way to a friend who had kindly agreed to put me up for the night, and rang my mother to see how she was feeling. Ever since she fractured her vertebra she has been low. So low that yesterday I mused out loud that I wasn't entirely sure what was keeping her and my dad in Leeds when they could move up to Northumberland. I mused on the understanding that I was musing, that they were not yet so decrepit they would have to come up to us, that even if my mother wanted to, my dad likes his independence too much and goes slightly loopy if he has to stay with us longer than four days. Well, bugger me backwards, no one explained the rules of musing to my mother, so she informed me that she and my dad had made a decision. A big decision. They were coming to live with me.

If aliens had landed their rocket in front of me, got out, waved and gone shopping, I could not have been more confounded.

My mother said: 'You're very quiet.' Because I couldn't find a cushion, my fist was stuffed into my mouth to stop me screaming. My dad chimes in – they always put the phone on speakerphone when I ring – 'I can't cope any more.' You can't argue with that one, can you? Oh my God.

Good deed no. 104.

Friday, 15 April

Had a lovely dinner with London friends, but spent the entire meal talking through the consequences of my mum and dad moving in. On the one hand, I love them to bits and this day was always going to come. On the other, does it have to come today?

What will go first?

- Bringing up three children who are now ten, eight and five and already engaged in a fight for light with each other;

- running the house (and my standards are reasonably low here);
- maintaining the semblance of a relationship with my husband (who is always on deadline and sometimes in London);
- caring for two elderly parents (one of whom is blind and frail);
- a writing/journalism career which brings in some money – not a lot maybe, but enough to make the difference between eating and not eating;
- working on a novel which doesn't bring in any money at all;
- my patience;
- or my sanity?

I love my parents. I adore my parents. But my prediction is I lose my patience first, rapidly followed by my sanity, then the novel writing, then the career, then the husband.

I was so subsumed by my proposed new role as carer of the elderly, I helped an old lady on the train back north to get her suitcase into the suitcase rack. When it was time for her to get off, I helped her with it then too. But she can't have wanted any more help, because she sort of wrestled it off me and was very grumpy, as if she suspected I was claiming the case as my own and intended leaping off the train when it drew into the station and running for my robber's den with her case of huge panties as my booty. The old can be very difficult.

Good deed no. 105.

Saturday, 16 April

The girls' dance school is in a former Mechanics' Institute which forms one side of a Georgian square, at the centre of which is the Catholic church. I am guessing the Institute has some link with the Masons because the doorway is huge and high and set at an oblique angle, and as I cross the threshold I always feel that my name is Alice and this another Wonderland.

The girls change in a large empty room to the right as you go in, with chairs set out around the edges on which proud maternal posteriors perch to supervise tiny, rose-cheeked ballerinas as they don tiny, pink-kid ballerina slippers. What I normally do then is speed-walk into town, buy a newspaper to read the property porn in the *Journal*'s Homemaker section, down a scalding coffee while they are having their modern dance class and speed-walk back to be there in time to change the girls into their black tippety-tap shoes. Because the dance studio is directly above the waiting room, once they stomp back upstairs for tap, I sit for forty-five minutes with my fingers in my ears to avoid another migraine. Very occasionally, like today, they have a fund-raising coffee morning, which means I get to eat cake and call it a good deed. Result. Apparently the money that is raised is going towards paying for the older ones to go on a cruise. I am guessing they dance on the cruise, so presumably they get a good rate. Young dancers and their mothers on a cruise ship – I so want to go.

Good deed no. 106.

Sunday, 17 April

With the lack of recent rain, the rugby pitch was ridged and pitted and rock-hard. Once a year the club holds a rugby tournament, and we spend most of the day cheering on our eight-year-old son. When we first moved, the ten-year-old took one look at contact rugby, uttered the words 'Never in a million years', went back to his Nintendo, and that was him and rugby done. But the eight-year-old enjoys it. I pointed out the concrete hardness of the ground to the rugby coach and he sent me off for Vaseline at the supermarket. Being a natural pessimist, I got Vaseline and plasters and antiseptic spray and Savlon for all those bony little-boy knees.

I smeared gloop over my son's knees and the coach's son's knees, and then other boys came up to me and stood around expectantly, and I kept saying, 'Who's your mum and dad? Where are they? Oy, Mum, can I Vaseline his knees?' I'm not entirely sure what the Vaseline was supposed to do – help the child slide over ground that might otherwise take the skin off his knee, I guess. But the coach used to play for Scotland, so he had to know what he was talking about. Having said that, I didn't ask to see his knees.

Good deed no. 107.

Monday, 18 April

Al is working late every night in the utterly insane way he does when approaching deadline on a project. Sometimes, when he is up against it, he listens to the music of the 1970s as he works. Tonight I traipsed through the study on my way up to bed, and there was bouzouki music playing as he worked. 'It's Tacticos and His Bouzoukis,' he informed me, glancing up briefly from his screen of numbers, the plinkety-plonkety crescendo of 'Zorba's Dance' building. I had this vision of him waiting till I'd gone to bed, the creaks and groans of the oak bedframe settling into silence, then standing up from his desk, stretching out his shirt-sleeved arms, kicking out one leg and then the other, crossing, bobbing, turning, dancing round the piles and files of paper, the BT Home Hub, his fingers clicking, his spirit free, Zorba on his mind.

Good deed no. 108: advised the food blogger on her blog.

Tuesday, 19 April

Good deed no. 109: checked on the expat after his hospital appointment.

Wednesday, 20 April

Bearing in mind my mum and dad might well be moving in, I consulted an expert.

Stephanie is, like me, an only child. When she can, she runs away from real life and hides away in her cottage along the row, painting and felting and walking the lanes listening to birdsong. This is her sanctuary, her holy place. Stephanie is about to turn sixty with two grown-up children and a 93-year-old mother, and because she's been there herself, this friend doesn't judge when I say how I fall short over and over, caught between kids and parents and work.

She used to spend more time up here on her own; more recently, though, she arrives with her mother in tow. She scoops the old lady out of the car, helping her into the cottage and over to a sofa. As a special treat she carries up hot and salty chips, splattered over with shop vinegar, from the village, and on trips out, pushes her around in a wheelchair, her mother all wrapped up in blankets. Twenty-seven years ago, her mother and father moved into the ground floor of a three-storey house while Stephanie and her husband took the other two floors. Her mother helped with Stephanie's two children while she pursued a career as a consultant anaesthetist. Fifteen years ago her dad died, and very slowly her mother became more and more dependent, a dependence exacerbated by a gradual slide into dementia. Shopping, her mum would buy the same soap or shampoo when her cupboards at home were full of them, while her repertoire of recipes faded back to a boiled egg and what she could put in a microwave. 'My husband, who has always been lovely with her, asked my mother to make some Yorkshire puddings for us one day and she said she couldn't remember how.' Stephanie shakes her head. The memory problems were diagnosed six years ago, but may well have started earlier. 'We had a couple of close shaves when she nearly burned down the house – she let an egg boil dry in a pan one time and she forgot to blow out a bathroom candle and the wax set fire to the carpet.'

Stephanie fought for the help her mother needs – help dressing, washing, bathing. She has to be given her meals and snacks and tea, is helped out of bed in the morning and put back to bed at night.

Her shopping, washing and housework all have to be done, but there is no resentment, only a daughter's steady and loving conviction that a fundamental obligation is being met. 'What goes around comes around,' Stephanie says. Her mother reared Stephanie, and helped rear her children. Now shrunken, and frail, and dear, it is her turn to be cosseted, to be held in stronger arms, to be a child again. 'I wouldn't be where I am today without my mother, so I think for me to turn my back and not help her would make me a bad person. I am simply doing what needs to be done. It's what families do.' Not all families, though. 'I see a lot of miserable people when their parents are in intensive care and are dying. They come in and want us to pull out all the stops to save them, and it is because they feel guilty. They'll never be able to think that they did all they could for their parents, but I'd like to think I could.'

Good deed no. 110: checked on a friend who has had an operation.

Thursday, 21 April

My parents are with us again, and after I put the children to bed, Al made up a fire in the living room where they're ensconced and I made cups of tea for them. Briefly I considered tea for Al and me; instead I pour us both a stiff drink to talk through my parents' move. That's not entirely true. I pour a stiff drink, then make it stiffer.

My mum and dad are waiting. She is sitting in a wrap-around bishop's chair, my dad on the sofa nearby. I suspect they have been waiting to have this discussion ever since they arrived this morning. I hand Al his gin and tonic, and he winks at me. There are some men who would run screaming at the thought of elderly in-laws moving in; Al just grinned and said, 'We're an attractive package' when I broke the news.

I sit down and my mother opens fire. 'You seemed surprised,' my mother says, 'when I told you we'd decided to move in with you. You did offer.' She sounds slightly offended and slightly amused.

The thing about mothers is they know you better than anyone else in the whole world. Know you and love you. Did I offer? I did, didn't I? In a roundabout 'God, you're getting old – I wish I could do something about that – and you live miles away – you could always move up here' kind of way. My mother is perfectly happy in my house. She listens to her audio books because she can't see to read any more, 'watches' TV soaps with the volume turned to levels that make my ears bleed, and when my dad wants to watch football (which is always), she keeps me company in the kitchen. Here, there are children and conversation and life, which is all any of us really want. My dad is also happy in my house. I have Sky Sports. He doesn't have to cook or wash up. But he has his own way of going on at home: his daily shopping trip up to Asda; no small children pleading to play Xbox on his television; a weekly trip over to the same church they have attended for more than forty years; handy doctors; and, best of all, no one trying to make him eat pasta.

My dad watches me struggle to find the right thing to say. Right morally, right by them, right by me. 'You can relax. Your mother and I have talked it over and we're not coming.'

I shake my head from side to side in case my mother's deafness is catching. 'You said you couldn't cope.' It is my turn to sound accusing.

My mother waves her hand dismissively in my direction. 'Of course your father can cope. I'm not that much of a burden, am I, pet?' She turns to him and my dad reaches out to take her soft hand in his. 'We're allowed a bad day now and then, you know. We're feeling much brighter and we've decided we'd rather keep our independence and stay in our own little house.' I bow my head. Somehow my glass is empty. 'Of course that might always change,' she adds, and when I look up again, she smiles innocently in my direction.

Good deed no. 111: hospitality and care of the elderly.

Good deed no. 112: aired and gave quick once-over to the next-door neighbour's house.

Good deed no. 113: arranged for transport of a second-hand TV to the expats as they haven't shipped over their stuff yet.

Glorious sunshine today, and after an Easter lunch for thirteen in the garden we took the kids to the beach so they could roll their hard-boiled eggs down the dunes. There are a couple of steep-sided hollows off this particular beach which we sledge down in winter when the snow comes, and the original idea was to race one egg against the other. (They were dyed with onion-skins and food dyes so we could tell the difference between them; otherwise, racing eggs is tough. 'The egg has it by a nose. No, it's the other egg, with yet another egg coming down the inside on the final straight.') For some reason, though, my boys preferred to treat their eggs like marbles, with the added satisfaction that when the red one smashed into the green one, hard-boiled eggs exploded across the sand, making the most fantastic mess.

After I had finally had enough of picking sandy yolk, rubbery white scraps and multicoloured shell-shrapnel out of the sand, we headed back to the car. Doing up their seatbelts, the kids bickered delightedly among themselves as to whose egg had made the most mess while I brushed yolk crumbs from my fingers, wrinkling my nose in disgust. I was just thinking that it would be at least September before I could face another hard-boiled egg, when through the windscreen I spotted a distracted granny supporting her wobbly granddaughter who was roller-skating along the sandy road ahead of us, the granddaughter scissoring like Bambi, leaning, bending this way and that, while passing cars heading home from the beach trundled by. Granny was concentrating hard on not letting the child fall; I, however, was concentrating on the younger girl walking alongside them. I don't know what was in her mind – how many chocolate eggs waited at home perhaps, or the fact her sister's flailing arms and legs were getting in her way, but all of a sudden she stepped out and around Granny and her sister and into the road – all oblivious to the cars coming up behind them. I started to open my door while wildly gesturing that she go back to the side of the road, willing her to step back. Still propping up one girl by her elbow, Granny turned back to see the trouble, hurriedly reaching out to bring the younger girl to safety. I shook my head as if to say 'What can you do?' as I pulled my door shut, and Granny thanked me as they passed on by.

Good deed no. 114.

Monday, 25 April

My best gay boyfriend originally comes from Tyneside and his parents still live up here. This is a good thing because it means once in a while I get to see him when he comes up to visit them. At Christmas he brings a huge bag of perfect gifts which you didn't even know you wanted till you pull at the spiral ribbons and tear at the hospital-bed corners of the wrapping; while if he comes for supper he brings pointy crimson tulips and smooth crimson wine. When he came over today, I made him tea and he said his dad had suggested he bring over a spare lemon drizzle cake his dad had in from the supermarket. The kettle was on the hob for tea. I reached for a cake plate from the overhead cupboard and pulled out a knife from a drawer and put them ready on the table. I said: 'Hand it over.' My best gay boyfriend laughed as if I'd told a particularly good knock-knock joke, and said he had informed his dad that there was no way on this earth that I wanted a plastic-wrapped cake with a topping of skinny white icing and yolk-yellow dribbles, soggy with E numbers and trans-fats and gritty white sugar. It had got quite heated between the two of them. Yes I did, I said. I'd three children and a house full of guests and it so happened that I was particularly partial to cake I didn't have to make, bake and mourn when it got ate. 'I got that wrong then,' he said wonderingly. He doesn't get things wrong, my best gay boyfriend.

The older I get, the more convinced I am that we don't say 'I was wrong and you were right' often enough. But life is surely too short for hurts to linger, for grudges and fond affection to wither for want of a deep breath and that single word 'sorry'. I have known his parents for as many years as I've known him, and they are lovely. I said he had to tell his dad that he had been right and my best gay pal wrong. 'I do, don't I?' he said, dismayed.

He rang me just now. He said he had fessed up and made his dad happy. 'Happier than he would have been if you'd taken the cake?' I asked. 'Don't push it,' my best gay boyfriend said.

Good deed no. 115.

Tuesday, 26 April

The other day I was considering counting lunch for everybody as my good deed, bearing in mind I shopped for it, paid for it, cooked it, served it in the garden and cleared up after it (not to mention six guests were staying over). But as I had placed the roast chicken and its companion duck, crisp and bronzed like poultry gods, onto the table one brave soul said, with due respect, that he didn't think I should count it because I'd have been laying on lunch anyway. It turns out that everyone has an opinion on my good deeds – whether I am doing enough, whether I am doing too much, whether I should be doing it at all.

But what happens if I as the 'doer' regard something as a good deed, but the 'done-to' does not consider the action a good deed at all, arguing it is more a matter of duty or obligation and should be done out of love or blood, morality or common humanity?

The doer believes: 'I'm doing a good deed. You should watch me, praise me, thank me.'

While the done-to believes: 'You're doing neither more nor less than you should.'

The doer believes: 'I'm going the extra mile for someone else.'

While the done-to claims: 'Can't you see me standing here? That's not far enough.'

And of course, according to the doer: 'I'm doing this for you.'

But the done-to argues: 'And so you should, my dear, because I'd do the same for you.'

It's a strange currency, this good deed. You give it, and hope you give it freely. But when it's given, is there public gratitude? Should there be? Or is there secret resentment on the doer's part that there is need at all – resentment too in other quarters at the obligation it places on the needy to smile nicely and say thank you? And we aren't any of us paragons – can there be tolerance if the good-deed doer fails to do the right thing by the needy another day? Surely we have to be our own moral arbiters in this life. We can't impose expectations one on the other or we can be certain only of disappointment. We have to make an agreement with each other that I won't judge you to be failing if you don't judge me to be falling short. These are complicated transactions. All I really know is that when I do something for someone else, I strike a match and with that tiny flame light up the waxen taper of my soul.

Good deed no. 116: made welcome 85-year-old Aunty Effie, who has arrived for a few days with her chihuahua. (Not the bitey one, she got rid of him. This is not the new chihuahua, this is the new, improved chihuahua.)

Wednesday, 27 April

THE VOLUNTEER

I am such an amateur good-deed doer next to Aunty Effie. Even at her age, with a bad knee which means she can't climb stairs, she volunteers every day of her life. Once upon a time she was a policewoman and in later life she was a court usher. Before her knee went, she used to offer victim support and act as a lay visitor in police cells, but 'that had to stop' because of the stairs.

Nowadays she works in a charity shop once or sometimes twice a week, and visits those who don't have any other visitors in hospitals, along with her 'oldies' in the old people's homes. When I said, 'How old are your "oldies"?', she said, 'Seventy? Seventy-five?' And I said, 'Younger than you then?', and she said, 'Technically . . . You were always a very rude sort of child.'

Like my mum and dad, she is very holy, and takes Communion round to the elderly and infirm in their own homes. She puts priests up when they come over from India, and when she was eighty-two she went to India on her own and rode an elephant. I wondered why she didn't sit at home and watch television. She said: 'I feel as if I'm earning my keep – as if God is keeping me alive to do it, and when I get to bedtime, I thank God for what I have been able to do today.'

Across the kitchen table, my mum nods in agreement. A complete life is a life of service – to one's family, to one's God, to one's church and community, and to one's fellow man. When my mother started losing her sight, the first thing she did was set up a support group for other people with macular on the grounds that many were living on their own or fearful.

'You're all too busy,' she said, 'your dad and I hadn't any money, so we gave our time, but to people this day and age, time is a very precious commodity.' And as the two sisters chat, I am aware that this generation is distinct from mine in its eagerness to give. I do two things with my time. I look after my children and I work. That is pretty much it, because if I am not doing one of those things, I am sure I should be doing the other. Many women are caught between that rock and a hard place, trying to do their best for their children and trying to keep their job. And if they're not working, if they're full-time mothers at home, then the pressure is on to do it all perfectly. Our children are our gods and they are demanding gods; our home is our church. Who has time to volunteer when you are a member of that religion? Who even wants to? And what does it mean when the old folk die out? Will each generation do less and less?

I tune back in from my rising panic that society is on the point of disintegration, and my aunt is telling my mum how the nurses and carers are always pleased to see her, because they say when she leaves someone's bedside, she leaves them cheerier than when she arrived. But she doesn't believe her volunteering is a one-way street, that she is giving and others are taking.

'If I had to sit on my bottom day after day, I would die, I couldn't do that. This way, I'm not just letting life pass me by and I get as much out of it as they do because I spend enough hours on my own, and this way I don't feel lonely.'

My mother nods. 'You put something in, and you take something better out.'

'Surely not,' I said.

'Just wait,' she told me.

Good deed no. 117: hospitality and care. OAP count: three. Good legs between guests: one (if you don't count the chihuahua).

Thursday, 28 April

Unimpressed by husband, to put it mildly. I was trying to make a call and the phone kept ringing out before I could complete the number. Al went very quiet and then he said there was an outside possibility BT had cut us off because we hadn't paid the bill. A possibility! Apparently we owe £600 – which is interesting because we have absolutely no way of paying. My overdraft is bust. Al is bust. Worse yet, Al informed me that even if we pay it straight away, it takes twenty-four hours to restore the service, which takes us into a bank holiday, through into the weekend and out the other end into another bank holiday. Which means there is a chance we won't have the phone, or indeed the Internet, restored till Tuesday. Or maybe Wednesday. Al, however, who is on deadline and thereby useless for anything other than meeting said deadline, announced he would have to go to London and work from there. A London with phones and an Internet connection.

Because I had three elderly relations sitting round my kitchen table waiting for the tea and hot buttered toast I'd promised them, I could not actually say how I felt about the fact we had no phone line any more. Every couple of minutes Al walked through the kitchen with a face like thunder and added something to the pile of belongings he was building up on the sofa, and the four of us watched him in silence. It was a Russian play. Two wise old women, a wise old man and a resentful wife watch as a husband prepares to depart for Moscow, the cow having died that morning.

My mother slid Al her Visa card so he could pay the phone bill, I gave him what cash I had in my handbag, and my dad and Aunty Effie drove him to the station. I slammed the door after he walked out of it. Hard. As he chuffety-chuffed down to London, I brokered peace between my kids and three of their friends in a row over a computer game, while working alongside Dr Will's teenage daughter Jess designing the Jam Jar Army poster. (Jess, of course, had to know we hadn't paid our phone bill, as presumably did her mother and father who were up in their cottage for a few days, as did my mother and father, and my elderly aunt and Aunty Effie's effing chihuahua.)

Finally, the poster was done, the children were playing nicely, the elderly parents and aunty nursing her chihuahua were sitting in the sunshine in the garden, when my blind mother stumbled to the doorway yelping because my dad had fallen in the garden and hit his head. Thank God Dr Will heard the commotion. He dashed out of his cottage, I sprinted down, and my dad had a nasty gash on his head and had to be guided back to a chair and cross-examined about whether he had tripped or fainted. My mother then edged her way back into the garden, arms outstretched, hands groping, having forgotten her white stick in her anxiety to get help, and started breathing as if she was going to dive head-first into a panic attack, so she needed hosing down. I wouldn't mind, but my dad is the good one: my mum can't see and can hardly walk with her bad back, and Aunty Effie can't feel her leg below her knee; he was supposed to be the one at the front of the queue of elderly ducks guiding them from one place of safety to the next.

Chaos. My life is chaos. I am sliding into lunacy on a tin tray and hitting the humps so hard, my teeth hurt.

Good deed no. 118: worked towards the launch of the Jam Jar Army.

Friday, 29 April

Since everybody is up in their cottages, they have organized a barbecue. There is a genuine communality about this place when everyone is here. Women who are busy with careers in real lives share chit-chat morning coffee on wooden benches and along the stone wall to the grassy green, and bring each other up to date on the doings of their children; men help each other saw wood and mend bicycles; while little ones trail after big girls, and boys play football with each other.

'This must be how people lived in the 1930s,' I said to Stephanie, and I thought of women in red-brick back-to-backs warning each other to bring in the washing before the coal man came, and leaning out of windows to talk across a cobbled alley.

'On a Sunday in Birtley when I was a girl, my grandmother used to cook her own joint and the joints of neighbours in her oven, so they could save on fuel,' Stephanie said. 'Then she'd carry across two plates of lunch from her own joint for old folk who'd have otherwise gone without.'

And I wonder if kindness is in the genes or whether it is taught.

Quite often, I don't go to the barbecues. Because all I do is write and bollock children, sometimes I struggle to have anything interesting to say. Tonight's barbecue was most astonishingly brilliant, however, because I didn't have to shop for it, prepare it, cook it or wash up after it. We ferried in sausages and burgers and potatoes for my parents and aunty, and the kids ate God knows what. Dr Will, who had earlier in the day come in to check on my dad, leaned over and poured wine into my empty glass and I sat smoked to death by the fire pit, wrapped in two cardigans and my puffa coat, with the cold north wind blowing against the green tarpaulin of the gazebo so hard I thought it would lift it up and ferry us all to Oz, and it was wonderful.

Good deed no. 119: gave my next-door neighbour a roll of toilet paper. (If only all my good deeds could be as simple.)

THE DOCTOR

Dr Will is tall and powerfully built. If he goes down to the village, he pops in to my kitchen and asks if I want anything brought back, a paper, a pint of milk? Occasionally, when he is up here, I drag one child or other in front of him and say 'That rash . . .?' or 'This sprain?' and he'll lift an arm, wriggle fingers, say 'How about United, eh?' then say 'They're fine' and pat a head and they'll skip away, all hurts forgotten. 'Why did you become a doctor, Will?' I asked.

It turned out that his grandfather had been a GP in the Wirral with a surgery in his own house, and was still working as a locum up to the age of eighty. As a boy, Dr Will would visit his grandfather. 'We'd be out and about together and he would bump into his patients in the street and I'd see the kind of relationship he had with them. He'd tell me stories – not so much about their medical conditions but about who they were and how they linked into the community.'

For Dr Will, medicine, and more particularly general practice, is more than a family tradition, it is a vocation. 'I truly turned up to my interview and said I wanted to help people – I wanted to help make things better – and I was the first person at med school who, on day one, admitted to wanting to be a GP. I took a bit of grief for that.' I pictured Dr Will, twenty-five years younger, amiable, charming, and burbling with enthusiasm about the joys of general practice to glory boys intent on royal colleges, surgery, consultancy and their very own spotty bow tie.

I asked him whether most people became doctors to help people, and he looked thoughtful. 'Quite a few go into it for status, whether that's to do with self-esteem or financial status. We were told by the Registrar at medical school that they used to oscillate between setting the academic bar quite high one year, when they'd get a lot of academic people who were a bit stiff, and lower the next year when they'd need more people-people, or GP types.'

Nothing is harder than holding true to the dreams you have when you are young – particularly when the dreams are ones of virtue. But working as a GP for more than twenty-one years, at fifty-four hours a week, Dr Will clearly remains a believer. 'The thing in it for me is the thank you. That's the drug. Several times a day, a patient says, "Thank you for your time, Doctor." I keep reminding them I do get paid.'

For Dr Will, the art to doctoring lies in wanting to be useful and, most of all, in listening. 'It gets easier once you know the patients better, because then they are more comfortable with you so they open up. I just seem to connect with people easily – I am very lucky in that. Somebody said on the radio the other day that if you shut up and listen, patients will tell you what's wrong with them, it's not difficult.' Even with the most chronic cases, there is always something new to try. Dr William Carson Dick, consultant rheumatologist in Newcastle while Dr Will was a student, died in 1995. Towards the end of his career, the consultant held weekly open-house sessions where patients and their relatives, doctors and medical students met together for a glass of wine and a sing-song. According to one obituary, after Carson Dick's death 'many of his patients claimed [these get-togethers] did far more for them than any of the drugs prescribed for their diseases.'

Dr Will admitted that there is a danger in his full-on, give-all style of doctoring and 'take your time' approach. Not only do queues build in the waiting room, but ten years ago he burned out. He blames the burnout on giving too much, and is wary of it happening again. 'I was giving too much, so this year I made a resolution to be less tolerant. It is a marginal switch on the setting – maybe I say no a bit more. But I just love it. If I won the lottery I wouldn't quit. The worry is the patients become my family, my friends, but I'm not sure that's such a bad thing. It is a drug, I'm sure – the sense you are helping and the feedback you get; and it is often the most vulnerable that give you the best feedback of all.' I smiled at Dr Will as he left to go out on a run along the lanes, and felt . . . uplifted. You want your doctors selfless and quietly heroic, to feel that they have your best interests at heart, that they work relent-lessly to make you better and the world a better place. You want them to carry a battered Gladstone bag at all times, to work in grainy monochrome, wear tweed and tip their hat, you want to feel all doctors are like Dr Will.

Saturday, 30 April

Waved goodbye to the old folk, who drove off in convoy, my mother all teary. She can't leave without crying, which makes me cry, which makes her cry more. I have no idea how my aunt man-aged to drive off at all bearing in mind she can't feel anything below the knee – I must ask her. She can move the leg; she just can't feel it. It's the left one anyway, so at least it isn't the accelerator foot. It's been nice having them: you know where they are – lying on the ground in my father's case – so you don't have to worry. As she walked out of the door, my aunt said: 'It's been lovely, pet, but it's too much work for you with the three of us. I'm coming on my own next time.' I've got these really itchy bumps on my back and I can't decide if they're mosquito bites or shingles. The fact I am even thinking shingles says my aunt might be right, but even my parents plus the kids are too much for me. Even the kids are too much for me sometimes. Even I am too much for me sometimes.

Apparently in Buddhism you get more brownie points if you perform meritorious deeds for holy people, the needy or your par-ents. That is some comfort, because I have now made so many cups of tea for my aged relations that I don't only have itchy bumps but my repetitive strain injury has come back. I am hoping Buddha might make it go away again. The problem is that I have an Aga, which is a vast cast-iron contraption that you cook on and that heats your kitchen and dries your clothes and makes you feel like life is worth living on a wet and wintry day. The hobs are covered by heavy round lids like giant tiddlywinks. They are not a good combination with ancient Irish DNA, on which scientists with microscopes can read, 'I drink tea, therefore I am.' To make tea on an Aga you have to lift the lid of the Aga, lift the kettle from its place by the Aga, fill it, lift it back onto the Aga, pour the boiling water into the cups, place the kettle back in its place and then shut the Aga lids. Farmers' wives must have arms like ham hocks. I am rolling up her sleeves and looking next time I meet one.

I am feeling so stressed, I am nauseous. Stretched like cling film ready to tear over a glass bowl that's ready to shatter. I have too much to do. I have so much to do I cannot even remember what I have to do. I should write a To Do list, but I can't because my arms hurt and anyway I would lose the list and then I would have to add 'Find the To Do list' to my To Do list and I wouldn't be able to. God. Don't have children if you seriously want to do anything useful with your working life, and don't try to do anything useful with your working life because life itself is too damn short anyway and you should be spending it with the kids. I am losing the plot. I am:

- bringing up three children while husband works far too many hours and occasionally goes insane while he does it;
- preparing to teach a university short course on blogging;
- doing a good deed a day;
- trying to launch a major fund-raising initiative;
- and writing a novel no one wants to read.

Plus my laptop now has thirty-one vertical lines running down the screen, one of which flashes all the time. I'm hoping it doesn't make me have a fit.

For ten minutes when the oldies had gone and before the next lot of children came along to play with my children, I sat out in the soul-drenching sunshine of the garden in the chair my mother had been sitting in. A chaffinch sang in the branches of the blossom-heavy cherry tree as I sipped my black coffee. I peeled off my cardigan and lay back in the chair; it was warm in the sun, but every now and then a fierce wind from off the sea slapped up against the cherry tree, knocking the blossom from the branches and, sitting in its lee, it was as if pale pink snow fell on me.

Good deed no. 120: checked Holy Island crossing times on the Internet for Dr Will.

Sunday, 1 May

Good deed no. 121: bought blue, bubblegum-flavoured ice cream for a friend's three boys we bumped into.

Monday, 2 May

Lovely sunny day again, so the children and I pootled into the market town and bought a box of ice creams from Iceland. Mums love Iceland, as they say. But even after we had all had one, there were ice creams left over. There was nothing for it but to give them away to strangers. The best one had to be as we were driving away. A family were wandering the streets. I imagine they had come down into town after looking round the castle. The child with them wore a helmet and was carrying a sword, which he was waving ferociously like the best knights do. I stopped the car and wound down the window to ask one of the grown-ups if the boy would by any chance like an ice cream. Who says never take an ice cream from a stranger? The grown-up nodded. From behind his visor, the boy stopped thinking where he might find a dragon to kill, and reached out for his Magnum. That family is going home thinking Northumberland really loves its visitors.

Good deed no. 122.

Tuesday, 3 May

Am abandoning the migraine medication which the consultant prescribed. All I want to do is sleep. How can I do good if I'm asleep? You could argue that while asleep I do no evil, but that isn't enough. I will have to rely on the good deeds to get me through the pain.

Good deed no. 123: bought expats a bread bin.

Wednesday, 4 May

I have all these great ideas that pop into my head – I should leave them there in the darkness to shrivel and die. Currently, my head is threatening to explode while I figure out how to set up a website for the Jam Jar Army. Not to mention the fact that one of the headteachers we approached to get their school on board wants a letter to make sure 'we are who we say we are'. He is not getting the letter. How desperate a fraudster would you have to be to set up a con involving collecting coppers in jam jars? I would be the worst criminal mastermind ever.

Good deed no. 124: edited the school admissions appeal for a place at grammar school for my Yorkshire cousin's eleven-year-old daughter.

Thursday, 5 May

Good deed no. 125: advised wildlife sanctuary on a prospective donor. (I had approached them to take Titty the Lamb, but they can't because they are so cash-strapped. Poor Titty. I have also asked a city farm, but they say they have 'as many sheep as we can accommodate'. It's not like he needs an en suite.)

Friday, 6 May

Good deed no. 126: rang Kirsty re knee.

Saturday, 7 May

Good deed no. 127: kept Ellie for lunch and afternoon play.

Sunday, 8 May

Good deed no. 128: dug out contacts for someone who wants to illustrate kids' books.

Monday, 9 May

Good deed no. 129: toing and froing between illustrator and potential contact.

Tuesday, 10 May

It is strange living by the coast. Turn your head one way and there are green cropped fields hedged round with dense hawthorn, grassy pastures where sheep graze, woodland with roaming deer, and in the background the swell of the Cheviot Hills. Turn your head the other, and it is all sea: endless, ever-changing greys and blues, washing in and out across the sands. For me the land is how we live: fixed and steady, managed and understandable; the sea, though, is who we are: changeable, immense, relentless and hard to comprehend. We come from it, walk by it, swim in it, admire it, and fear it because we have no mastery over it. Years past, those who lived here also worked it for the fish, though there are few enough left do that today. And it was the sea that gave me the idea for another good deed: I could join the crew of a lifeboat. The shame is that I seem to be the only person in the world who thinks this is a possibility.

We live a couple of miles outside what used to be a fishing village and which now makes most of its money from tourism. The village still has its own lifeboat station, however, which sends out lifeboats to rescue bendy divers or those foolish enough to drive over the causeway between Holy Island and the mainland in the belief they can beat the tide. Joining the crew seems an entirely logical choice to me. Why then when I mentioned it to my husband was there a telling silence before he said: 'Why don't you volunteer in a charity shop, darling?'

I rang the local lifeboat operations manager and he said they had a training exercise this evening, so along I went. I walked into the lifeboat station past the little shop selling model lifeboats and teddies, then along a metal gallery; to the right there are crew rooms, and to the left the space drops away to the boathouse where the lifeboat sits in dry dock looking huge and orange and brave. Wooden plaques line the walls with the names and years of the former lifeboats and coxswains and all the rescues that the lifeboat has gone out on. A bearded chap who helps launch the boats took me through to the room where the lifeboat men were gathered. They were ranged in seats around the room chatting to each other, and silence fell as I walked in, which was the right moment to be a foot taller and ten years younger with a willy to call my own.

The operations manager was lovely and cuddly, like a cut-out-and-keep grandad, but he wasn't exactly biting my hand off. I may not be the ideal candidate. A five-foot-two, forty-something woman isn't exactly poster material for the lifeboat crew. Grandad starts talking about training and the sea survival test you have to go through at the Royal National Lifeboat Institution in Poole where they throw you into a tank of choppy water and see if you drown. Physically, I'm not sure I'm up to it. I'm a terrible swimmer with a bad back and a tendency to migraine. I'm short-sighted and I never lift anything heavier than my handbag or a glass of Chablis. I wouldn't want to get to someone who needed rescuing in a stormy sea, decide, 'Do you know what – that looks like far too much trouble,' lean over the boat and, instead of reaching down a hand, shout into the wind, 'Any last words? I'll be sure to pass them on.'

But I can't blink. I'm here to join the lifeboat crew. Grandad meets me halfway. He offers me a ride.

First things first. I climb into the yellow rubberized boots and trousers and enormous jacket. The trousers aren't too bad because the boots stop them trailing on the ground, but the boots must be at least two to three sizes too big, which means I have to throw one leg up into the air to clear the boot before it comes to rest on the ground, then throw the other up in the air to keep the momentum going. Another woman turns up, a young teacher in the local high school, and I breathe a sigh of relief that I am immediately less of an oddity.

We walk from the gallery straight onto the boat deck before the boat trundles out of the boathouse pulled by a tractor. I am jacketed and booted and helmeted. The tourists lining the harbour taking pictures are firmly of the opinion I am a hero. A short hero, admittedly, but a hero nonetheless. One of the guys I am standing next to is six foot five if he is an inch, and I move away from him because he is making me look teeny-tiny. My fellow female lifeguard kneels by a massive metal chain, which is held in place by a metal bracket. When the alarm sounds, you hit the bracket with the hammer as hard as you can, the bracket lifts, the chain falls away and the boat slides from its metal bed parked on the slipway and into the sea. The only problem is there are two chains and two brackets. I kneel by the other chain, take the hammer from its box and raise it over the bracket. The vision of one chain falling from the boat while I repeatedly bash away at my bracket as the boat lists to one side and lifeboat men fall from its deck like passengers from the *Titanic* starts playing on the YouTube channel that is my brain. The alarm goes, and I hammer the bracket so hard I'm lucky I do not go through the plank beneath. Suddenly we are in the water.

The helmsman guns the boat and it begins to plane, its pointy bit raised at a thirty-degree angle as it cuts through the water. The training exercise involves taking the boat across to Holy Island, opening up the engine, practising tying her up at the harbour and checking the shifting sandbars. Occasionally, spray hits me across the face and I try not to mind, like a real hero. The sea cuts Holy Island off from the mainland twice a day, flooding its causeway and occasionally catching strangers and the certifiably stupid off-guard. Only the month before, a car with four adults, two children and a dog had to be rescued by the lifeboat as they attempted to cross the causeway against the tide times.

I wonder why they do it. I'm out with a crew of seven and there are twenty-four volunteers in the village, including the chap who owns the crazy golf course, an IT technician, a college lecturer, a teacher, a plasterer, a plumber, a welder, a barman, a BT engineer, a few boatmen and one fisherman. I understand the boatmen and the fisherman, but everyone else? Why do they put their lives on the line? Because that's what you do. They help the divers who get the bends or who push themselves too hard and run into trouble, surfers who get too ambitious, motorists who get caught out – like the man who took a drink too many one night and parked his van where the tide came in and was plucked from the roof of his van dressed only in his pants and shame. Occasionally, tragically, there are bodies; more often there are rescues.

I enjoy the sea journey out to the island; the problem comes when we moor. The boat is tied up against the harbour wall and a wet iron ladder set against it. We are distinctly lower than I would like us to be. I eye the ladder distrustfully and wonder whether, if I slip between the lifeboat and the lichened wall, I would be pressed flat and dead or would instead slide straight down into the waiting waters and drown beneath the boat. I sling my leg with its over-sized boot over the side of the boat, step into oblivion and hope desperately that somewhere my boot will find a rung. I immediately start to dread climbing back in.

I climb up and down the ladders from hell three times: once onto the island, where we stretch our legs; once off the island back onto the boat; and one final time from the boat back into harbour, which is the very worst time, and I am certain I am not the only one envisaging me slipping between the boat and the dock. Still, there is the consolation of the admiring glances of spectators. It is almost enough consolation for having to heft two of the heavy rubber skids that the boat slides up stern-first out of the water and onto its carriage. These are so heavy, I can barely lift them off the ground let alone into the trailer to clear them away once the boat is free of them. I am useless at shifting the rubber beams but, given a hose, I excel at washing the saltwater off the lifeboat. This has to be the biggest thing I have ever washed. It just doesn't make me look much like a hero.

Good deed no. 130: wrote a press release for the village middle school on its Ofsted inspection report.

Wednesday, 11 May

We live a couple of miles outside the fishing village and a couple of miles outside a village with its own castle. The castle village is picture-postcard pretty with a shady green grove at its heart and an ancient church which tradition tells is built on the spot where a church was founded by St Aidan in AD 635. St Aidan was a genuine good-deed doer and patently my kind of guy. According to the Anglo-Saxon ecclesiastical historian and scholar the Venerable Bede, St Aidan was a man who 'loved to give away to the poor who chanced to meet him whatever he received from kings or wealthy folk'. I haven't actually met a king, but even so I am sure I would give away whatever treasures he gave me. Probably. Unless the treasures were really good treasures, when it might seem down-right rude to give them away. My youngest son persuaded me to go into the ice-cream parlour in the castle village, so as my good deed I cleared the window of the cups and dirty crockery for the very nice shopkeeper which another customer had carefully shifted to one side as he sat down at a bar stool. The shopkeeper said, 'Do you want a job?' and I need the money so much I almost said yes. I have no scruples whatsoever about getting my hands dirty, I just need more hours in my day. I have always thought that the answer to the question 'If you were hungry would you prostitute yourself to put bread in the mouths of your children?' was a pretty resounding 'You betcha'. At my age and in my condition, I'd fetch about £2.50.

Good deed no. 131.

Cryssie's legs turn inwards slightly and if she loses muscle – as she did recently when her foot was in plaster after an operation – she won't ever get it back. Her face is also constricted in its movement, which means she can't smile. I was particularly worried I might not understand her because her speech is similarly constricted by her frozen facial muscles. But she wants to be a writer. And I'm supposed to help. The physical aside, what I didn't know was how severe her learning difficulties were. For a brief moment I thought of Christy Nolan, a genius trapped in a massively physically handicapped body; and at the idea of releasing that, a Pulitzer dangled in front of me – not one for me, but one for Cryssie, which she could hold proudly as my own eyes misted with tears of a teacher who had changed a child's life. But according to her mother she has moderate learning difficulties, so the Pulitzer's off then.

I have never been a teacher. I do not have the patience. So it's strange I am teaching Cryssie in the morning, then going into the university and teaching blogging in the afternoon. I must be one of the least-qualified teachers ever. What a fraud. I had to google 'how to write a children's book' while she sat next to me. I told her that to be a writer she needs to read, and she does read, which is good, but she reads the animal books my five-year-old daughter likes, which is bad. Admittedly, Cryssie is actually reading them and my daughter is having them read to her, but nonetheless I am pretty sure they are way below Cryssie's abilities. She had three ideas for stories – one for a dog, one for a kitten and one for a rabbit. They all involved the animals getting lost or hurt and ending up at the vets or safe at home – cut-outs of what she is reading, I'm guessing – but on the bright side, she did have three ideas. She picked the rabbit one to develop, and what was interesting was that from the ideas of titles we worked up together – 'The Lost Rabbit', 'The Rabbit Who Got Lost', 'The Rabbit Who Got Rescued' and 'The Rabbit Who Needed Rescuing' – the one she picked was the last one: 'Bunny's Bad Day'.

I talked to her dad when he came to pick her up. She had given up computing, but needs to learn to type so we found a programs to practise on, and we talked about finding a more challenging book to read, and I gave her some homework – to sum up 'Bunny's Bad Day' in one line, then in three paragraphs. Carefully, she lifted one leg over the lintel, balanced herself, then brought the other one to join it. She picked her way through the back door and across the yard to her car, her dad close behind. The lesson was not much in the scheme of things, but it was a start and I felt OK: that a good deed meant something.

Good deed no. 132.

Friday, 13 May

I was shattered last night driving home. It was very weird teaching at a university when I have never taught before. I felt like an ancient bluestocking bag-lady walking through the university dragging my little black wheelie bag with my enormous knack-ered laptop in it. It made me remember my friend who used to be an academic and who said what was strange was the fact you got older and fatter and balder as the years passed, while everybody around you stayed young and beautiful.

It was the second session of the six-week course on blogging which I'm tutoring along with Tyneside IT genius Oli Wood. At least three people on the course have been blogging very personal stuff – one, who has chronic ill-health and blogs about her condi-tion, was wheeled in by a friend who had brought her out of hospital for the evening, and a first-aider sat behind her in case she suffered an anaphylactic shock at any point. Another girl had writ-ten about recovering from a massive tumour in her chest when she has three tiny children, one of whom has haemophilia. And the third had written about being married and fancying a married man with whom the blog would have you believe she had shared a drunken moment, along with her apparent desire to do more. All of them write really well but, speaking as a blogger, even I am taken aback by the confessional nature of some of it. I know blogging can act as therapy because I've used it myself that way, but I am taken aback to see it from the outside.

Good deed no. 133: recommended one of the students (keen to find a market for her writing) as a potential contributor to a women's online magazine.

Saturday, 14 May

Ellie was good today. I kept her for lunch and play. Lily said she has been testing me with her attention-seeking behaviour. She advised me to take a tougher line with her, and it certainly means less faffing about. You say no as firmly as you would to your own child, and the child might ask once or twice more, but not a dozen or two dozen times till you want to say 'OK – whatever' or shoot yourself.

The kid is gorgeous with her dangling ringlets and those vivid round eyes. You can tell something is amiss with her sight, though, because she stares in a fixed manner. She also falls over all the time because, however beautiful her eyes are, they only work at 30 per cent capacity. She is prone to kidney infections too, and before she gets the kidney infection, her behaviour goes downhill. What do these women think when they are pregnant and they are drinking or on drugs? Don't they think of the consequences, the love they owe that unborn child, the care? Do they scratch at the tracks on their ruined arms with bitten-down fingernails and figure the consequences will drive on by, that there won't be the sound of a car drawing up outside their house, and a rapping at the door, that the hoodied debt-collectors of their own addiction won't force their way into the darkness of their womb, slip on knuckledusters and beat on the innocent, curled-up child that's growing there?

Surely, if there is one place a child should be able to trust their mother, it's inside of her. But then something went wrong in me when my child died – so who am I to talk? A mother who let down her child and didn't even know it. Perhaps that's why I get mad. I do not know what went wrong when my child died in utero – it wasn't drugs or drink, or pesticides on food, or lack of yoga or green tea – but these greasy-headed girls pour poisons in their bodies and make their unborn babies drink it.

And then afterwards, when the babe is born, and offstage the social worker types 'At risk', the doped-up mother turns neglect into an art form. Her itch for oblivion. The conviction that there is nothing like that feeling on this earth, nothing makes her feel that good – not even the smell of her baby's head, the curl of her fingers. Leaving her babe unchanged, alone, hungry, thirsty, in the dark – forgotten. A mother who makes promises that this wrap will be the last, just one more time but never again. Telling herself, 'She's quiet . . . asleep . . . won't wake up for hours.' But yelling, screaming, cursing when they come to take the babe away. Shouting of love and 'You've no right' and 'She's my baby'. Now she's your baby, is she? This limp and damaged child. Bad decisions; bad company; bad, bad mothers. Lily doesn't judge, but if I had Ellie's natural mother here, I swear by that child's green and poorly eyes I'd slap her till she wept and wept some more.

Good deed no. 134.

Sunday, 15 May

My good deed was ringing Merry. I haven't sent her a book in a while. I must look one out for her. She sounded in good fettle, though. She is still getting counselling to cope with the extent of her grief after her one true love died, which is obviously helping, and she has set up her own gardening company and is working thirty hours a week. The anniversary is next weekend, so I must remember to send something. A card saying I remember? Flowers? A book in which nobody dies?

Good deed no. 135.

Monday, 16 May

Last night as I was reading to her, my daughter started bouncing up and down, and when I asked her why, she pleaded for a telescope or binoculars. She loves animals, loves birds. I thought she must want to spot a finch, a tit, a red-breasted robin. She said: 'That way I'll see the aliens when they come.'

I was not quite sure what to do for my good deed. This happens a lot less often than I expected. In fact, there are times I believe the good-deedery is out and out compulsive. In the end I decided to write to Diane's oldest son, who is away at boarding school. He loves it there. He went when he was eight. And now he's nine. Old enough then to be away from home? Almost a man? Maybe at eleven. Maybe at twelve. When they're so old they do not want the kissing and the closeness and the mummying. It is a class thing. I am too working class to put my child out the door at eight. 'Bye now, see you on your exeat.' Genes tell me that when hard times come, I'll need that child. I want him handy to send down the pit or up the chimney to earn the cash to keep me in my gin. I've written before – three times – like a distant aunt, to ask him how he is. I tell him news of me and mine, which doubtless he has no interest in hearing, and I draw him little pictures of my world – sometimes I crayon them in. His mother tells me he thinks my letters mad. I enclose slim bars of chocolate, which make them better reading – bet he doesn't tell her that.

Good deed no. 136.

Tuesday, 17 May

We've sent our eldest to the middle school in the village, and our younger ones are at a church first school a couple of miles away. Both are lovely, excellent schools, but is there anything you worry about more than your children? Their health, their happiness – present and future. School, college, career. Whether their hearts will get broken. How they'll cope. Whether they'll have children, and if you'll be there to help. In my saner moments, I consider how happy my boy is right now – genuinely, beautifully happy. He swings his rucksack onto his back, quick-kisses me, goes out for the school bus with a smile and comes in with a smile, and I think, 'Stop fussing, you neurotic piece of baggage.' Then the chilled-as-chilled-is eight-year-old got up on Monday, came down to breakfast and while pouring out the Weetabix Minis into his bowl, pronounced with due phlegm: 'Five more days of misery then.' Today, though, my eldest boy burst through the kitchen door waving a scrappy piece of paper on which he had scribbled his results for an English test, and he scored level 5C – better than his target and better than I'd expected – and I thought, 'Good for you. I'll wait until tomorrow to worry some more.'

Good deed no. 137: worked on Jam Jar Army.

Wednesday, 18 May

Cryssie arrived with a much more suitable children's book than the books about kittens and puppies she has been reading. It is interesting to watch her write because she settles to it and there's a sense of rightness while she is working. She says she feels 'engrossed' when she writes. The fact is her physical disabilities are such that movement and exertion have to be restricted, and I don't think she realizes yet where she can go with her writing. That if we can lift the latch on her imagination and push open the door, she can swim with mermaids, jump from star to star, that she can be and do anything she wants. For now, though, we are sticking with 'Bunny's Bad Day', a tale of a young and curious rabbit who cuts his paw on broken glass and is rescued by a little girl and taken to a vet. It is almost certain to contain universal truths.

That was the good thing about the day. The bad thing was apparently I live too far away to join the lifeboat crew. I am both secretly relieved and horribly disappointed. Now I'll never know if I'm made of the 'right stuff' – then again, that might be just as well.

Good deed no. 138.

Thursday, 19 May

My geek friend Oli and I spent the day at his place building the website for the Jam Jar Army. To be strictly accurate, Oli built it and I spent the day picking my way through cables and asking whether he had any food in and if I should make another cup of tea. He said he just gets into work and looks up and it's four in the afternoon. I'm not like that. If I don't eat, I want to kill those puppy dogs Cryssie likes to read about. He did me a big favour by doing it because I was struggling and he has done a really good job. What is terrifying, though, is I will have to go back in and finish it off because it is only halfway there, I'll also have to drop in the words and pics, and I don't have the skill-set. Positive thinking. With experience I will acquire the skill-set.

Good deed no. 139: advised a blog-course student (who wants to write a book) how to write a synopsis.

Friday, 20 May

It has been the best part of twenty-five years since I started work for a regional newspaper. I wore ra-ra skirts and shoulder pads, clacking out my first stories on typewriters, working in an office with strip lights and a coffee machine which piddled coffee into plastic cups so thin they scorched off your fingerprints. I was grown-up. I shared a flat with my best gay boyfriend and ate vinegared chips in bubbling, spitting, green curry sauce for tea. I was an official member of Her Majesty's media. When I walk into the flat-fronted Georgian pile that is the offices of the *Northumberland*

Gazette, I want to be twenty-two all over again. It smells of paper and deadlines, the oak panelling sucking away the light in the hallway as I push down the shiny brass bell to tell the nice lady behind the counter that I have an appointment with the editor.

Paul Larkin is a tall man in his late forties with a wide smile and preternaturally white hair. He exudes calm as he tucks himself behind a desk in an empty office and listens to my burble. I have an idea. I speed-walk him through the Jam Jar Army and astonishingly he bites. Not literally. He is way too chilled to bite me. He bites on the idea. The *Gazette* will get behind the Jam Jar Army to raise £10,000 for the hospice. When he moots ten grand, my pleasant smile spasms into a rictus and a nervous tic starts up in my left eyelid.

'Is that too much?' he asks, and I make a rapid calculation. If I yelp and say yes, way, way too much, the cool dude will think I don't have faith in the project, so he will lose faith in the project. I swallow and it sounds loud in my ears.

'Nooooo,' I say, trying to sound as cool as him and sliding my finger up to my eyelid to hide the tic. 'Sounds good to me.'

Outside, I put one hand against the stone wall and one hand on my chest and try to stop myself from hyperventilating. Is that doable? It's madness, isn't it? At £3 a jar we will need 3,333 jars out in Northumberland. I am going to look chronically stupid if this comes to nothing. What if we get back twenty jars? That's £60. Larkin wants some *Blue Peter*-type thermometer to judge how much money they are getting in. Apparently, he used to be deputy editor on the *Sunderland Echo* and they raised £90,000 for charity. He said he hasn't ever done a charitable appeal on the *Gazette*, so I had excellent timing.

I am now officially terrified at the prospect of looking incompetent in front of the entire county. What is going to persuade people to 'fill a jar with change'? Why would they? Will they if, week after week, they are reading about it in the local paper? I am going home to ring round some more schools – somebody has to fill these jam jars. Perhaps Al will let us take another mortgage out on the house.

Good deed no. 140.

Saturday, 21 May

Ellie got in the car and announced yet again my daughter wasn't her friend any more. What is it? I wonder. Is any attention better than no attention? My daughter ended up sobbing, and I ended up bringing the car to a dead-stop as we pulled into the churchyard and instructing Ellie very firmly that enough was enough. My daughter promptly announced she felt sick and Ellie said she felt sick too, and my daughter said she didn't want to go to dancing and Ellie said she wasn't going either, and I marched into Wonderland anyway.

Buying them both a bag of chocolate caramels for the return journey was not straight out of the parenting textbooks, but it is astonishing how chewy caramels occupy little mouths for extended periods. Once they'd finished chewing, they were sufficiently blissed on a sugar high that together they sang songs from musicals and hymns from school all the way back. Consequently, when we pulled into the farmyard, anyone watching would have thought I had a real gift with kids. Yep, a real gift and two bags of chocolate caramel chews.

Good deed no. 141.

Sunday, 22 May

It is a year ago exactly since Merry's partner died. I wasn't sure what to expect when I called. I thought she might end up sobbing down the phone because her soulmate had been swallowed up by death. In reality, I felt better when I came off the phone, because she was strong and together and laughed – even at some psycho-babble rubbish I spouted at one point. I know she misses him terribly and thinks of him every day – God knows how many times, as many times as there are breaths in her body probably – but she was centred and peaceful even. Her gardening business is doing well, she is managing her money even though she hasn't much, she has her three boys to love, and there was such devastation when he died, such grief and terror at his loss, that I want to hang a 'Well Done, You' golden medal shaped like a sunflower around her neck and say, 'Congratulations on your survival. For pulling through, we would like you to have this medal as a token of our esteem, to mark the small miracle that you are still you.'

Good deed no. 142.

Monday, 23 May

I invited myself over to Diane's farm for coffee, and as my good deed picked up another mother who I know likes company and brought her along with me. Diane's little girl took me upstairs to see her plump, purring cat, which was curled up in high comfort on her brother's duvet, and asked me to read her a book, so I lay next to her and we read stories together. Diane said she slept right through the night for the first time in months. She shouts out at night wanting to know where she is, and if she's not persuaded, the shouting slides into hysteria. What handbook is there for mothers? *My child is different. Just how 'different' is she? Is she different like this? Or like that? Try this approach. Try that. This 'How to Parent' manual worked for me.* And people are so quick to judge. I had noticed myself that the child roams, that Diane will be talking and her little girl will be away, and occasionally someone rounds her up and brings her back. Do they wonder why this child doesn't cling, doesn't hang off Diane or hide behind her skirts? But she's in a world where noises crash and bang, where no one speaks her language, trying to find her way.

Good deed no. 143.

Tuesday, 24 May

Al asked me how I felt and I said, 'Like I'm standing on a cliff top screaming,' and he backed away and said, 'I'll make you a nice cup of tea.'

On the upside, the headteacher at my eldest son's school has rung with a whizz-bang idea for the Jam Jar Army. She has got 104 jars of jam coming from the local and very public-spirited Sainsbury's to give out to her children, and her Year 6 (thirty-three kids) are going to walk along the coast from one village to the next – around eight miles – to raise public awareness of the Jam Jar Army. Which is astonishing. The head is doing this totally off her own bat as part of the kids' community week. I'm amazed and delighted and worried that people are taking me seriously and it may all come to naught. My son clamped his hand to his forehead when I told him. 'Because of you, they're all going to blame me for having to go on a mega walk in the rain,' he said. He's ten and about to disown me. Welcome to my future.

Good deed no. 144: toing and froing between the school and hospice over the Jam Jar Army walk.

Wednesday, 25 May

Despite the fact the RNLI turned down my kind offer to be a crew member, I filled in a nomination form at the supermarket for them to be a Sainsbury's community charity. Maybe they'll change their minds if I tell them?

Good deed no. 145.

Thursday, 26 May

Cryssie's lessons are taking on their own shape. We start by talking about the book she has just read. She read two this week, both of them historical. Then we do a bit of research on those books and their authors, after which we turn to her homework and finally get her to take on the planning of her story. I'm trying to pin down what she is capable of and what if anything I am capable of passing on. I don't think I can be doing any harm because at the very least she is going to walk away with a better understanding of how to read, if not to write.

One of her books was based on New Lanark, the new town set up by social pioneer Robert Owen which educated children and which housed its mill workers in decent homes, and the other was based on the Irish potato famine. Cryssie wasn't aware of either New Lanark or the potato famine, so we researched both on the Internet. We found a documentary about Robert Owen and an interview by the author of the potato famine book, Michael Morpurgo, about how he writes. He bases his books on an element of truth and builds from there, and he advised doing lots with your life to give you plenty of material and trusting your heart. I was critically aware as I sat next to Cryssie, who moves deliberately and slowly as if her frail legs were trapped in metal braces, that her disabilities would limit that life experience, but she loves greatly and is greatly loved in return, so that box at least she can mark with a juicy fat red tick.

After seeing Cryssie, I drove down to Newcastle for a pre-session meeting with one of the students about her writing. She married when she was just out of university, and had her kids early. Now they are grown and she is wondering what to do. It's difficult, I think, for a woman to get to her forties and start over. Middle age is a hard place to be without that silk and goosedown cushion of 'potential' the young carry so casually tucked beneath their arm. This woman is smart and talented but sensitive to criticism, and cyberspace can be a hard place for the soft of skin. She badly needs to decide what she is willing to put out there and whether she is going to write as she wants to write, or whether she is going to write looking over her shoulder, waiting for wounding words to fall. There is no one-size-fits-all for women. But if you have a career and then the family, although you might exist in a state of permanent exhaustion, at least you've been there and done that in terms of ambition – there are no what-might-have-beens and I'll-never-knows as you cook the tea. Either which way, children first or children last or children not at all, criticism is surely no stranger by the time you hit your forties. But so what? Because by then you have decided who you are, and for those who don't like you, those who don't get you, those who claim you disappoint them or argue you should change to suit them, well, you can shake their hands, say 'Each to their own' and 'It's been a pleasure meeting you', tip your hat, and carry on past regardless.

Good deed no. 146.

Friday, 27 May

I rang Kathryn for Diane, who is about to go on holiday. She hadn't asked me to, but I know she's daunted because the nights are so bad at the moment – let alone climbing on a plane to Portugal. There is no doubt about the child's autism, and I figured Kathryn would have travelled often enough with her own autistic daughter to hand on some wisdom.

She answered the phone, and in the background I could hear a sheepdog barking. We talked it through and she advised taking an extra bag of toys and pens and paper to keep the little one thoroughly engaged and locked on to what she is doing so she doesn't get mesmerized or upset by the hustle of the airport or the strangeness of the aeroplane. The toys would also comfort her in a strange bedroom. Later, I googled 'holidays with autistic children' and emailed Diane what I found. The advice on the Internet was pretty similar to Kathryn's, basically 'Don't get stressed' and 'Keep a sense of humour'. I imagine that's easier said than done.

Good deed no. 147.

Since it was half-term, I expected the girls' tap and modern dance class to be cancelled and I breathed a sigh of relief I would not have Ellie for the morning. Al brought me up a cup of tea and, still yawning after I drank it, I broke through a skim of snowy bubbles to slide my weary bones into a boiling-hot bath smelling of lemons, which was the natural cue for the phone to ring. Lily was calling to say dancing was on even though it was half-term and wasn't that good? I stood there, naked – that part of my body which had been beneath the water a riotous fleshy red – dripping steadily onto the stripped wooden floor, staring hard at the footprints from the bath to the bedroom phone, and thinking that if I was a genuinely good person I would dry myself with a rough white towel and drive the girls down to dancing, and not mind the bickering that starts up, and the incessant pleas that she come back to my house and play, or that we go to the café and drink hot chocolate.

I am not a genuinely good person. I am no better than ever I was. I said, 'Let's skip it, shall we?' ignoring the silent disappointment down the line. I followed the trail of footprints back into the water and slid back beneath the waves in shame. I wonder, were there many leggy fish who crawled on up the beach out of the roiling, bucking, funky stew, thought better of it and crawled back down again?

Kirsty and her husband arrived, which would have been great but for the fact he too is a fan of Manchester United, so the evening consisted of sitting round the telly watching Man U's chance of one cup or another swirl down the drain. I just about managed the first half when there was some prospect of victory, but had no interest in the second half at all. Al let the boys stay up to watch it. It is difficult to teach them to lose with grace when their father is patently gutted whenever his team loses. Perhaps I shouldn't try. Perhaps I should take the view I am breeding winners who do not have to learn to lose with grace because it will never happen. I was taught to 'play to lose and win if you can', which is Delphic but basically means you treat losing with the same grace as winning, and I still regard myself as competitive.

Kirsty is using two sticks after the operation to replace her knee. She came off her rheumatoid medication for the op and has been vomiting and nauseous with the painkillers, so she has had to give them up too. Her hands, feet and knees are swollen, and you want to scoop her up and hold her till she's better. She is resolutely optimistic: she says she is looking forward to the swelling going because the new knee will make a big difference to her quality of life. Everybody has their own story. With Kirsty it is all about grace under pressure.

Good deed no. 148: had a neighbour in for the football. He told a very bad joke: how many Manchester United fans does it take to change a light bulb? Two to hold the ladder, one to change the bulb and one to drive them back to London afterwards.

Sunday, 29 May

Al always takes the children to his brother Rob who lives in Wales for this half-term week and leaves me to work. Since I wasn't travelling with them, I did not have to jump up and down on the same spot yelling 'Look at the bloody time!', which meant Al left for Wales at 2.30 p.m., approximately four hours late. If I had been going, the fact he disappeared into the study to 'finish off a bit of work' in the morning instead of herding the children into the car and setting off would have hacked me off no end. Instead, I inhaled deeply, let it out slowly, and thought, 'Calm down, dear. You don't have to put them to bed at ten o'clock tonight and you don't have to be there tomorrow morning when everyone is grumpy as hell.'

Good deed no. 149: emptied out a neighbour's grill pan in kitchen cupboard, which was catching water from a leaking pipe.

Monday, 30 May

I ate my solitary breakfast today – poured my milk, spooned up my cereal and drank my tea – and there was silence everywhere. This is how it would be to live a single life: one bowl, one cup and emptiness.

Good deed no. 150: tipped out water from the neighbour's grill pan again and called them to say that the plumbers hadn't been.

Tuesday, 31 May

Spent all day on the Jam Jar Army website when I should have been writing. I kept setting myself deadlines: first noon, then 1 p.m., then 2 p.m., then 4 p.m. It's 6.30 p.m. and I'm still tinkering with the website. It really would help if I knew what I was doing. When I finally stopped working on it and sat down and closed my eyes, my overloaded brain fizzed and pulled a wobbly, and every single screen I'd opened up that day on the computer downloaded before my eyes, one after the other, at huge speed, like something from *The Matrix*.

It does me good to be on my own. You walk out and nothing seems to pass you on the road that runs down to the sea and on into the village. The only movement is that of the wind in the leaves of the banked trees; the only other sound, the chirruping song of birds; the only other sign of life, your own breath. It is nerve-wracking at night, though, as I bolt the doors against the darkness; and even when I am safe and locked-up virgin tight, the cottage is old so it creaks and strains, and above a pump roars into life all unexpected, which makes me jump and wake again. If I was in the city, I'd think 'thief', but in the country dark, with the silvery moon hidden away in the clouds, away from shining houses, far from streets of beery laughs and the tip-tap scurry of those late home, the thought 'thief' would be a light relief; I move straight instead to 'Maniac – there's a maniac in the house.'

Friends arrived next door at their cottage. He's a teacher, so they are up for a few days during half-term week – it is just as well because I started talking to myself this morning.

Good deed no. 151: let in the neighbour's plumber and made him a cup of tea when I was too busy to make myself one.

Wednesday, 1 June

Woken up at five o'clock in the morning by some stupid pigeon deciding to fly through my open window into my otherwise entirely silent house and entangle itself in my curtains. My windows were only open a hand-span for fear of psychotic murderers creeping in, so the damn bird must have limbo-danced its way in.

Thanks to the pigeon, I was half asleep when I stumbled across the 'World Giving Index' by the Charities Aid Foundation, which says in terms of money we are the third most generous nation in the world (equal to Thailand), with 73 per cent of people having given money in the last six months. Top came Malta and the Netherlands. The index also calculated the percentage of those giving time and helping a stranger. In the UK, 29 per cent had given time and 58 per cent had helped a stranger. Overall, in terms of these three factors, we ranked eighth below Australia and New Zealand, who came joint first, then Canada and Ireland, who came joint third, then Switzerland and the USA, joint fifth, and the Netherlands, seventh. Eighth came Sri Lanka and the UK, which is pretty good.

Apparently in Britain, according to some government white paper, we give more than £10bn a year. That is wildly impressive. It has flattened out in the last couple of years, so the government is trying to do various things to reinvigorate it, like mobile giving (on mobile phones) or rounding up your giving to the nearest pound. It all seemed very technologically cutting edge. Then there is me and a jam jar.

Good deed no. 152: drove into the local market town and left flowers on the Lovely Claire's door handle from the 'flower fairy'. Facebook said it was her birthday. She had ninety-five birthday congratulations and good wishes. That is not normal.

Thursday, 2 June

Glorious day. The heavy hum of buzzing bees through the nodding spindly yellow poppies, the imperial purple of aubretia spread along the stone walls, the do-or-die song of unseen birds, and a cashmere breeze and azure-blue skies, immense and wide, stretching down to the sea over the pastures. Even the ground beneath my stockinged feet is warm as I stand and listen to the wind moving through the trees. Some trick of nature makes that wind sound like the sea, and there are times when the seas run high and you hear the sea and the sea's impostor together. I like that best of all.

Good deed no. 153: lent a neighbour a body board and change for the parking machine.

Friday, 3 June

Good deed no. 154: had my picture taken for the Jam Jar Army in the Gazette. (I hate having my picture taken. I wonder if they can take a picture of me if I use both hands to hold back the fat, which would also have the effect of smoothing out the wrinkles. Or would that look odd?)

Saturday, 4 June

Good deed no. 155: boosted a local writer's new book on Twitter, Facebook and Amazon with a five-star review (despite acute attack of jealousy that I didn't write it).

Sunday, 5 June

I said bedtime prayers every night when I was a child – I had my own altar in my bedroom with prayerful statuettes glowing in the dark and a writhing silver Christ hung upon an oaken cross. *'Matthew, Mark, Luke and John, God bless this bed I lay upon, and if I die before I wake, I pray to God my soul to take.'* It's amazing I ever closed my eyes. My Irish aunty has come back from a parish trip to Lourdes. She spent two whole nights crying to herself once her friend had gone to sleep because she missed my uncle so much, and never told a soul. What's the point of saints if they only watch us while we weep? I'd rather those that stop up that weeping altogether.

Good deed no. 156: set aside £20 for raffle tickets for my eldest son's school fete in aid of the RNLI (despite the fact they didn't want me on their poxy life-saving boat).

Monday, 6 June

Week of the Jam Jar Army launch. So far today I have:

- given eldest a dozen DVDs for the school fete;
- paid out £20 to ice-cream parlour for ice cream (the shop-owner did it for me at cost) to be given out when the kids do their Jam Jar Army walk on Thursday;
- picked up leaflets at hospice and dropped them off at school for distribution on the walk;
- gingered up hospice folk re engagement/active partnership/ commitment with the newspaper appeal so that they are not just being passive recipients. The hospice must regard me as a mixed blessing: on the one hand, I am delivering publicity and the chance of cash; on the other, I am a pain in the arse.

Good deed no. 157.

Tuesday, 7 June

Al in London and my daughter down with stomach migraine.
I was literally hopping from foot to foot as I tried to figure out if
I had to cancel the school assembly I was booked in to do on the
Jam Jar Army, which the photographer was turning up to shoot.
I didn't have the photographer's number and there was no one at
the *Gazette* to call. I ended up getting in the expat to look after my
daughter while I went to the school. I made three platefuls of jam
sandwiches to give to the children at school on the premise that
the jam jars had to be empty before they could be filled with
money. No one threw anything at me, so it could have been worse.

Good deed no. 158.

Wednesday, 8 June

Another school assembly at another school. My daughter came
with me because she was so disappointed she didn't get to see me
yesterday at her own school. She sat like a mouse at the end of the
front row, and butterflies unfurled themselves from chrysalises in
my tummy and flew round and round at the thought of her watching me. This time I made more than a hundred jam sandwiches;
mid-presentation, I asked who would like a jam sandwich and they
all stuck their hands up, so I carefully jammed a piece of bread and
picked out a child to give it to. I looked at the few pieces of bread
I had carefully left out, asked who else would like a jam sandwich
and they stuck up their hands again; I gave another lad a jam
sandwich and they all sighed with longing and disappointment. I
said that luckily I had made some more earlier, and hauled out three
enormous plates of jam sandwiches. Everyone laughed and cheered,
but when I smugly handed the plates to the teachers to give them
out, one of the teachers suddenly shook his head and said the
children had better wash their hands first and wait till after lunch to
eat them. I just about resisted saying, 'You're kidding, right?' But

he wasn't. The poor kids watched with big round eyes as the three plates of jam sandwiches were put to one side and then watched me sorrowfully as I wound up the talk. Bet nobody ever sabotages Bill Gates or Al Gore when they're doing their big presentations. And I bet those kids don't get to eat those sandwiches either.

Good deed no. 159.

Thursday, 9 June

Launch date. Big splash in the *Northumberland Gazette*. Even better, the photo of me on page two is blurry. Result.

Ferociously busy day. The middle school were walking along the coast with their home-made Jam Jar Army banner and I went down to see them get medals from the hospice girls to thank them for their efforts. They even gave me one, which was nice – I'm too superstitious to wear it, though – maybe I will hang it round my neck if we actually make the £10k, and maybe, if we don't, I'll just hang myself with it. The kids seemed delighted with their medals and just as pleased with the chocolate ice cream I brought along as my thank you. I had to leave someone else to serve it because I had to drive down to Newcastle to do a radio interview to mark the launch. The interview was definitely my good deed. I was so nervous, I was virtually hyperventilating. I have spent so many years asking tough questions as a journalist that I am now almost catatonic with nerves by the time I do a broadcast interview and have to actually answer someone else's.

Good deed no. 160.

Friday, 10 June

I dropped off doughnuts at the *Gazette* office to say thanks for the way they handled the launch of the Jam Jar Army yesterday (doubled up as my good deed), and had a sit-down with their young reporter who is in charge of appeal stories. He did a degree at Durham, his masters at Sunderland University in journalism and has been with the paper since he finished his masters last July. He is probably twenty-two, which means I could be his mother. When does that suddenly happen? When do you suddenly become everybody's mother?

After I dropped off the doughnuts, I crashed and burned and went back to bed. It has been a hell of a week:

- My daughter got sick.
- I did two presentations to two schools, including preparation (and making a shedload of jam sandwiches).
- The Jam Jar Army was launched.
- And I had to go down to Newcastle for the radio interview and then teach the blog course (which entailed an hour's drive down there, the radio interview, an hour's pre-meeting before the blog course, two hours' teaching and an hour's drive back).

Of course, Al was away in London throughout.

I really should capitalize on the launch, and I had a list as long as my arm of things I should have done today. Instead I crawled into bed and stayed there till lunchtime. I am not a saint. I wonder if people reading the *Gazette* will think that I think I'm a do-gooder? Is it really middle class to exhort everyone to 'do their bit' and 'pull together' – it is, isn't it? I never realized it was. Am I about to come across as some middle-class, patronizing whatsit when that is actually what I am trying to get away from? Fund-raisers in ball gowns and grand auctions and gold credit cards.

A friend at school who used to be a council leader round here asked me what I was busy with the other day, so I told her and she got it straight away when I said I could have made more money climbing Mount Kilimanjaro and getting a few mates to sponsor me. She said, 'Yes, but you're trying to engage people, aren't you?' And I said, 'Yes. Big mistake.' Why didn't I just climb Kilimanjaro?

OK, I'd have had to do some training, and there'd have been a bit of preparation like buying a Thermos flask and a woolly hat. There's a chance my mates would have rolled their eyes when I emailed round my JustGiving page details, and when I droned on for the next three years about how I-haven't-recovered-feeling-in-my-little-toe-after-the-frostbite-but-it-was-worth-it-for-the-view-from-the-top-which-made-me-feel-like-I-was-entirely-insignificant-but-somehow-fundamentally-'connected'-to-the-bigger-picture. As it is, this Jam Jar Army thing could quite clearly eat up my entire life if I let it. I wouldn't actually mind letting it, but for the small matter of three kids, husband, elderly parents, house to keep, need to earn money, desire to write books and the fact I'm committed to doing a good fucking deed every fucking day.

Good deed no. 161.

Saturday, 11 June

Youngest son's first Communion class. During the parents' preparation, the TV preacher on one of the videos we have to watch spoke about how basic it is to eat with people. How it's one of the first things we say to someone when we are getting to know them and we want to know them better – come round to eat with me. And how eating together as a family or with friends is almost sacred, a celebration of love, and that Communion is an extension of that – a way of saying Jesus Christ is with me. We were allowed to comment during the breaks in the sermon this time (I'm guessing because I fed back to the nice catechist that this should be more of a conversation and less of sit there and listen to the TV preacher and then listen to the priest). I said how valuable I had found that: it's too easy to think of meals with the kids as being little more than catch-up and ketchup, a chore to get through before you move on to the chore of clearing up and washing up. Then one of the other parents – a dad this time – intervened to say they didn't even have a kitchen table because they had decided they didn't need one. That shocked me. They must eat on their knees. Maybe there's a breakfast bar the kids eat at? I wanted to run out and buy them a table. I wanted to say, 'You don't know what you're missing. Sit down and eat – together.'

Good deed no. 162: made cups of tea for the mothers and fathers at the Communion class.

Sunday, 12 June

Brought tray-bake and crisps along for younger son's football presentation. (I could have made a cake, but give me a break.) It took up the whole afternoon, but my younger son did at least walk away with three trophies. I have never won a trophy for anything sporty in my life. Nor have i ever won a medal or certificate – the medal from the hospice the other day is my first. The best I did in swimming was a certificate for three lengths – I never even got far enough to be trusted to come back up with a brick from the bottom of the swimming pool – so it is a constant source of wonder to me to have a child who triumphs on the field. I was proud of him, but I was prouder of his older brother, who loves football with a desperate passion and who watches while his younger brother picks up trophy after trophy and who never says a word other than 'Well Done' and 'Good for you – you worked really hard for that' and pats him on the back. And I know how very much he wants to hold that trophy and to score those goals, and I know too that his big brother's golden words mean more to his little brother than all the silver-painted football boots in all the whole wide world.

Good deed no. 163.

Monday, 13 June

A couple of months ago comedian Ricky Gervais 'died' as host to the Golden Globes; after Berwick High School, I know how he felt. I was due to speak at the Year 9 assembly of thirteen- and fourteen-year-olds. Around 180 teenagers sat slumped in their chairs in the hall. They had already sat through an in-house assembly on friendship after staff became convinced I might not show, or at least arrive too late for the assembly. I had 128 jam sandwiches wrapped in cling film ready for the kids (I hadn't realized there would be so many of them, but I reasoned that 128 was safe enough because not everyone would want one; how right I was). I'm standing outside the hall ready to go in when the teacher with me suddenly announces that the 128 jam sandwiches aren't a good idea. This potentially utterly wrecks the presentation. I am relying on the jam sandwiches as a way into the Jam Jar Army and because Sophie has assured me that if you are selling something (which I am), the best way to get someone to buy it is to give them something first (something like a jam sandwich). At the look of wild-eyed panic that moves across my face, she concedes I can give out one jam sandwich. I shake my head to clear my brain and start making rapid calculations about what I have left to say – which is basically, 'Give me your money' – and suddenly I'm on.

I talk about me. I talk about emptying a jar of jam and filling it with cash. I talk about the Jam Jar Army, and the good cause that is the hospice. I ask whether anyone would like a jam sandwich, and there is silence. The teacher has said I can make one jam sandwich and give it to someone. Nobody – not one kid among the 180 kids – wants that jam sandwich. I am dying. I hold fast to my conviction that someone will crack – there is a jam sandwich and 180 teenagers – someone is going to be hungry. It turns into a war of wills. I offer it along the front row. It is made of soft white bread and bramble jelly. There are half a dozen girls in front of me, and I offer it to each. The girl at the end of the row is not a healthy eater. I move swiftly on: there is no way a fat lass is going to say yes to the jam sandwich, however much she wants it. The blond boy next to her is equally large. I have great hopes of this lad. He bulges out of his blazer, his sizeable thighs spread as he leans forward. He shakes his head. His friend shakes his head. The boy next to him shakes his head and I eye the tousled-headed boy at the end of the row with the final shreds of hope. He looks at me. He looks at the jam sandwich in my hand – the purple jam shyly peeking from its white and doughy hiding place. He shakes his head. Not one taker. The teacher tells me she'll have one later. She says it out of pity. I shrug as if public humiliation was nothing new and say, 'Well, I'll have to eat it then,' and take a bite. I contemplate making them wait until I have eaten every scrap. I contemplate chewing slowly but I am unconvinced the staff will let me get away with this, so I decide one bite will have to do. The bread and jam immediately and for all time sucker themselves to the roof of my mouth. I try to scrape the bite of sandwich off the roof of my mouth with my tongue and fail. One hundred and eighty adolescents watch my jaws contort with what might be their first spark of interest that morning as my tongue does battle with the bread and jam. I shrug for the second time as if I have not been engaged in a public battle of wills with 180 adolescents and lost and am not now engaged in a battle of wills with dough and losing that too.

By the end of the assembly I have twenty-odd commitments from people (four of whom are staff) who claim they will start collecting in a jam jar at home. At £3 a jam jar, that is roughly £60. They troop out of the hall, leaving me humiliated and still the proud possessor of 128 jam sandwiches. I watch them go, and with my tongue finally prise the bread and jam from the roof of my mouth.

Good deed no. 164.

Tuesday, 14 June

One of the worst things about yesterday's humiliation was the sure and certain knowledge I'd have to come back today and do it all over again with Year 10. I decided against jam sandwiches. Instead, I boned up on some gen on giving and decided to blind them with fascinating facts about the super-rich – people like Roman Abramovich, the owner of Chelsea who is worth gazillions of pounds and has a super-yacht complete with a helicopter landing pad and a roof that opens to the stars in the master bedroom. After that, I planned to make the point that unfortunately we aren't all multimillionaires, which is why the Jam Jar Army is such a good idea because it means we can all afford to give what we can at a time when we can afford to do it. I expected them to stop listening round about the moment I stopped talking about Roman Abramovich and started talking jam jars.

To drive up to Berwick yesterday I had to drag in a neighbour who was up for a few days in her holiday cottage to see my eldest son onto the school bus, which allowed me to take the little ones to their school early. Last night, to complete my joyous day, both boys opted to take up projectile vomiting as a hobby. Unusually my husband was around, so he cleared up and I put one back to bed in our bed and slept with him while my husband camped out in the older boy's bedroom. Going to Berwick this morning consisted of bringing in the expat to take my little girl to school, delaying Al's plans to go down to London, and feeling very guilty at leaving him with two washed-out boys clutching plastic bowls who refused to budge from the TV on the grounds motion made them queasy.

I rehearsed all the way up the A1, trying for a Jerry Maguire cocktail of engaging sincerity mixed with a large dose of inspirational charisma. By the time I arrived at the school gates I was almost plausible. I sat in the car for a minute or two, breathing deeply as I clutched the steering wheel – a vision of 180 'go on then, impress me' adolescent faces swimming in front of my eyes.

I'd parked in a disabled spot because I couldn't see any visitor parking and I'm doing good deeds and I figured someone could cut me a break. I walked into the reception and the teacher who had witnessed my humiliation yesterday greeted me with the words 'Bad news'. I figured she meant, 'Bad news, you can't park there.'

She didn't. She meant, 'Bad news, bit of a cock-up, your assembly is cancelled.'

When I'm under a lot of pressure and have several zillion things I should be doing all running round my head screaming at the same time, sometimes I can't speak. I have never met anyone else who does the same thing – till I met this woman. Her words ran into each other, so that I could scarcely follow what she was saying. The assembly was booked out for me – she pointed at a piece of paper stuck to the wall – but the Year 10 kids were busy with an exam. It went through my brain that the assembly the day before had been so bad, they had decided to effect a mercy killing on today's, but she was so very apologetic that my ego and I opted to believe her. She'd rung home to tell me but I had left early in order to arrive in good time. She brought me up to the staffroom to meet the Year 10 teacher. I wheeled out my engaging sincerity and inspirational charisma, dialled it down and mixed in some outright pleading. I asked her if she thought the high school could deliver on a hundred jars and she said she would hope so. Many of the children taking exams aren't in school any more, but I calculate there are still more than 500 of them left; one in five seems like quite an ask from where I'm standing, but then I was at yesterday's assembly.

Aside from the jam jars, I'd also asked yesterday's Year 9 to 'Like' the Jam Jar Army Facebook page. Last night, seven out of 180 duly Liked it. My maths isn't brilliant, but I reckon that's 173 who didn't. I took comfort in the only one to leave a message who told the world 'I too like jam'. His profile picture, taken with a mobile phone, was of him with his third finger raised in salute. I'm hoping no one accuses me of grooming.

Good deed no. 165: helped Kirsty work out a plan to move from Edinburgh to Oxfordshire (where her husband has a new job). The plan is to rest up from her attack of severe fibromyalgia, stay in hotel, find house, pack up, move. At one point she said, 'What would I do without you?' I am absolutely sure she meant it.

THE PHILANTHROPIST

Youngest son now vomiting with stomach migraine triggered by the tummy bug. Since Al is now back down in London, the small vomit monster had to come with me to drop my daughter at school and to pick up some migraine medication at the doctors. Four bowls of vomit later, we got back home.

Al has been at an extraordinarily posh dinner down at the National Gallery, where a philanthropist called Michael Hintze has donated £2m to refurbish Room 8 of the Gallery. The room, with its grape-coloured walls, blooms with tender Madonnas dandling lustrous, fleshy, child-Christs, and boasts work by Raphael and Michelangelo, altarpieces and massive gilt-embossed frames – here a crucifixion, there an entombment and there a resurrection. I can guarantee Al was the poorest guest at the table – except, perhaps, for the priest from the Vatican Museums, who presumably took a vow of poverty upon his ordination. Apparently, one of the National Gallery people said when the dinner loomed into view that you never saw gilt capitals spelling out the names of Hintze and his wife Dorothy appear on a wall so fast.

So here am I on the one hand busting a gut to get everyone to put coppers in a jam jar, with a target of £10k, which we may not even make, while Michael and Dorothy Hintze plough millions upon millions into worthy causes. Because I have foundation envy, later I met up with Hintze myself. Philanthropy intrigues – not because of the noughts on the end of the cheques, but because of its contradictions, its tangle of the individual and the collective, personal ambition and sacrifice, acquisition and generosity, self-belief and altruism, of acquiring money only to give money, because it prompts both envy and respect. Hintze is worth £550m according to the *Sunday Times* Rich List, who have him as the joint 138th richest person in the country. He has given away £25m to good causes, much of it through the Hintze Family Charitable Foundation, and turned giving into an art form, as arresting and creative as anything on the walls of the Hintze room in the National Gallery. 'I give because I can,' he said when I asked him why he does it. 'I feel an obligation – it's something that's innate. Some people might feel an obligation to dance or to paint. I feel an obligation – and a desire – to give.'

Hintze's family lost fortunes partly down to revolutions. Fleeing first the Russian revolution and then Mao Zedong in China, his family settled in Australia. Now Hintze has his own hedge fund, CQS, managing £7bn in assets. 'I'm not saying I have been poor without being able to eat or that I didn't have shoes on my feet, but I haven't been able to have everything or anything I wanted. Now I can have everything I want, and one of the things I want to do is give it away. I'd like to change the world for the better. I'd like to be helpful.'

He wants to give back, to repay good work with his own good work. To that end, he has funded not only the National Gallery, but the Victoria and Albert Museum, the Old Vic Theatre, hospitals, a hospice, a cancer charity and the Vatican Museums – backing those he considers to have a vision, such as Prince Charles and Hollywood star and artistic director of the Old Vic, Kevin Spacey. 'And we're not stopping there. There's a lot more to do,' he told me. Faith is part of what drives him. He quoted the Bible, 'For unto whomsoever much is given, of him shall be much required' (Luke 12:48), and the parable of the talents (where a master gives a servant five talents and he makes five more, and another servant two talents and he makes two more, but it doesn't end well for the servant who was given one talent and who just buried it in the back yard and watched Sky Sports). 'If you've done nothing with your talents,' said Hintze, 'you haven't fulfilled your obligation on this earth or to your God. I am no saint – that said, I do try to do my best.'

For this hedge-fund boss (who is also a leading Conservative Party donor), philanthropic giving is part of civil engagement and something too which gives him pleasure. 'I feel good when I can see that I make a difference,' he said. Bearing in mind he gives a lot and makes a big difference, I'm betting he feels very good indeed.

He wishes everybody would become civilly engaged in some way, whether that is donating money, or contributing in some other way. 'I know I can make some more money. There are certain people who have inherited wealth who don't give much and the reason they don't give is that they don't believe they can make it again. All they are doing is holding on to give it to the next generation.'

I liked Hintze, and generally I don't like multimillionaires. They make me feel bad – like I made a wrong turn somewhere in the past. As he was talking, though, I wanted to clap him on the back or shake his hand vigorously up and down, I wanted to say, 'Good on you, mate' or pin a medal to his expensive, tailored shirt. I'm glad there are people out there who want to make the world a better place – even if they are Tory donors.

Good deed no. 166: lent a neighbour a cup of sugar (OK, it's not £25m, but I'm not getting the sugar back either).

Thursday, 16 June

A perk of teaching Cryssie to write is the fact I don't have to think about what good deed to do – but I had severe doubts that I taught her much today. I've been setting homework – practise touch-typing, read a book, keep a journal of 'moments' and do a writing exercise. This morning as I drew into the yard having taken my own kids to school, Cryssie arrived with a book on Noah's Ark that was far too young for her, which she had read any number of times, a pink Playbook-bunny book of 'moments' with only one recent moment in it, and absolutely nothing else written down.

I struggled. I sat with her at the kitchen table, bowls pebble-dashed with cereal and still full of milk slops piled haphazardly and reproachfully in the sink, and seriously wondered who was wasting whose time. Without her having read a proper book, I couldn't talk to her about the author or the author's style or the story or the history behind the story, and without her having written very much, I couldn't talk about how to improve her own writing. I'm noticing this with other people I've tried to help – there are some who impose their own limits on the help you give them. Karl never sent me his revised CV to polish, for instance; the arty girl I put in contact with an agent and a professional illustrator never replied to my message asking how she got on. Why? I wonder. Shyness? A reluctance to impose? A decision not to chase down that dream?

Cryssie and I were still trying to squeeze out 'Bunny's Bad Day'. I would cheerfully shoot this rabbit by now, and I'm trying to explain to her the difference between writing 'It was a lovely sunny day' and 'The morning sun felt warm on Bunny's soft, brown fur', and it's harder than you'd think. I said, 'Try writing something like "a butterfly landed on Bunny's whiskers and he sneezed, and he sneezed again",' and when I looked she'd written 'a dragonfly' rather than a butterfly, and I said, 'That's great – I love the idea of a dragonfly,' and she said, 'I saw a dragonfly on a bouncy castle. The other children were jumping and I was on the edge of it, and they didn't notice the dragonfly but I did.' And for a moment, I saw her standing by the edge of a bouncy castle watching whole-bodied children leap and scream and hurl themselves from rubber swell to rubber swell, and I felt her reach to catch the secret comfort of a turquoise dragonfly between her fragile hands and keep it there. And I thought, 'Fair dos.' 'That's what writers do,' I said. 'See things that other hurly-burly people miss and write about them. Now back to Bunny – how's he doing?'

Good deed no. 167.

Friday, 17 June

Met with a *Gazette* reporter to drop off the new posters and stickers and discuss this week's story, but since the Queen is about to visit Alnwick and wipe out the entire paper, there's little to be gained by agonizing over it. We will be lucky to get a mention.

He did say the first four jam jars from the general public have come in from a couple who were collecting for charity anyway and decided to donate via the Jam Jar Army. Plus the local Tory prospective parliamentary candidate, a clever, energetic woman called Anne-Marie Trevelyan, has agreed to get her local party members behind it – which is very Big Society of her.

I'm such a control freak, though. Who knew? I want to write the reporter's story, physically slap a poster in every shop window in Northumberland and draw up a Jam Jar Army strategy for the hospice to get them organized, and I can't, because I've got enough on. It's the eight-year-old's first Communion on Sunday and he hasn't got a white shirt, I haven't got any shoes, there is nothing to eat in the fridge, I suspect at least one of the three kids has nits again so I can't get their hair cut, and I'm about to be descended on by my extended family, all waving prayer books. What would it be like to have only yourself to please? This year I'll do good, and next year I'll do whatever I bloody want.

Good deed no. 168: picked up a child's coat and bags after she dropped them in the playground.

Saturday, 18 June

In town for coffee after Communion class and the sports shop had a Jam Jar Army poster, as did the café and the tapas bar. Jess has worked six days with me in total, ringing round schools and churches and putting up posters. I've paid her £300 for six days on the Jam Jar Army along with some blogging research she did for me. That means I've paid out £240 for the Jam Jar Army work she did, plus £30 for the first lot of posters, plus £138.72 for the second lot of posters and stickers, plus £100 for the domain name, plus £170 for the legal fees to establish the intellectual property rights, plus £20 for the ice cream the other day – a grand total of nearly £700. Gulp. To be honest, I wouldn't have dreamed of writing a cheque of £700 for a charity. But then, the hours I'd have saved. And I don't resent the money I've spent – not a penny, not a dime, not for one minute, no I don't. What could I have done with £700 after all? It's not like I could have asked for my name on the wall of the National Gallery. I'd have been forced to spend it on myself. And what is the point of that?

Good deed no. 169: bought wine for the catechists to say thank you for their work during the First Communion preparations.

Sunday, 19 June

We all had this very holy day. Thirteen of us were packed on a wooden bench and watched as my youngest son, dressed in white shirt, smart trousers, red polyester tie and a red sash complete with gold medal, took his First Communion. We managed to get haircuts for the kids after an emergency nit comb yesterday afternoon, and he did look very smart and remarkably happy. Children need time to shine all on their own, and this was his day. He made the Communion. He ate up the Communion breakfast (I provided the pizza), and he posed for the hands-together photos afterwards. Back home we had chicken pie, which I made last night, and salad and new potatoes for lunch, and after the kids ate, the adults went out to the garden to eat and talk. It was all very mellow and understated.

The cause of Catholicism was not helped this evening. Midway through the day, someone rang from London to tell us Father Kit Cunningham was in the papers. Father Kit prepared us for our wedding, concelebrated our marriage, baptized our boys, concelebrated our first son's funeral service and gave us solace throughout that grim time. The loss of our son, he said, was the suffering of a crucifixion. When we lived in London, we worshipped at his church, going to Mass every two to three weeks – Latin, because Latin was at eleven o'clock and that's about as early as we could manage. I even cleaned the church with yellow dusters and with polish – my token for what he had done for us – and he said that I was too clever to clean a church and I said that no one was too clever to clean. Father Kit, of course, was himself a clever man, his sermons erudite, the Masses beautiful in the ancient church of St Etheldreda's in Holborn, all oak – and polished – wood, stained glass and carved wooden Catholic martyrs watching from up high, from plinths that took them closer to heaven than to earth. There's a tradition in Fleet Street that St Bride's is the journalists' and writers' church, and St Etheldreda's served a similar purpose for Catholic journalists and writers. I took a certain pride in my attendance at such a place, in the fact that I was known, and I shook the hand of a friend when I shook the hand of Father Kit when Mass was done, felt a simple pleasure when his hand rested on my son's head in blessing.

He had died in December. I had found out too late to attend the memorial, but it turns out that the glowing obits had brought out a less than palatable truth: Father Kit had been a paedophile. We liberals do not like to judge – but still, there are exceptions. In a Tanzanian school in the 1960s he had preyed on young boys, and these young boys are now men, and men are not so easily silenced. When Father Kit was confronted before his death, he admitted his guilt in a letter to the victims, and sent back his MBE to the palace – without explanation. To say I am gutted is putting it mildly. The harm done to those boys is horrific, and the betrayal to his congregation pales into insignificance set next to it. But betrayal and wider harm there is.

How does a man – any man, let alone a man of faith – abuse a child? How does he read 'Suffer little children to come unto me' and not fall down dead from shame? How does he gaze upon a crucified and bleeding Christ in private prayer and not weep to know the pain he caused? As years go by, does he forget? Does he confess to himself in a darkened box behind a metal grille, repent, mutter 'Hail Mary, full of grace' awhile, till 'Peace – that's enough. I was a different man and those were different times'? Sitting old and roly-poly fat in his chair by a fire, does he draw comfort from the tracts that talk of those without sin and stones to throw, the word 'forgiveness' written there on his Bible's page, illuminated by his need? Or does he sleep, the holy book falling from old man's lap to floor, and wake to find the smell of scorching flesh and sulphur in his red-veined nose? Then, caught between sleep and waking, does he remember all too well his guilt, their childish anguish, thorns he wreathed round each boy's head, and nails he hammered into each boy's hands and feet?

Good deed no. 170: helped my child make his First Communion, thereby making my parents happy.

Monday, 20 June

Good deed no. 171: did a radio interview for Jam Jar Army.

Tuesday, 21 June

I've crashed into a brick wall. Maybe it's the aftermath of the Communion, or the news of Father Kit Cunningham, but I am suddenly and profoundly bored by the monotony of goodness. Does the deed still count if I resent it? I have spent all day on the Jam Jar business and I'm raving with the dullness of setting up some website that hardly anyone in the Web's Wide World will read. I talked to the village priest about the fact we have to go to London at the weekend and so can't make Mass, which we were supposed to go to as the final step in the Communion journey. I like this priest a lot: he is a gentle soul of great humanity. He was as understanding as ever, but he had little to say when I told him how betrayed I felt about Father Kit Cunningham. He advised me to pray to the Virgin Mary. Seriously, that's it? The Virgin Mary? Does she wash whiter? Will she kiss away the hurt, betrayal, crimes?

Good deed no. 172: recommended a local singing farmer's wife who has her own flock of sheep and who is desperate for more bookings as a possible story to Radio Newcastle.

Wednesday, 22 June

The Queen came to town. As a republican, I debated whether to go, but I thought, 'What the hell?' We stood waiting for her with two other families we know, and I sent Al for flowers because I figured that was our best chance of her coming over to the children, and lo and behold she did. She appeared at the end of the street in a pink coat and an elegant pink straw hat with a green quill, and my eldest said, 'She looks just like Granny' (my mother would be delighted). When she got to our part of the crowd, she said to my daughter in her poshest, Queeniest voice, 'Are these for me?' Stunned silence, and I bent down and whispered in my child's ear, 'Yes, Your Majesty,' thinking, 'I am the worst republican ever.'

So the children got to meet the Queen, and do I have a record of it on film? I do not. I was filming on my Flik camera, but I am short so I could not see very much. My eldest son, however, leaning over the metal barricades was also filming on his iPod. A perfect position to film his sister's brush with royalty. Does he film his sister's brush with royalty? No, he films footballing legend Alan Shearer (former Newcastle United striker and current Deputy Lord Lieutenant of Northumberland), who was standing in the royal party, clutching a golf umbrella and waiting for it to rain so he could get a knighthood. Great one for my daughter's scrapbook: 'Alan Shearer and his brolly on the day I met the Queen.'

Good deed no. 173: gave flowers to the Queen (they'll end up in a hospital – so it counts).

Thursday, 23 June

The Queen's visit infected all and sundry with a devout love for the monarchy. Andrea, who was introduced to her as an official carer, arrived to pick Cryssie up from the lesson and was positively burbling with love of the monarchy, and she is normally quite a sensible woman. Cryssie hadn't done her homework. Again. She had read a Philip Pullman book, which was good, but she brought along last week's homework, so everything we had learned and I'd hoped to build upon went by the board. I am getting her to lift her game with reading, but I'm unconvinced that anything on the writing is sticking.

Good deed no. 174: gave away a newspaper (complete with royal supplement) to Cryssie's mum.

Friday, 24 June

Good deed no. 175: helped an old lady and her husband off a train. She had a white stick – next time I help a blind person off a train, I am checking they know which station it is.

Saturday, 25 June

Breakfast in London with my little girl and my best gay boyfriend at the patisserie I went to with my publisher after she read the first draft of my novel. It is dark and the tables in this particular French café are very close together. Consequently, other customers went monastically quiet as they listened with interest and some degree of *Schadenfreude* to my editor list, in loud and excruciating detail, exactly what was wrong with the novel. I'll always associate the words 'and another thing . . .' with the taste of hot chocolate and shame.

My best gay boyfriend is a child psychotherapist. His partner is a consultant psychologist. Occasionally they throw each other meaningful glances while I'm talking, which is generally my cue to stop. I asked him why he thought we do good deeds. He sat back in his chair and smiled dazzlingly at the white-aproned waitress as she placed his Earl Grey tea in front of him, and she retreated blushing. 'Fundamentally, we are nurturing and we do like to look after each other. We like to be kind and generous, though we also feel guilty and sad and regretful sometimes. Being good to someone else is a way of treating the pain of your own situation as well as demonstrating your genuine appreciation of someone else.'

As he is talking, I think of my lost son and wonder whether the consolation and comfort I offer the bereaved consoles me, whether the support I am offering the children who are damaged or different is because there is nothing I can do for that missing child of mine.

My best gay boyfriend's hand stole over to my daughter's plate to filch a piece of pain au chocolat and she giggled furiously as he swiped it. 'You develop your capacity for empathy and compassion working as a psychotherapist, and you need to do that because the children you're working with can be very challenging. Kids who've had difficult experiences become in their turn difficult to look after – for instance they can become more aggressive or withdrawn, or they can be harder to reach. Kindness is important but it's not enough on its own.' He held the pastry scrap out to her in the palm of his hand and she took it.

My best gay boyfriend works with the most vulnerable children in society: the victims, the unfortunate, the troubled. 'What these children need is help to understand their experiences and their potential – not forgetting that it's also important to support the parents or carers because they're the ones at the sharp end, day in, day out.' I regularly witness this friend's charm and patience with my own children, and think of him walking patiently alongside those others, through the dark, tangled places where they have lost themselves or been abandoned, nudging them towards the grassy path, towards the sunlight and away from prowling, yellow-eyed and mangy wolves. He dismisses me as I get misty-eyed about what he does for others in his day job. 'I don't feel any more compassion, don't feel any more benign than anybody else. I get a lot of satisfaction from what I do, a lot of fulfilment when I see myself being useful – I enjoy that more than I enjoy other things.'

My daughter leans against me, pulling at my sleeve, her face looking up at me, her voice low. She wants me to stop talking about anything other than her. She wants me to tell him about her dancing lessons. Her godfather stops talking to me, puts his elbow on the table and leans his handsome head on his hand. He is all attention as she begins.

Good deed no. 176: bought a friend coffee.

Sunday, 26 June

Good deed no. 177: sent a whodunnit to Merry.

Monday, 27 June

Good deed no. 178: picked up change which had fallen from a man's pockets as he sat in a deckchair by the sandpit at the Museum of Childhood (and gave it to him).

Tuesday, 28 June

I love the virtual world. Someone I know from Twitter alerted me to the fact that Karen (who is someone she knows from Twitter) was coming up to Northumberland and would be staying up here on her own. As my good deed, I have invited this stranger to my house for coffee tomorrow morning. I am hoping Karen isn't a nutter, and doubtless Karen is hoping the same.

Good deed no. 179.

Wednesday, 29 June

One year, I will actually arrange something for my birthday. I mean to every year, and each time it manages to creep up on tippy-toes and yell 'Surprise!' very loudly in my ear. On the upside, I am still only twenty-four. (It is entirely legitimate to lie about your age – mine is now forty-seven – if you don't feel the same on the inside as you do on the outside.) My ever-helpful daughter pointed out I was 'twenty-four' last year too, but birthdays are like that – magic.

I got a card from the village priest who had advised me to pray to the Virgin Mary. In any event, his thoughtful card acknowledged the 'sadness of recent days' and wished me a joyful birthday with love and prayers, which was nice of him. At first, I panicked that I hadn't set up coffee or lunch with girlfriends. Usually I go shopping on my birthday, but courtesy of the state of my finances that's not really a goer. Despite my lack of planning, though, the birthday turned out great. My little girl gave me a kids' DVD she wants to watch with me, my younger son a pencil sharpener 'Because you always get so cross when you can't find one, Mummy', and my eldest a bag of chocolate-covered coffee beans. Oh, and my husband gave me a battery for my watch. But I love those gifts. I wanted all of those things, to sit with my daughter in front of the TV with a sharpened pencil in my hand, eating chocolate espresso beans with a tick-tock watch. Hurrah. And best of all, Karen (from Twitter) arrived and turned out to be completely sane and entirely lovely.

THE CARER

Karen works for a wholesale bulb outfit based in Urmston, Manchester, and was up to talk to the Duchess of Northumberland about a daffodil grown especially for Alnwick Garden called Alnwick Magic. We got to talking, as women do, and it turns out that she is one of the most caring people I have ever come across – and God knows she has had to do more than her share. She first started caring for someone when her 36-year-old mother was diagnosed with breast cancer and had to have a mastectomy. Karen was ten at the time. A year or so later her mother had to have a hysterectomy, and throughout that time Karen helped around the house, went shopping and did what a child could to make things easier. Ten years after her mother was first diagnosed, when Karen was twenty, the cancer came back worse than ever and her mother was given only a year to live. With her father poorly and unable to cope, Karen started doing the night shift, drinking tea with her mother, trying to ease her pain and breathing, while the rest of the world slept. 'I regret the things I could have done better, but you do what you can do at the time and hope it is the right thing,' she said, and I struggled to grasp how you believe you could have given more, when you have given all you have.

She might have cared for her mother and thought herself safe, that she had done her bit, but within six months of her mum's death her dad was diagnosed with Parkinson's disease, which went on to ravage him. 'He didn't like to speak because he felt we couldn't understand him, his walking got worse. They changed his tablets and he started having hallucinations, didn't recognize us, became incontinent. I had to hand-feed him. I became a mother to my own mother and father. That was a hard time,' she told me, shaking her head at the memory. Things weren't all bad, though: when she was twenty-six – five years after her mother had died – Karen fell in love and got married to Rod. 'But it broke my dad's heart. He told me I was doing the right thing, but bless him, in the Rolls-Royce he held me and cried all the way to the church the day of my wedding. I felt as if I had betrayed him.' Karen moved out, and her brother and his family moved in to care for her dad. He died two years after her marriage.

Rod was everything Karen needed; a handsome engineer, she adored him and loved his parents, both of whom suffered from angina. She checked on them every week. In 1991, when she was thirty-three and Rod was thirty-seven, he was knocked off his motorbike, shattering his knee. The car driver, taking part in a treasure hunt, had turned his head to talk to a backseat passenger – having missed his turning – only for his car to veer across the road, straight into Rod. Over the next ten years Rod was in and out of hospitals for more than a dozen gruelling operations and bone grafts, in constant pain and prone to infections. 'I'd leave him a Thermos of hot water in the living room because he would be too bad to carry anything. I'd come home at lunchtime to check on him. Sometimes he could walk, sometimes the pain was so bad he would cry in his sleep. I'd wake him and we would talk for hours to try and take his mind off the pain. There was one night he was screaming because it was so bad and the knee was huge because there was an infection. All this time, he begged them to take the leg off, but they wouldn't.'

Things got worse when Rod's mother was diagnosed with Alzheimer's, and Karen spent her fortieth birthday in Wythenshawe hospital after her mother-in-law fell down the stairs from a brain haemorrhage. Every night after work Karen went round to her in-laws; every Saturday she took her mother-in-law shopping. By the end she was feeding her with a syringe, and when her mother-in-law died after pneumonia set in, she died in Karen's arms. 'I never thought in my life I would be able to do that,' Karen told me. 'I felt guilty that with my own mum, I wasn't at her side when she died, but that was the first time somebody so close to me had died. This time, I found the strength from somewhere.'

She didn't get that chance with Rod. In 2001, at the age of forty-seven, Rod died from a blood clot from his knee. 'He phoned me at work on a Friday and said, "I think I'm dying" and then put the phone down. I said, "I've got to go home," and when I let myself in, Rod was dead on the living-room floor.' But Karen's caring still wasn't over. There was her father-in-law to visit every other night and every weekend, easing him through emphysema until his death from an aneurysm a few years later.

Toileting, bathing, feeding, medicating, barrier nursing: spread across decades, these are a powerful testament against sentimentality and mawkishness, against those who say, 'I'm sad to hear that' and turn on their heel and walk away. I am looking at this short, pretty 53-year-old bundle with her round, smiling face and wavy, silvering hair, and I am wondering how she has the energy to get up in the morning. 'I never felt caring for the people I loved was a duty, it was a pleasure,' she explained as she sipped hot water. She doesn't drink tea any more – she drank too much tea as she sat through those long nights with her mother, the lights turned down low, the bedroom more like a hospital ward. 'Because you love them, you want to make it easier for them, you want to pro-tect them and you want to help them keep their dignity.' She went on: 'You do grow, you can cope with things differently, and when someone is ill there is a different sort of love, a deeper love – you cherish them more deeply.'

Is there consolation in knowing that you cared for them? That you eased the suffering of those you love best in the world? That your constancy and devotion were ranged against their indignity and pain, your humanity taking on their mortality in a battle you can never win but one which you have to fight. Because it is hard to lose those you love the best. 'There are times that I do feel like I'm the only per-son left in the world – times when the loneliness can totally crush you,' she told me. The husband she lost. The children she never got to have (she herself had to have a hysterectomy only weeks after her husband died). 'On a girls' weekend, they're always phoning their husband to say they've arrived safe or "How are you?" – you miss that, because you've got nobody to phone and say, "I've arrived."'

Later, when I check her Twitter profile, it describes her as loving friends and family and explains that she is 'trying to make life easier for others'. I hope, I sincerely hope, trust and pray that she too is cherished as she deserves to be, that she is honoured as an aunty and as a most decent human being, that the love she spent so freely comes back to her a million times over from her sister and her brother, her sister-in-law and her nieces and her friends, that when the time comes she is carried and her feet not allowed to touch the floor, that a mirror is held up to her and she sees beauty there.

Good deed no. 180: emailed three people to try and get work experience for the media student.

Thursday, 30 June

Some of these good deeds are a complete pain in the arse. I have a grant application form to fill in for the local Citizens Advice; I have a letter to write to the trading standards people on behalf of

Karl's mam about her car, which keeps breaking down; and today I was supposed to take Cryssie for her writing lesson. Which I did. Her dad arrived with Cryssie at 9.45 a.m. and said he would be back at 11 a.m. Since it was a public sector strike day, I already had my youngest son off school pleading for a game of tennis. I couldn't manage the game of tennis with Cryssie here, so I said, 'Later' and, grumbling furiously, he went to slump in front of the telly. The problem was that no one picked her up at 11, or at 11.15, or at 11.30, or at 12. Finally, about 12.10, I rang her mother and Andrea said hello in her usual friendly sort of way, and I said hello all friendly back, and there was a silence, and I said, 'I still have your daughter in my kitchen.' And there was a gasp of horror, and Andrea said, 'I'm so sorry, I completely forgot she was there.' And I said, 'It's fine – don't worry about it.' I absolutely didn't mean it.

I got over myself when I opened up my email inbox. Yesterday, I emailed round contacts pleading for work experience for the media student, and somebody has agreed. Truly excited. This kid is the first in her family to go to university (way too distant a relationship to count me as true kin on this). This kid is clever and beautiful with long, shiny dark hair and a wicked sense of humour. She also has a dad she hasn't seen since she was two, a brother who died of cancer at seventeen and a mum with poor health – and she has kept going, kept wanting, kept pitching. I am proud of her. Up the revolution.

Good deed no. 181.

Friday, 1 July

Things are reaching the point of no return. This evening, I picked up Al from the railway station and the first two carrier bags of change people have brought into the *Gazette*. We then called in at a friend of a friend's house for jam jars she didn't want any more. The lady makes jam but needed her spare room clearing for family who are visiting over the weekend. I was expecting a fair few jars – we counted 481. All shapes and sizes – not just jam jars, but empty jars of Nescafé, gravy and baby food too. She virtually cheered as we drove away. The car isn't running properly at the moment and is driving really slowly, so there were five of us in the car with a boot full of spare change weighing it down. The boot was also full of the jars, which were also rammed into any and every space between children and onto laps and under legs. At one point my eldest son said, 'Seriously, I can't feel my legs any more,' but we just kept driving and the strange jingling, tinkling noise almost cloaked my screams entirely. There are 481 jars in my kitchen.

Good deed no. 182.

Saturday, 2 July

I am more than halfway through my year, which is a strange thought. How am I doing? On the downside, it is hugely more effortful than I expected. On the upside . . . actually, I'm not sure there is an upside.

Good deed no. 183: counted one of the bags of money. (£41.70 counted in 1 hour and 40 minutes. Counting is the worst job ever – my brain stopped using numbers and used shapes instead.)

Sunday, 3 July

Al counted the second bag of money (which took him less than half the time it took me; then again, he can add up). We have a grand total of £88.80. That's £88.80. Our Jam Jar Army target is £10,000. That's £10,000, not £1,000 or £100 – £10,000. Oh my God. There is no silver in the money coming in. Everything is twopence pieces. If this doesn't work, I'm going to be known as the Tuppenny Tit. On a more positive note, staff at the local Bar-clays bank in Seahouses have agreed we can bring the money into them – which is incredibly community-minded of them – despite the fact the hospice doesn't bank with them. It strikes me there are 'bankers' and then there are sensible people of goodwill who work in banks.

Good deed no. 184.

So six months of good deeds and I am the perfect citizen – you just wouldn't want to have me to dinner, I am so effing worthy. Today I did so many good deeds, my sandalled feet are in danger of lifting off the ground and my entire physical body ascending straight into the heavens.

- I put the last touches to Karl's mam's letter of complaint over the car for the trading standards people.
- I asked a café owner to take nine jam jars for her tables (£88.80 keeps going round my head, and not in a good way).
- I stuck labels on a couple of dozen more and popped into the community centre to talk to them about publicizing the Jam Jar Army, which they agreed to do.
- While at the community centre, I offered to put the organizer in touch with someone who could help them on a heritage project they have going on (thereby potentially earning my history friend some dosh).
- I liaised with Berwick Citizens Advice Bureau re the grant application.
- I advised Lily on publicizing the IT company she is working for.
- I discussed work experience with the media student.

I am ready to kill.

Good deed no. 185.

174

Tuesday, 5 July

Good deed no. 186: bought a photo from the Gazette *of my son and a friend's son together at the royal visit and framed it for his mother.*

Wednesday, 6 July

It can be a tricky business being a good-deed doer. I duly advised someone who had asked me for help, which required in total asking favours from one mate, one acquaintance and one total stranger, but when I actually checked, the girl who had originally approached me hadn't done anything much at all with the help I had given her. This means:

a. I wasted my time

which means:

b. I feel like only helping those who help themselves

which is to say:

c. The project is turning me into a Tory (runs screaming into the distance).

No, I won't let it. I will be compassionate and empathetic and charitable. I will not judge. Repeat after me: I will not judge.

Then again, it is hard not to.

If the recipient does little or nothing, the good deed having been done, that is at least relatively straightforward. Account closed. Once you help someone and they act according to your advice, however, it turns out there is an absolute obligation on you to help them again. I have a CV to revise for the media student (who needs it for the work experience), and a feature to edit for one of the students on my blog course (having helped her get a magazine commission). Not to mention the grant application which is still outstanding for the local Citizens Advice Bureau – oh, and the fact my friend rang for a briefing about that heritage job and, laughing, said, 'You should be my agent' and, laughing, I said, 'Actually there's a price – I want your school to do jam jars,' which is when she stopped laughing.

When this year is over, I am not helping anyone ever again, ever.

Good deed no. 187: arranged jam jars in two cafés by the till and took a dozen to the local village shop for distribution to regulars.

Thursday, 7 July

Good deed no. 188: took thirty-five jars round to Lily for distribution in holiday cottages and local shops.

Friday, 8 July

For the very first time I felt today that I was making a difference. Perhaps it was because I got thanked and most of what I'm doing is thankless. I also got to feel lucky. A local Citizens Advice Bureau gave me their annual report so that I could draw up an application for a competition to win some money for them. I have been putting it off because I expected it to be so dull; what became clear was the reality and scale of the problems and the effectiveness of the service.

This particular CAB helps all these people who come to them with employment problems and debts, or who are sick and don't have the money to drive down to hospital in the south of the county or into Tyneside for a chemotherapy appointment. Their workers are handling cases of more than £3m of debt – more than a hundred people had to go bankrupt, according to their latest figures. And alongside the annual report was a spreadsheet on the causes of problems last year. Fourteen were down to bereavement as clients struggled with something as basic as the cost of a funeral, let alone the emotional toll of their wife's death, or their baby's, which was also listed. Debt was another significant problem: some were harassed by debt recovery agencies, some had their benefits stopped for one reason or another, while those in jobs suddenly found themselves redundant or working in jobs with their wages unpaid. And, in black and white, diseases: strokes, leukaemia, non-Hodgkin's lymphoma, spinal degeneration, breast cancer, cancer of the oesophagus, head injury, terminal cancer, Alzheimer's, and some sectioned under the Mental Health Act. People's stories, their lives, their deaths.

The CAB caseworkers can relax. I read through the feedback forms. There were comments like: 'Without your help and advice I would be in a mess' and 'Gave me hope' and 'I was treated with dignity and respect once again' and 'Words cannot describe the courtesy meted out to me' and 'We would have given up without you'.

Good deed no. 189.

Saturday, 9 July

Good deed no. 190: gave money to dance school's coffee morning.

Sunday, 10 July

Good deed no. 191: worked on the media student's CV for her.

Monday, 11 July

I slogged round a couple of the local villages planting another eighteen jars around shops and cafés. It turned out that quite a few people, although they had been given posters and a sticker, didn't actually stick the sticker on a jar. 'Sticker' – the clue is in the name. I am having to go round all over again at a time I thought we would be doing a first collection. Had a couple of world-class miserable responses, including one local shopkeeper who pronounced gloomily, 'There are too many charities,' while a local pub owner rejected the jar because he had other collection tins. That is absolutely fair enough, but when I offered him a jar for home, he said he didn't 'do charity' other than wine at Christmas for a local school. He eventually softened enough to let me put two jars on the mantelpieces, while warning me it was 'at my own risk'. Anyone who wants to steal a glass jar with a few coppers in it needs that money. It is far more likely that the glass jars will get knocked off by someone's elbow on a Saturday night. And he wasn't the only misery: another hotel manager up the road turned down the idea of a jar on his bar because they had a collection tin already, and no thanks, he didn't want to put them on the tables. In fact no one wants to put the jars on tables, so that particularly brilliant idea went down a storm.

Even more of a shocker: Berwick High School (of 128-uneaten-jam-sandwiches fame) hasn't done it. Seriously? I rang to talk about collecting the jars, and the assistant head told me that it's been very busy, and they didn't get round to the jars but would give them a go in September. And they are not the only ones. I rang another school and they haven't done it either. And another, and they haven't done it either. At this rate we are going to bring in a couple of hundred quid and count ourselves lucky.

Good deed no. 192.

Tuesday, 12 July

I spent an hour and a half reworking a letter of complaint over the crocked car after Karl's mother came to pick it up and found a few errors in it, but at least she bought me a bottle of wine as a thank you, which was kind of her. Her grown-up daughter asked me if I enjoyed doing it. Enjoyed writing other people's letters of complaint? As an alternative to a crossword? I said no, it was excruciatingly dull, adding (because I felt I had to) that it was worth the time and effort if it helped someone out.

Fate must have taken me at my word because the son of our

lovely elderly London neighbour who died earlier in the year phoned again. His mum had been cremated, and the family wanted her ashes scattered over the ground where her husband's ashes were and a memorial rose already grew. Unable to face dealing with the ashes themselves, they had trusted the crematorium staff to do it on their behalf.

Despite being told it had all been done, when they went to visit the plot nothing had changed – there was the rose tree and the plaque to their dad, but there was no joint marker for their mum and dad. Initially, they were assured they were at the wrong plot – despite having visited their dad over nine years. It turned out they were not at the wrong plot: their mum's ashes had been interred in someone else's plot with a similar name across the crematorium. Understandably, the son is distraught. The family do not know what to do. The crematorium says they need them to sign the official documentation before they can move the ashes from the wrong plot across to the right plot, but understandably the family are worried there's been heavy rain and there won't be any of their mum's ashes left (plus they might get some of the other guy). They have been to see a solicitor at the CAB and, such is the upset, they are even contemplating suing the crematorium.

What can be done to make it better? Even if they scoop up the ground and bring it across, the danger is the family will be wondering how much of their mum's ashes is there every time they go and visit. They are sending the correspondence.

Good deed no. 193.

Wednesday, 13 July

Good deed no. 194: gave one of the expats a lift to the garage. (They cut their hair and take their car to the garage more often than anyone else I know. We cut our hair when we can't see out from underneath it and take the car to the garage when it won't start. Planning ahead? Hmm. I didn't know you could do that.)

Thursday, 14 July

Took round 110 washed and re-labelled jars to Ally, who has agreed to give them out for me at something called a 'puppy show'. I went to one a couple of years ago. All the hound puppies from the local Percy Hunt are shown in a ring. They all looked identical to me. My friend is incredibly sociable – she knows everyone. I'm hoping there is alcohol to soften people up and that she'll shift the lot. She said the master of the hunt said I was welcome to come along too, which was very nice of him, but it's events like the puppy show that make me realize that, however settled we are, I will never belong. If I went I would only know about three or four people there and everyone would be talking nineteen to the dozen with immense vigour and animation to everybody else about things like horses and harvests.

Good deed no. 195: taught Cryssie writing. (I am coming to the conclusion I'm not that good a teacher, though she seems happy enough sitting at my kitchen table writing away.)

Friday, 15 July

The correspondence arrived about the mistake at the crematorium, including a Ministry of Justice form which is necessary because Section 25 of the Burial Act 1857 states you cannot remove a body or the remains of a body which have been interred in any place of burial without a licence from the Secretary of State.

A letter of the 20th May assures the family the ashes were interred that day and a double plaque (for the mum and dad) placed at the rose. Which was nice to know. The follow-up letter on the 16th June from the chairman of the crematorium confirms an 'unintentional error', offers 'sincere and heartfelt apologies' and blames 'human error' for the fact the ashes were buried in a stranger's plot. Both plots bear the same surname (although not the same first name), and are in a row with the same alphabetical letter (although in completely different parts of the crematorium from each other). Classic cock-up.

The crematorium letter asks the family to sign the form necessary to obtain a licence and move the remains. It goes on: 'for practical reasons this needs to be done without delay . . . I would stress that any delay renders the process of reburial more difficult.' Signed by the chairman of the cemetery and crematorium, it says: 'I hope you will understand that this type of mistake can always occur, although thankfully very rarely in my experience. We are reviewing our procedures to try to ensure that it does not happen again, but I do appreciate that this will be of no immediate comfort to you.'

The letter offers a refund of £181.50 for their mum's burial and double plaque, alongside the offer 'that the rose be yours for life with no further payments being made to the cemetery for the upkeep of the rose'. (Every ten years you pay for the upkeep of the rose, which seems odd enough in itself, frankly. This costs £450.) Doubtless they mean well by the offer of the refund, but £181.50 and a pot plant for burying your mum in the wrong place is brutal in print. The form they want the family to sign admits 'cemetery error. Cremated remains buried at wrong memorial'. I talked to the cemetery manager, who seems keen to resolve it, and so she should be.

Good deed no. 196.

Saturday, 16 July

Good deed no. 197: took Lily's daughter to dancing lessons and lunch.

Sunday, 17 July

The expats came along for tea, and their gorgeous, glossy, black and white springer spaniel promptly went into the lounge – which is, I might state for the record, one of only two rooms in the house with a fitted carpet – and promptly shat on it. I went in to bring out an empty glass, and there in the middle of the carpet was an enormous and gently steaming pile of dog poo. I contemplated saving the expats embarrassment and cleaning it up as my good deed – frankly, I couldn't face it, so I went back out and told them and they did it. The woman was mortified. They treat the dog like a child. I would be equally mortified if one of my children shat on their carpet.

Later, we went for a walk along the beach, the tideline high with twisted, bubbled heaps of chocolate-brown seaweed and silvery driftwood, while out at sea the wind planed the swell of the water, the parings curling and twisting away from the blue. Beautiful – then my husband ruined my mood by ordering me to stop saying hello to people. Beach etiquette dictates you raise your eyes to the people passing you and if they do likewise, you say 'Good morning' or 'Hello' or, at the very least, you nod or smile. That is just what you do. It is not me – I am not a nutter. Greeting your fellow man is a good thing: it helps connect us to each other. It isn't as if I yell at them in a 'I've got better manners than you, matey' way in the event they stride past on some rainy ramble from hell or they are concentrating on rescuing their dog from drowning. Occasionally, you make a mistake and they glance your way and you give someone a cheery hello and they don't know the rules so they are past before they get to say hello back – but all you have done is give them a nice warm feeling that someone out there cares. He made me stop doing it.

Good deed no. 198: gave out twenty stickers and three posters to an RAF contact for the Jam Jar Army. (I am trying to do a ripple effect. It is like pyramid selling: find a contact, then let them spread it through their own community.)

Monday, 18 July

We have tipped over the £1,000 mark for the Jam Jar Army, which is great – only £9,000 to go, which is less great. I am in a cold sweat about not making the target. I can come up with the idea, I can get the local paper involved and do media interviews, I can set up a website and a Facebook page, tweet about it and get labels and posters printed up at my own expense. I can hand them out to whoever will take them and get schools on board. I can slap labels on jam jars and give them to shopkeepers. But I can't put a jam jar in everybody's house in Northumberland – at a certain point, people have to engage with the process and decide for themselves to do it. Will they, though?

Good deed no. 199: handed out jam jars to fellow parents at school sports day. They've already filled them once, but hey, no harm in repeating yourself. I said there's no harm in repeating yourself.

Tuesday, 19 July

I am fed up with good-deedery. Any spare minute I have, I am soaking jam jars to get their labels off them or sticking my labels on them, or super-duper helpful people are suggesting things I might do to bring in money. What they don't realize is the Jam Jar Army is me. I want to say, 'Thank you for your idea. Yes, of course I've thought of involving the Scouts/the WI/the Rotary. The problem is I haven't the effing time. How about you do it for me?' But of course I can't say that, so I have to play dumbstruck, as if it's an idea of sheer genius and the first time anyone has ever suggested such a thing, and thanks very much, and I'll get straight on it, and their idea will make all the difference between success and failure. Good on you.

Good deed no. 200: bought end-of-year gifts for teachers and staff.

Wednesday, 20 July

Good deed no. 201: arranged coffee morning between three parents with autistic children.

The family rang back and have decided not to sue about the cemetery mix-up, which I think is the right decision. The most important thing has to be that their mother's remains are laid to rest alongside their dad's. His mum's illness, her death and now this has made this poor man think the pain of losing his mother is endless. My friend is sleepless with it; he said that he feels as if they got it wrong last time when they left it to the crematorium, and now he is torturing himself with whether he needs to be there in case they get it wrong again when he simply can't face it.

I told him I would witness it. Al and I loved his mother. She was more than a good neighbour. She was our friend. A tiny, busy, immensely kind Cockney through and through. We couldn't be there when she died, but this is something I can and want to do for her. I can stand by and watch while they move her from a stopping-off place to a resting place. I can make sure they take every last scrap of ash, every ounce of soil that she might have touched, that they place it in a wooden casket and carry that casket with due reverence to the rightful plot and bury it there. The cemetery manager isn't keen on the whole thing being witnessed – apparently it is 'against regulations'. As is piling someone's ashes into the wrong plot in the first place, I imagine. But she understands why the family feels the need for it to be witnessed, and we have made an arrangement for a week on Monday, by which time the paperwork will be through and I'll be down in London on holiday.

Good deed no. 202: wrote and printed out sixty-odd letters for potential Jam Jar supporters from the puppy show.

Friday, 22 July

A nice woman called Sharon Williams has seen the Jam Jar Army in the paper and started marching round her village giving out jam jars. How amazing is that? She has a holiday cottage and saw the piece last week on the cottages Lily had managed to get the jars into. Sharon has had friends die of cancer in the last five or six years so was happy to put a jar in her cottage, then she did one better and took it upon herself to go round her village with them. She has also been decent enough to start going round the shops in the market town giving them jam jars too. My only concern was that, as with the local villages, some of the shops in the town took posters and stickers a month ago and with a few exceptions didn't get round to sticking the stickers on a jar and getting the jar out by their tills. Small, screaming noise. Never mind, they're out there now.

Good deed no. 203: picked up 2,000 more labels for jam jars (at a cost of £78.72. This charity thing is making me a pauper).

Saturday, 23 July

Good deed no. 204: made a 'thank you' jar for hospice supporter Stephen Waddington's five-year-old son Dan, who had squished £136 into their jar. I painted a jar gold, stuck gold stars on it, bought a sheriff star and decorated it with gold stars, bought three Freddo chocolate bars (at seventeen pence each) and popped the sheriff star and chocolate in the jar. I told him I had made him a star in the Jam Jar Army. Hope his dad doesn't think they were the most expensive Freddo bars ever.

Sunday, 24 July

Good deed no. 205: washed labels off a dozen jam jars and stuck on my labels. My kitchen is now like the cottage industry of a jam maker who keeps forgetting to make the jam.

Monday, 25 July

There's interest from a Sainsbury's store down south in taking on the Jam Jar Army. Apparently, the local Sainsbury's community relations lady up here (who has given us 225 jars of jam for schools) has put details up on an internal fund-raisers' forum. Whoop-whoop noises.

Good deed no. 206: offered a cousin's daughter and her kids our house for a week while we're away in London in someone else's house.

Tuesday, 26 July

Opening up the boot of the Ratmobile has to be done with immense caution now as there are always a few of the bolder jam jars perched on the edge, ready to make a break for freedom. I trailed round one village like a Bible salesman. Knock knock, big wide trust-me smile, *I'm going to let you into a secret which guarantees eternal salvation, my friend.* It must be hell to be in sales. I have no idea how you keep it up. You put yourself on the line every time. I was trying hard to keep the kids outside one café where I expected to be rejected, and they insisted on coming in because, as my youngest son said, 'I want to be there when they say no to you.' I got a good reception, though, from a pub and the café that looks onto the golf course, who agreed to put them on their tables – in fact I gave out a huge boxful of jam jars. But today's good deed is buying a stranger a parking ticket. I had driven through to the market town and parked up, I had paid for my ticket and then put the money in again for another ticket. The stranger was standing behind me and I turned and gave the ticket to him, explaining, 'It's my good deed for the day.' He looked puzzled but very pleased. A few minutes later, after I got the kids out the car and we were walking down the road, he was standing in a queue for money from the cash machine with two teenagers and as we passed he said, 'I've told them we all have to pass that forward today,' which was really nice because that means there will be another good deed floating around the world and I didn't have to do it.

Later I checked out his comment about 'passing it forward'. I wasn't entirely sure at the time if he said 'pass it on' or 'pass it forward', but it turns out there is a heart-wrenching movie where a small boy decides to change the world by doing good, the under-standing being when you yourself benefit from a good deed, you have to do good to someone else, and so it goes on.

Good deed no. 207.

THE HERO

Another branch of Sainsbury's, this one in Scotland, has been in contact and might be interested in using the Jam Jar Army to raise money for an ex-servicemen's charity called the Mark Wright Project. It reminded me how Professor Wilkinson, the animal biologist, said humans were the only creatures on this earth willing to sacrifice themselves for their fellow man. Mark Wright was a 27-year-old corporal in the 3rd Battalion, Parachute Regiment, who was awarded the George Cross for gallantry. The George Cross is the highest bravery award possible when not in the face of the enemy. According to the citation published in the official government newspaper the *London Gazette*, on 6 September 2006, while serving in Kajaki, Helmand Province, Afghanistan, Corporal Wright 'made a con-scious decision' while 'fully aware of the risks' to enter a mined area in order to help a colleague who had been severely injured in a mine explosion. He made this decision knowing that waiting for a mine clearance team to arrive would take too long and that the soldier was likely to die before it was completed. Exercising com-mand, Corporal Wright directed two medical orderlies to treat the injured soldier, ordered all unnecessary personnel to safety and then began organizing the casualty evacuation. He called for a helicopter and ordered a route to be cleared through the minefield to a landing site. Unfortunately, the leader of this task, while moving back across the route he believed he had cleared, stepped on another mine and his leg was blown off. At enormous per-sonal risk, Corporal Wright immediately moved to help the new casualty until one of the medical orderlies could take over. He again ordered all non-essential personnel to stay out of the mine-field, sent an accurate situation report to his headquarters and ensured that additional medical items were obtained to treat the wounded.

The words in the *Gazette* are cool and clinical, spelling out the risk and command structures, and leaving out the dust, terror, comradeship, smell of blood and courage. More mines, more wounded men – Corporal Wright among them – till there were seven casualties in the field, three of whom had lost limbs. The cit-ation reads: 'Despite this horrific situation, his own very serious injuries and the precarious situation of the others in the minefield, Corporal Wright still strove to exercise control of the situation. He did this despite being in great pain and fully aware that he was in danger of bleeding to death.' Eventually evacuated by American helicopters with winches, Corporal Wright and his men remained in that minefield for three and a half hours. He remained conscious for the majority of the time, continually shouting encouragement to those around him, 'and several survivors subsequently paid trib-ute to the contribution this made to maintaining morale and calm amongst so many wounded men'. Corporal Wright died of his wounds on the rescue helicopter. 'His outstandingly courageous actions and leadership were an inspiration to all those around him during an extremely precarious situation. His complete disregard for his own safety while doing everything possible to regain con-trol of the situation and to save lives constitutes an act of the greatest gallantry.' That's a man you call a hero.

Good deed no. 208: gave lifts to the expats from the garage and into work (their car is in the garage again).

Thursday, 28 July

Excellent day. I wrote a Jam Jar Army letter for holiday cottages because the company Lily persuaded to put jars in their cottages said that the jars haven't got any money in them yet, and they wanted their visitors to have more of an explanation. In it I said: '. . . to let you into a little secret – we don't have many people living in Northumberland, and frankly we need your help too . . . We hope you have a wonderful holiday. Welcome to our Northumberland family.' I have no idea whether it will work. Holidaymakers might just feel they are on holiday and would rather spend their loose change on fish and chips than cancer. But as they say up here, 'Shy bairns get nowt.'

Later on, Duchess High School in Alnwick rang and told me they had around £200 for the Jam Jar Army. This is excellent, not least because staff had said they couldn't take it on because the school was fully stocked with charitable stuff. Apparently, the kids raised the money on some non-uniform day and when they were asked what they wanted it to go on, the children themselves said the Jam Jar Army. Good on them. Plus the hospice emailed to say they had banked another £192 in Jam Jar Army funds. Plus I've got around £100 in jars on the floor of my kitchen, so I reckon that is around £1,500 in total so far. (Not panicking just yet about not meeting the target; I figure I can do that later.)

Good deed no. 209.

Friday, 29 July

I am wondering if my mother is right and you do indeed get back more than you put in. I am only just coming out of a migraine, which can leave me feeling low, but if I'm honest I have felt better thanks to the good deeds: trite, but true. There is an emotional return in giving – who cares if that sense of well-being is down to your own body chemistry or evolution? When I rang my seventy-year-old cousin to see if her daughter wanted my house for a week, she sounded delighted that I'd thought of her, which in turn delighted me. There have been tangible returns too: flowers and chocolates and wine sent for sorting things out with the crematorium, seeing the forty-something's feature I'd advised on printed in the magazine and knowing how delighted she would be, even that stranger telling his sons we'll each of us have to pass the good deed along the other day.

Good deed no. 210: pulled together artwork for the other Sainsbury's branches in case they do want to go ahead.

Saturday, 30 July

Summer this year is ten days in London staying in a friend's house while they're away and a few days in Suffolk in another friend's cottage. Thank God for friends who holiday abroad. We left our own house looking incredibly clean and welcoming (including a 'Drink Me' bottle of wine in fridge) for Worcestershire cousins who are staying there for a week. It looked so welcoming once I had finished cleaning and polishing and artfully arranging, I decided that I actually wanted to spend my holiday in my own home. Why can't we really live like that? In a note left for my cousins, I have implied it is take-me-as-you-find-me – in reality, I have worked like a navvy to get my home looking this good.

Good deed no. 211.

Sunday, 31 July

Good deed no. 212: took a photo of an American tourist – a teacher carrying a cardboard cut-out of Flat Stanley around with her on her travels for her pupils – with the Paddington Bear statue at the railway station.

Monday, 1 August

I changed my clothes about a dozen times today before we set out for the crematorium. What do you wear to an exhumation? I settle on a French navy linen skirt, a white T-shirt and a white linen shirt. Sensible without being too formal, with due allowance made for the steaming heat. I'm not used to summer in the city any more. The weather in London is killing me, it's so hot.

Manor Park cemetery and crematorium on the outskirts of London, opened in 1874, boasts of 'serene locations both for burials and cremated remains' with 'open and secluded areas for private graves, a woodland burial site and a children's private garden for burial'. As you walk in through the massive wrought-iron gates, the memorials are all desolate angels and oversized monuments to boys lost in war, like John Travers Cornwall, VC, who was sixteen when he died from his wounds after saving many lives at the Battle of Jutland in 1916 and is the youngest recipient of the Victoria Cross.

I picked up a pot of African violets, which my gran always loved, pausing in my purchase as a hearse drove through the gates followed by a cortège of mourners. Truth to tell, I was slightly hysterical at the thought of it all, which was strange because I'd been perfectly OK about it up to then. I took a deep breath, and the African violet and I went into the office.

As I waited for the manager, I skimmed the brochure they have – *Hello!* magazine it isn't. Graves are sold for fifty years, with further extensions 'available on application'; traditional grave space starts at £2,900, while reopening a traditional grave comes in at £1,400. Even in death, there's a price to pay. Ironically, the literature reassures the reader that staff understand 'the importance of choosing the final resting place for your loved one'. That question – where will I lie when I'm dead but not quite gone? It made me wish I had a family vault of marble with carven skulls and crossed bones for me and mine. My son is buried in an Essex grave with my husband's parents. I'll never lie there. My natural father, who died when I was a baby, is buried in a Yorkshire cemetery; my mother's already said there won't be room for me once she is down there with her second husband. Who'd want to live with their parents when they're grown and dead anyhows, Ma? We don't even share the same taste in music. No, I need a marble vault with my name inscribed upon the stone – that or immortality. I'll take either.

The cemetery manager was an efficient, kindly woman in a white blouse and a dark skirt, so at least I'd got the right dress code. We sat down in a little room decorated with illustrated pages from the Book of Remembrance and a warning to visitors to watch their footing because of ground subsidence. She had the official paperwork which gave her permission to move the ashes, and the first thing she did was apologize, all over again, through me to the family. As a result of the mistake with my neighbour, they have changed the way they document things. More importantly, in future there will be checks on the neighbouring plots, and two people rather than one will check the ashes are indeed going in the right place. You make a mistake, you make it better.

She brought in a small oak casket with my neighbour's name and age and the words 'In Loving Memory' engraved on a small plaque. Outside the office was a little buggy which we climbed into, putt-putting through the cemetery, careful to avoid the mourners heading into the chapel, the empty oak casket resting on my knee. The gardener was already waiting for us at the 'wrong' plot when we drew up. Introductions made, he spread out a large piece of AstroTurf and dug in his trowel. The earth was dry with the recent warm weather. He dug in the trowel again and lifted the soil out onto the fake grass. I began to panic that the rain might have washed her all away, but as he lifted out his trowel again, along with the soil was ash. Not ash like cigarette ash, but grittier – white and grey, like something you might dig into the soil to make your flowers bloom. My lovely little neighbour. I felt like saying, 'There you are, pet.' She'd have been so pleased to see me, and I was pleased to see her too. The gardener eased the trowel into a large brown paper bag resting in the small casket, and dug again, again and again. They don't scatter ash, haven't for forty years – it gets everywhere I understand; instead, they dig a hole and bury it. The gardener kept digging till the hole was more than a foot deep, and not till he had scraped every scrap up did he stop. Then I took the trowel and scraped some more. 'There's no chance we are getting any of the other chap, is there?' I asked, looking up – a fair question in the circumstances. The cemetery manager said no, the other chap had been buried in 1997 and the ash disperses without trace after ten years. The gardener gathered up the ash and soil on the bright green turf and carefully poured the last bit into the bag. The cemetery manager folded over the top of the bag, and as I thanked the chap whose eternal rest we'd so invaded, they carried the casket across to the rightful plot.

A hole had already been dug. It was deeper than the hole we had just dug – this time, there'd be no coming back. The cemetery manager drew my attention to the plaque with my neighbour's husband's name on it, and I went to confirm the number of the plot. No more mistakes. I said I would like to pour the ashes into the newly dug plot. One last act of neighbourliness for the best of neighbours. I wasn't sure they'd let me, bearing in mind I shouldn't have been there at all, but the cemetery manager agreed, so I moved around the rose bed, took the brown bag from the gardener and knelt to pour the bodily remains of my one-time little friend into her final resting place. Her final resting place. And I tapped the bag and flicked it with my finger so that nothing stayed where it should not. I lifted the AstroTurf and tipped the soil that had been dug out over the ashes. The gardener tamped down the earth and covered it over with the scraps of bark they use to keep the weeds down, and I leaned over to slide the plaque into the earth that linked her with her husband and stood to say a prayer. And I thought of her harvesting hops in Kent, the pictures of her grandchild cherubs in the living room, the names of her sons like blessings in her mouth, and I thought how simple life is, how you love whomsoever you love, and how you die, and how in the end peace comes.

Good deed no. 213: helped a friend rest in peace.

Tuesday, 2 August

Good deed no. 214: took another photo – of Italians this time, climbing the hill to Greenwich Observatory. The father wasn't at all grateful but then his face was puce.

Alert though I am to the opportunity to do good, there are occasions when I do the deed and then think there is more I should have done. Today on the street a girl was allegedly collecting for a £600 plane ticket to get her home to Australia to visit her mother, who has breast cancer. She had it all written out on cardboard. Was she a panhandler, or was the story true? If it was true, I realized only afterwards that I should have done more. If it was a lie, can it count as a good deed if the intention to do good was there? It has to, because no one knows the consequences of a deed at the moment it is done. You might help an old lady to cross a road only for her to be mugged, help someone to a new job only for them to be miserable. Someone else's lie or misfortune cannot negate your own good intention. But can you do a good deed accidentally, without any intention to do good? Can you be an accidental good-deed doer? I am struggling to think how, but maybe. Can a good deed come back and bite the good-deed doer? I have to hope not, but of course it can; I just wouldn't want to think it has to.

Good deed no. 215.

Thursday, 4 August

Good deed no. 216: made a donation to the British Museum (already having paid the exhibition ticket price).

Friday, 5 August

Good deed no. 217: sponsored Dr Will's son in his first marathon. The only problem is he is running for the League against Cruel Sports. The website says the charity 'works tirelessly to put an end to animal cruelty through "sports" such as hunting with dogs, live game-bird shooting and trophy hunting abroad' and relies on animal lovers nationwide. If they find out in Northumberland, they'll feed me to the hounds.

Saturday, 6 August

Had one of those serendipitous moments today when I rang my best gay boyfriend to try and arrange to see him after *The Railway Children* and it turned out he was going to the actual performance with his partner and his nieces. Of all the theatres in all the world you had to walk into mine.

It transpires that there are lots of good deeds in *The Railway Children* – including the fact the children's mother takes in Mr Schepansky, a Russian refugee and dissident who is lost and ill and trying to find his wife and children. (It made me think that I should find a refugee and offer them a home.) I loved the performance – partly because it addressed the fundamental human need for kindness. For instance, when the children's mother catches influenza, 'the old gentleman' from the train sends them a hamper of beef stock and foie gras, and more importantly works to free the children's father, who has been the victim of a miscarriage of justice. Yet kindness is so often overlooked as a motivating factor in literature – or for that matter in life. Love, yes. Money, yes. More kindness, that's what I say.

Good deed no. 218: bought ice cream for someone else's nieces at The Railway Children *(hardly on the scale of taking in a refugee, but ice cream cannot be overlooked as major contribution to making the world a better place).*

Sunday, 7 August

Good deed no. 219: invited teenage god-daughter to Northumberland for a week so her mum and dad can work with an easy conscience.

Monday, 8 August

Visited my son's grave in a chilly English churchyard on a grey and washed-out day, the grass long and wild across it and its unkempt neighbours – Mother Nature claiming what's hers. The cheek – when it is me he should be calling 'Mam'. Perhaps it is as well we live so far away. Perhaps otherwise each week I'd manicure the grass with gilt, curlicued scissors meant for a baby's nails, or graze the grassy grave myself, biting and chewing and swallowing up what grows there. Death keeps us shackled to God. Someone you love dies. Are you willing to accept they are lost and gone for all time and for ever more? Or do you choose faith, the miraculous, the mysterious? Do you choose the trumpet sound on Resurrection Day and a sometime-someplace reunion for the innocent, the deserving, for anyone with a golden ticket and a *What Would Jesus Do?* button? Once upon a time in a land called Eternity, the good and righteous met again those they had loved the most in this whole world, and knowing them again, holding them again, smiling on their beloved faces, together they lived happily hereafter. So endeth the sermon. The End. Or maybe not. Maybe this here is the end, this earth mound, filled up with child bones, wild and unmown grass, this lichen-covered headstone written over with his name and gouged-out promises of forever love.

Good deed no. 220: filled and set right a vase of gladioli on some other child's grave which had been knocked over by the wind.

Tuesday, 9 August

Good deed no. 221: now in Suffolk, offered an old lady some blackberries from a raffia punnet as she sat on a wooden bench in the evening sunshine outside the village hall with her glossy spaniel at her feet. When I'm old, I want to sit in the sun with a spaniel at my feet, lips stained with brambles, a tincture of bobbing ice and stiff gin clutched fondly in my liver-spotted hand.

Wednesday, 10 August

I have competition from chimpanzees. Research published in the journal *Proceedings of the National Academy of Sciences* by a team from the Yerkes National Primate Research Center at Emory

University, Atlanta, found that chimps will do things for each other even without direct benefit to themselves. According to the primate scientists, this confirmation of chimpanzee altruism suggests that 'human altruism is less of an anomaly than previously thought'.

Apparently animal behaviourists had observed chimps acting altruistically in the wild and in captivity, but such behaviour had not been replicated in scientific conditions. Chimps, then, had been regarded as 'reluctant altruists' who only acted 'in response to pressure and solicitation'. But in this latest test by the primate researchers, seven female chimps with three different partners got to choose between taking a token which meant a treat for them and a treat for the partner chimp, or a differently coloured token which meant the treat was only for themselves. Most of the time they took the altruistic route and chose the win-win treat, doing their chimp buddy a good turn. The chimps weren't related to each other and there was no immediate reciprocity involved that the scientists were aware of, which does not follow the normal way of things for altruistic behaviour among non-human primates. I expect Helena Bonham-Carter will lollop along with a banana for me any minute.

Good deed no. 222: signed up for the online organ donation register.

Thursday, 11 August

What happens in this part of Suffolk is that the men go to sea in small wooden boats while the women trail round a string of Boden-dressed children for activities such as crabbing. I have been crabbing – that is to say, I have sat for an hour at the quayside anxiously holding on to one or other of my children who threaten to fall into the sea below in their anxiety to pull up a bacon-laden hook, complete with clinging crab. I have also been for a walk en famille and taken the kids out to lunch. I've played witches with my five-year-old girl and been to the park for a game of cricket.

I've put my wet and muddy and exhausted son in a bath, flannelled a bloody knee clean and found chocolate to help him recover from the hurt. I've set my girl up with painting by numbers and ignored the mess. Tonight I still have to make tea and wrestle them into bed, and I'm already planning a trip to Edinburgh next week so my Harry Potter-loving god-daughter gets to see a comedy about Harry Potter at the Fringe and I get to see Kirsty. I am happy. I am exhausted.

Good deed no. 223: wrote a letter to the Catholic Church telling them to compensate the victims of child abuse.

Friday, 12 August

Popped into an art exhibition in a Suffolk chapel which held out the prospect of art activity for the kids. As they painted paper bags, I looked around the chapel walls. Someone had done a modern twist on the Ten Commandments, with the emphasis on positive thinking. The first, 'You shall have no other gods', had been converted into 'Live by priorities', while 'Remember the Sabbath Day' was 'Catch your breath', 'You shall not commit adultery' had turned into 'Affair-proof your marriage' and 'You shall not steal' into 'Prosper with a clear conscience'. You believe God goes to all the trouble of burning a bush and writing out the rules in longhand on a couple of pieces of rock, then he gets Moses to carry them back down the mountain, and you think to yourself, 'Times change: I'm not that fond of rules. I could do it so much better.' If only God had hung on a couple of thousand years, he could have tweeted. It's the age of the Internet, we have the attention span of gnats. 'Do good' would have covered it.

Good deed no. 224: paid a glazier to mend a broken window in a friend's cottage. (I originally blamed the kids for breaking it playing cricket, but it turned out to have been broken already. Kids are unbearably smug about it.)

Unsurprisingly, the children squabbled ferociously in the back of the car driving home from Suffolk, but I can't say I blame them – we set off at 2.30 p.m. and got home at 10.45 p.m. The A1 was closed, and around Middlesbrough my husband began to fantasize about having a drink when we got back. I said, 'We've no wine in,' and he said, 'Your cousins will have left a bottle.' This was on the grounds that we had borrowed a house in London and left six bottles and a bunch of flowers, and had borrowed the house in Suffolk and left two very expensive bottles, country market jams, tea, coffee and flowers. Wind forward the clock several hours later to the stage directions: *Family collapses through the back door, wild of hair, red of eye, white of lip, husband carrying sleeping daughter and a large number of bags. Wife chases the two boys up the stairs to bed, and after a few minutes, the adults return to the kitchen.*

On the kitchen table were three very charming thank-you notes, one from the grown-ups and two from their kids. The house was sparkling and the notes lying flat on the kitchen table were beautifully written and suitably grateful. One of the boys had counted our DVDs and informed us we had 124 of them, which is always useful to know. Al picked up the notes and peered underneath them in puzzlement. 'Your bloody, bloody family,' he muttered as he put the kettle on for tea.

Good deed no. 225: gave £1 to an East Anglian cancer charity at a country market.

Sunday, 14 August

It is bliss to be home in my own bed. The children are so taken with the novelty of home they have forgotten to squabble with each other.

Good deed no. 226: took in Dr Will's washing as it started to rain and dried it in my squeaky tumble-drier.

My fifteen-year-old god-daughter arrived from London, thereby allowing her parents to work (for this week of the summer holidays at least). Her mother assured me that I don't have to entertain her and she will help me with the kids. I'm unconvinced she is aware of this arrangement.

I want to work, but I want to be at home when the kids come in from school; I need to earn money, but I don't want to care about money. Summer holidays and working mothers are certainly not an easy mix. If you take a fortnight's holiday together as a family, that still leaves four weeks with the children at home. What are we supposed to do in that time? Abandon work? Call in grannies and grandads – who in my case need more looking after than the kids? It is not like we still have that mindset where we can in all conscience turn them out to play in the woods with a doorstep of bread and beef dripping wrapped in brown paper and expect them home only when dusk falls – exhausted, grubby and dangling a glass jar of tadpoles. It is bad enough for me, and I work at home. Friends who work in offices confess to passing children round grannies and aunties and sending them to football academies or to learn circus skills they don't want just to fill up one more week. We're breeding an entire generation of kids who can juggle swords. I Box and Cox. That is to say, my husband goes into his office and closes the door seconds before I throw something heavy at it, then I give up on work. Not today, though. For some reason today I thought I would try to get something done. Fool.

After lunch I set up my laptop on the kitchen table. Within three minutes, my daughter came in having scraped her knee and elbow falling over. Cue clean-up operation and three chocolate fingers each for her and her pal. I sent her back out with her friend. Two minutes later they were back because my daughter was complaining of pain from elbow and knee. Cue a pink milk bribe to make it feel better, and back out they went. Seven minutes later they were back in, wanting to play on the iPad. They played on the iPad and I managed fifteen minutes of work before I remembered the Sky Box Office movie all the children were supposed to watch so that I could work undisturbed. I set them up with it and made popcorn. When I took the popcorn in, it turned out one of my children's friends doesn't eat sugared popcorn. I made admiring noises at her strength of character and quality of her strong, shiny teeth while inside cursing because all the popcorn was sugared. I went back out to the kitchen to coax unpopped kernels at the bottom of the pan to pop, and cobbled together a small bowl of unsugared, virtuous popcorn which I duly carried back in. Cue ten minutes work before my daughter and god-daughter carried out empty bowls saying the boys were demanding more popcorn. I shoved two popped corns into my ears and feigned deafness.

Good deed no. 227.

Tuesday, 16 August

When we got back home from a day at the Edinburgh Fringe and lunch with Kirsty, there was a hamper waiting for us. From the cousins. For the loan of the house. It was an 'ultimate indulgence hamper', complete with not one but three bottles of wine – a Shiraz, a Sauvignon Blanc, a sparkling brut – alongside cheese bites dusted with Parmigiano-Reggiano, a jar of gourmet baby beets in red wine vinegar, handmade all-butter lemon curd, cocoa-dusted truffles and after-dinner coffee. 'That's my bloody family for you,' I told my husband.

Good deed no. 228: bought lunch for a friend.

Wednesday, 17 August

My god-daughter lost a plaited leather bracelet on the beach and however hard we looked, we couldn't find it. She had tucked it into her jeans, which she had left on the shore as we waded into the

North Sea, and when we came out it was gone. There were hardly any people on the beach; perhaps a dog snuffled around and carried it off or it dropped to the sands as she folded the jeans and an ambitious wave took it. It fell down a crack and disappeared from sight as lost things do, as lovers do, as life itself does sometimes. You forget, though, how seriously teenagers take these things. If I lose something, I shrug and count my children and reach out to feel my husband's heart, take hold my parents' hands, and, if all are present, I shrug and say, 'Ah well – that other thing is lost to me. We'll get by without it.' For her, the sky grew grey and sadness came upon her, and I rejoiced – that a cheap keepsake could mean so much, that she didn't know what true loss was, and I prayed she never would.

Good deed no. 229: bought my god-daughter a new leather bracelet.

Thursday, 18 August

Good deed no. 230: gave a neighbour toilet roll (I love this good deed – I'd do it every day if I could).

Friday, 19 August

Forget trying to do any work, it is really hard to do good in the holidays. Who has time to be good when you're a mother? Not bloody me. We are wandering round the genteel Alnwick Garden before we put my god-daughter on the train home, and there are late summer roses, and smiling elderly visitors, and giggling tots standing in puddles of sunshine and the rainbow spray of the fountains, and my eldest is in his hoodie with his football socks around his ankles, and he is going one way when I say 'Come the other' and splashing his brother with water even though I say 'Stop that' and walking up the cobbled rills to the fountain when I say 'Don't do that' and lifting up the mesh grilles to see if he can get the money out people have thrown in to make wishes, and

I say, 'Stop behaving like a yob.' He stops – armies would have stopped on hearing my voice – and he swivels his sun hat back to front and turns to his eight-year-old brother with his little finger and his index finger stuck out, grins and starts pimp-rolling out the garden.

End of week 4 of the summer holidays and I came home from our day out, shovelled them out into my own garden so I could decompress with a cup of tea and strict instructions not-to-speak-to-me-at-all-not-one-word-not-even-if-you-break-a-leg-I'm-not-interested-you-understand, in order to recover from my children's ability to drive me insane.

Good deed no. 231: bought Worcestershire cousin's son a new Harry Potter wand (him having left it behind after the stay at my house, and my house having eaten it). I've bought him a wand because I'm guessing he is that kind of kid – the kind who sits and does magic and reads books and occasionally picks up a rubber dinosaur and says, 'Mummy – look, dinosaur does roar.' My kids would use a wand to stir up noxious potions made of mud and smells to splatter on their siblings, or sharpen it for pokes and warrior javelins: 'See how high they fly? We didn't mean to kill that cow – seriously, how were we to know?' Or just sit upon each other's heads and use it to beat out the rhythm of their joyful hearts.

Saturday, 20 August

Good deed no. 232: lent a neighbour a bag of pasta.

Sunday, 21 August

The present from my cousins has given me the idea to buy one nice thing a week and fill the hamper for Christmas for the expats. I would do it for my mum and dad, but they'd just say thank you very much and promptly give it all away because they think mustard a bit racy. I grew up on meat and convenience: fish on Friday, otherwise it was sausages, pork chops, lamb chops and Sunday roasts alongside Findus Crispy Pancakes so hot they melted the roof of your mouth on the way down, Smash – mashed potato pellets you poured boiling water over to make mashed potato – and Fray Bentos steak and kidney pie with suet pastry, which you cooked in its flat, round tin in a saucepan of boiling water. Ah, the 1970s – it's a miracle we made it out the other end. It's a miracle anything made it out the other end.

Good deed no. 233: re-gifted a bottle of red wine from the holiday thank-you hamper.

Monday, 22 August

Good deed no. 234: lent butter to a neighbour. (I should wear pin-curls and a floral pinny and set up one of those turn-of-the-century shops with wooden shelves and a lift-up counter for the holidays when my neighbours come up to their houses. 'Ah'll put it on yer tab, Mrs Broon – ah knows yer good fer it,' I could say, smiling at them gummily. Actually, we borrow stuff too. Usually when they're not here, which is technically burglary, but hey, what's a bit of olive oil between friends? About eighteen months with good behaviour.

Tuesday, 23 August

Good deed no. 235: let out, played with and fed the expats' dog while they spent the day in Newcastle. Bearing in mind that the last time I saw this dog, it shat on my carpet, this good deed proves I do not bear a grudge.

Wednesday, 24 August

I suspect it might be time for the holidays to draw to an end. Massive row with Al today, during which I shovelled the children into the car (one of them in floods of tears), swept out of the house and drove off into the distance with absolutely no clue where I was going. I'd have driven to Paris I was in such a bad mood, but I didn't have the kids' passports and even if I did they're out of date. Al had got fed up with them squabbling and decided unilaterally, even though I was in charge and he was supposed to be working, that my daughter was going to a friend's and my sons were going to a football camp. I'm clambering out of the bath, and first my daughter comes up to tell me Daddy has rung her friend and then my eldest boy comes up to say Daddy has gone down to the village to buy them food for their packed lunch. I would have put them all in the car at that exact moment, but a. I was naked and b. my husband had the car.

We ended up at the shopping nirvana that is the Gateshead Metrocentre, where the kids strapped themselves into some bungee contraption and bounced up to the ceiling and down again. While I watched my middle child, there was a moment at the top when the ropes slackened off and he sat there with his legs crossed, beaming and as content as any genie. The guy doing the bouncing up and down unstrapped him, and I said, 'How was it?' My son said, 'I thought my stomach was going to come up my throat and out my mouth – brilliant.'

The good deed was easy-peasy, though. We are wandering through M&S and I'm wondering just how middle-aged you have to be to wear one of their blouses when a scruffy blonde girl of about six, dressed in a black puffa jacket, comes up to me. 'I've lost me nanna,' she says, and takes my hand in hers. It is disconcerting when a strange child puts her warm and sticky hand in yours, not least for your own children. Of course, there is no assistant in sight, and I have no idea where there's a till, so we start wandering round and I'm calling for the nanna, thinking if this woman sees me with her granddaughter in tow, she is going to think I'm kidnapping her. So I start yelling louder, and people's heads are beginning to turn because I've four children around me now and I am calling out like I'm away with the fairies. The granny appears but she's not looking at me, she is looking at the granddaughter, and she doesn't speak to me, so I say 'She got lost' in explanation. She doesn't so much as blink at the sight of the child's hand in mine, she just takes the kid, and another woman who looks just like her but twenty years younger and is pushing a pram nods at me.

Good deed no. 236.

Thursday, 25 August

Good deed no. 237: sent Jam Jar Army artwork over to the mental health charity Derwentside Mind, who want to raise money for themselves.

Friday, 26 August

Good deed no. 238: Dr Will and his son washed up very forlorn, having been caught in terrible traffic en route to the Edinburgh Fringe, so I invited them to share our roast chicken dinner. (The son is a gluten-free, dairy-free vegan – he shared our vegetables, our air and our conversation.)

Saturday, 27 August

Mum and Dad arrived yesterday morning. My mum's back is really bad – she is walking very slowly and carefully as if she were some novice in a martial arts film training to walk with light and spread toes over a fragile carpet of white chicken eggs without cracking one. She manages the pain when she is sitting, but any sort of movement hurts. Why can't we just go on and on and then stop? Why do we have to fall apart first and then grind to a halt in the middle of the traffic where juggernauts of pain are sure to run right into and over us?

Good deed no. 239: put money into jam jars in shops in the market town. (Worryingly, none of the jars looked that full. When I say 'looked that full', I should say that they 'looked distinctly empty'.)

Sunday, 28 August

Horror. My neighbour down the lane is on some pavilion committee and a couple of months ago asked me to organize and run the tombola for the summer fete. I wrote it in my diary. I forgot to read my diary. I spent the day down in Newcastle buying clothes for the kids to go back to school. Oh my God. Have they had a fete without a tombola? Is that even possible?

Good deed no. 240: sent a fantasy adventure book to Merry.

Monday, 29 August

Shamefaced, I rang my neighbour about the tombola. He let me crawl in apology for a couple of minutes, then said he had forgotten to pass on the fact I'd volunteered for the tombola anyway, so someone else organized it. Big fat phew.

Good deed no. 241: attended Lifeboat Day in a local village, despite the fact they didn't want me as a coastguard (I bear no grudge, not one bit. Instead I paid a pound to have a go on one of those metal loop-the-loops that bleep when you brush it with a metal ring, navigating my course from the jolly blue and orange lifeboat across a painted plywood sea to a sinking ship, and hardly got a bleep at all. I rest my case).

Tuesday, 30 August

The end of the holidays is almost in sight. I took the children to a bouldering wall in the sports centre so that the three of them could scramble up it. Naively, I assumed they would be harnessed to a beefy young man and guided up and down the rocks. Instead, it was up to them to move from rock to rock. My little girl traversed a curved rock face like a goat, while the boys attempted the riskier vertical climb, competing against each other to see who could get highest. At a certain point, my eldest would stop, cling to the wall and then leap off and away onto the deep foam mattresses that lined the floor. He did it again and again and again, his awareness that he might fall if he climbed further pipping the urgent desire to get that bit higher. He did not appreciate my five-year-old daughter's advice as she hopped from rock to rock, 'You have to believe in yourself.' She watches too much Disney.

Good deed no. 242: agreed to take Lily's son on Thursday, so she can meet a deadline.

Wednesday, 31 August

My dad asked me to speed things up for my mum re her referral to a consultant for her back. They mentioned it a couple of weeks ago and I uttered platitudes along the lines of *Let's see what happens, she is in the system and I'm sure it won't be long*. This morning, though, before she tottered into breakfast, he said how very bad she was. I know he's right, and God knows they would do anything for me. My only hesitation was that I went through this last year for the operation on her spine, and it worked and the consultant was lovely throughout, and you don't want to be seen special-pleading all the time. But scruples seem ridiculous when your aged father is telling you the poor state your blind, pain-wracked mother is in.

Good deed no. 243: rang the consultant's office re mum's referral for a cracked vertebra (they checked and hadn't had it), rang GP's surgery to arrange a fax of the referral (they claimed they'd sent it) and emailed the consultant twice to explain the situation. He said he was sorry to hear about my mum and he would do what he could. Mum promptly bollocked my dad when she realized what he'd done.

Thursday, 1 September

There are builders in the farmyard at the back of the house renovating an old cart shed for my Yorkshire cousins, who bought it off the farmer because they want their own holiday cottage. The disruption hasn't been too bad, but after my mum and dad left this morning and Lily's son arrived, one of the builders started using a nail-gun to construct a complex framework of wooden struts to lay the plasterboards against. Whenever he shot a nail into the wood, there was a loud boom, and whenever there was a loud boom, it set his Jack Russell dog off barking – loudly. I let it go, and I let it go, and the noise was tipping me over into a migraine so I went out and suggested they might like to tie the dog up at the front. As I'm talking to them, the damn dog makes a beeline for my kitchen door and suddenly he is in the house, but I think that's OK, I'll let him out the front myself. As I'm thinking that, he cocks his leg and wees in the hallway. I'm looking up 'Dog Stew' in Delia.

Good deed no. 244: took kids' stuff that's too old for the charity shop to the recycling bin at the tip.

Friday, 2 September

Took the boys down to see the latest Harry Potter movie and bought a bucket of popcorn and water for them and a coffee for me. They went to the loo and I left them standing in the foyer while I went. I was away two minutes. Two minutes, and when I came out two cinema attendants were standing over them at the edges of a popcorn sea that surrounded the waste bin and my two boys. They had decided to have a popcorn fight. Seriously? I wouldn't mind, but there were roadworks and it had taken two hours to get down, I'd had to beg a favour to get someone to take my little girl for the day, and we were trying to be discreet because I wasn't entirely sure whether they were allowed in at their ages. Not a good start to the movie. I should really have marched them straight back out, but I couldn't face another two-hour trip home again with hysterics in the back of the car, so we compromised on them picking up the popcorn piece by piece by piece. So much for me setting a good example with my virtuous life. If I was a good example, I'd have set them a fitting punishment like giving their bucket of popcorn to a hungry child without one.

Good deed no. 245: gave a cupcake to a neighbour.

Saturday, 3 September

Good deed no. 246: took some of my sons' stuff to Sue Ryder.

Sunday, 4 September

Good deed no. 247: overnight hospitality to an unexpected visitor.

Monday, 5 September

An entire day of good deeds. I sorted out my daughter's bedroom yesterday afternoon, and this morning I took school pinafores and old toys into Sue Ryder on my second drop-off of the week; I gave my cousin a bed for the night again; I brought out tea (twice) and iced buns (once) to the builders (bearing in mind they are not even my builders); and I gave someone directions for the fish shop and picked up a baby's Tupperware bowl and lid in M&S – I am sooooooooo virtuous.

Good deed no. 248: gave away a wooden rocking horse to Sue Ryder. (I wanted to give something of proper value, having been seized by the sudden conviction that the stuff I was giving away was helping me more than it was helping the charity shop.) NB: I have discovered it is very liberating to let go of things. I have also discovered my children have far too much of everything.

Tuesday, 6 September

Manifold good deeds again today, including taking a photo of ramblers on a sand-blasted windswept beach, picking up jam jars, and making tea for the builders working outside, which makes me wonder if it is all becoming a bit compulsive. You definitely get a buzz from good-deeding, but I see no evidence to date that doing my good deeds is making me a better person. I am no more patient, no more kind, no less selfish. I have made small differences to other people's lives for the better, but no great difference to my own – other than to complicate my life considerably, according to my husband. I am going to up my game and do some proper volunteering.

Good deed no. 249: picked up jam jars in one of the villages (including big coffee jar, which the ten-year-old promptly dropped – glass shards and splinters and coins all over the road, bringing traffic to a standstill. Helped by three good-deed doers: a nice lady who helped us pick up coins and glass, a builder who shovelled up the last of the glass and coins so traffic could start rolling, and a holidaymaker who gave us a plastic bag to put the broken glass in and then gave us a pound when he realized it was for the hospice.

Wednesday, 7 September

I dropped the children off at school for the first day of the new academic year and the usually smiley mum with the crutch said forlornly, 'My, that summer's gone quickly' as her little blond lovely skipped off into class. I watched as she hung his coat on his peg, blank and outright disbelief flooding my veins, and groped for any response that wouldn't incriminate me as a bad mother who didn't love her children enough to want to spend every waking moment of her entire life with them. 'You have to be kidding, right?' wasn't going to cut it.

Swallows are everywhere, swooping and diving round and round like autumn leaves caught in gusting wind, ready to fly to winter haunts. Outside, there is windblown sunshine; inside, there is nothing. Letting myself back in after the school drop-off, it was as if nobody lived here at all – apart from the smell. Unfortunately, the kitchen resembles the boudoir of an aged and painted harlot: it smells of roses, bunches and bunches of roses – warmed because the air is warm from the Aga. Reaching for a cup last night, I managed to knock a full glass bottle of perfume from the mouth of the cupboard onto the black granite kitchen counter and smash it. I used to like the scent of roses, but you can have too much of a good thing. I've mopped the floor, wiped the counter and everything that was on the counter, antiseptic-sprayed both, wrapped up the broken bottle in newspaper, emptied the kitchen bin, thrown out the cloths I've used and washed out the mop – and still it is like living in a bowl of potpourri.

Perhaps, though, the smell is the reward for my good deeds? It reminds me of a fairy story I read as a kid with a good sister and a bad sister, and wherever the bad sister walked there were poisonous toads and green slime and snails and vicious rats, and wherever the good sister went flowers grew in her wake and bluebirds sang and small silver bells tinkled in a gentle summer breeze. Perhaps now wherever I go the smell of roses will linger? Shame it is making me gag. Although I can live with that if the smell is a foretaste of what life would be like as a saint.

In Catholic theology there is such a thing as the 'odour of sanctity' – a phenomenon known as osmogenesia. Padre Pio, for instance, was a priest born in 1887 who died in 1968 and was canonized by Pope John Paul II in 2002. Reports have it that he developed stigmata (which hardly seems fair), could bilocate (that is to say, could be in two places at once, allowing him to be twice as holy), has a thousand miracles attributed to him and gave out a 'very intense and pleasant fragrance, similar to the scent of the violet', according to a bishop sent to investigate him. Other witness reports mention the smell being of roses, jonquil, lilies or incense, sometimes from his wounds and their dressings, sometimes from his clothing or left behind where he had walked. To judge by my kitchen, that may be the reason he was in two places at once: maybe one of him was trying to get away from the heady floral notes surrounding him. I love the stories to do with Padre Pio. One of them involves American airmen during the Second

World War abandoning attempts to drop bombs on his hometown of San Giovanni Rotondo after seeing a floating, bearded, brown-robed friar above the city.

A whole host of Catholic saints and holy types allegedly give off this smell of virtue, including the Little Flower or St Thérèse of Lisieux, often featured in statues clutching a crucifix and a spray of roses. 'What matters,' she said, 'is not great deeds but great love.' In 1897, shortly before the 24-year-old Carmelite nun died of tuberculosis, she said: 'After my death, I will let fall a shower of roses. I will spend my heaven doing good upon earth. I will raise up a mighty host of little saints. My mission is to make God loved . . .' At her death a strong scent of roses was detectable for days after, and many of those who have asked for St Thérèse's intervention believe they have received not only the grace of God but a symbol of it in roses or the smell of roses. She'd love my kitchen.

Good deed no. 250: rang and listened to a friend whose husband has been made unemployed.

Thursday, 8 September

Good deed no. 251: took Cryssie for the first lesson of a new term.

Friday, 9 September

I am in major need of a kick up the backside as far as the Jam Jar Army goes. It seems like so much effort. I figure we stand at around £2,100, which is good. I'm not knocking it. It is 20 per cent of the target, but I need a major brainstorm and push to bring in another £8,000. If I had £8,000 I would just write a cheque and be very happy if I never saw another jam jar in my entire life.

According to the latest official figures, around 25 per cent of adults volunteer formally once a month, with interest in volunteering growing (attributed to rising unemployment). I popped into the local Salvation Army shop on the high street of the local market town and asked about volunteering. It was very busy and very brightly lit. There were at least half a dozen elderly folk picking thoughtfully through the racks of clothes and buying second-hand cookery books. The manager was out, so I have to phone her tomorrow. Perhaps she will give me a trombone and try to recruit me to the Salvation Army. Perhaps you have to be able to play the trombone before they let you work there.

Good deed no. 252: picked up jam jars from Gazette *offices for counting.*

Saturday, 10 September

If you have not done a good deed during the day, one of the hardest things is to make yourself think about someone else at exactly the moment you have put the children to bed, washed up, tidied up and are crawling hopefully towards the TV for an hour's respite sprawled on the sofa before you go to bed. Yet at that exact moment, when in other circumstances your day is virtually done and you are utterly exhausted, you have to start thinking about someone other than yourself. Bizarrely, however, I have discovered that when you do make time for someone else, there is a return, and when you're done, there is revival.

I rang to check up on my Irish aunty who lost her husband earlier in the year, and she sounded positive and together and looking forward to a trip home to Ireland with her daughters. Aside from her two grown-up daughters, she has a son who is an engineer in America. Years ago, he was diagnosed with a very severe cancer but made it through. My aunt told me he used to wear a Padre Pio medal pinned to the inside of his shirt. I wonder if he smells roses?

Good deed no. 253.

I have set the kids a challenge of a good deed a day for a week. They were not thrilled at the prospect – I am pretty sure my eldest rolled his eyes. An easy thing to do would be to be kind to the younger children who have just started school, I explained. Now all they have to do is remember.

Good deed no. 254: opened the door out of a restaurant for a mother with a baby in a pushchair and a toddler.

Monday, 12 September

My neighbour down the lane who knows I am doing good deeds emailed saying he is away but he put his bin out and would I go 'rescue it if it falls over in the wind'. We are at the tail end of Hurricane Katia, with winds forecast to be gusting furiously and weather reports warning that trees could be brought down. His bin is probably in Moscow right now and I am wondering who will rescue me if I fall over in the wind, but I'm going.

Good deed no. 255.

Tuesday, 13 September

Good deed no. 256: took Lily's son after school while she drove the little one down for a hospital visit for her eyes.

Wednesday, 14 September

The hospice wanted me to write a piece for their magazine asking for jam jars to be returned. I wrote: '. . . the Jam Jar Army is about all of us – the shopkeeper who puts up a poster, the café owner who puts jars out on her tables, the little old lady in the retirement home with a jar filling up with tuppenny bits and the child who puts in his week's pocket money rather than spend it on sweets.' We have around £2,700. Only another £7,300 to go then, but the Jam Jar Army is about us, so I can stop worrying. Can't I?

Good deed no. 257.

Thursday, 15 September

Cryssie hadn't read a novel this week when she arrived for her lesson. Instead she had read a Christian book described as a 'Young person's guide to knowing God'. Usually we have a chat about whatever novel she's read the week before, but there was nowhere I could go with this one. A guide to knowing God? You have to have some self-belief to write that. To 'know God' – what does that even mean? If someone says to me they think they really know me, I think, 'Honestly? You know nothing, mate' and I'm just me. I bet it hacks God off when his faithful claim to know him. I bet it makes him want to beat on his white hairy chest and bellow, 'I am Yahweh the Unknowable.' Did Cryssie really read it? Or did she think it was the sort of book I would approve of her reading? It is certainly the sort of book her parents would approve of her reading, but their job is to lead her into faith; my job is to lead her into make-believe.

I have told her I want her to go away and finish writing a story. I have no idea how much she is absorbing. She nods a lot, but I can't tell from her writing whether she's getting what I'm saying. When I began teaching her she told me she wanted to write stories about dogs and cats. I asked her again today what she wanted to write and she said, 'Stories about dogs and cats.' I tried coaxing: 'You've had a go at an adventure story and a ghost story and you've read all these other books now, is there anything else you might be thinking of writing about?' She looked at me for a long moment and said, 'Giraffes.'

Good deed no. 258.

Friday, 16 September

Good deed no. 259: returned woman's suitcase to her after she had left it at the café counter in Durham railway station – I knew she would. I was right behind her and in a steaming hurry and she couldn't have been slower if she tried. The pull-along bag had its handle fully extended and kept falling over, so she plonked it against the sandwich display before she bought her coffee and a whole selection of food, paying for it with a card which for some reason took the attentions of both assistants behind the counter. Then she walked away. Piously, I wheeled it over to her as she stood with her coffee and her food and her handbag and her other bags, and instead of saying thank you she just said, 'Oh. My. God' in a horrified way. 'You're welcome,' I said.

Saturday, 17 September

On the way down to the mini and junior Great North Run, I asked the children how their good deeds had gone this week. The eldest claimed he had no memory of any such conversation over breakfast or the challenge ever being set, although my eight-year-old boy and my little girl said they had both been kind to the younger children. Then my eldest said, without lifting his head from his iPod, 'But we are doing the Great North Run, so give us a break,' which was true.

Watching them run inspires me. Not just my kids – all of them: those grinning, tiny, pink-winged fairies running alongside a huffing, puffing daddy; cowgirls in glittering Stetsons; three-legged teenage racers, their arms wrapped around one another, a paper explanation of her fund-raising pinned to one girl's T-shirt: 'I'm doing this for my aunty'. Can that aunty see her do this? Is she proud? If she can't, I'll be proud on her behalf. Proud too of those kids in wheelchairs pushed up steep banks by gritty mums and dads – faces ablaze with sweat and loyalty; a teenage boy with muscular dystrophy surrounded by his family urging him on, willing him on, as he leaned into his walking frame, frail legs twisted under him, moving on and on to the finish line. The generosity, the energy, the purity of the young. Their willingness to own up to their love;

their readiness to struggle, to climb the hills and make it to the end for us. This week my children – all those children – they did enough.

Good deed no. 260: facilitated £250 in sponsorship for the hospice through the Great North Run.

Sunday, 18 September

Good deed no. 261: brought along an apple pie to the village priest's retirement do.

Monday, 19 September

Good deed no. 262: mentored the media student on behaviour and approach during her work experience. Best advice: get everyone coffee, get everyone lunch, get there early, leave late, take out the nose stud and don't sleep with anyone unless you have to.

Tuesday, 20 September

Karl, my radio wannabe, has finally been back in touch asking me to help with his revised CV (which I asked for in February) and an application letter, having stumbled across something on the Internet about a radio work-experience programme for students. (We're ignoring that bit on the grounds he does a programme for community radio, which is far more important than being a student.) Where has he been all this time?

Good deed no. 263: worked on radio wannabe's CV.

Wednesday, 21 September

I got quite low this morning trying to add the final details to Karl's CV. He had tried his very hardest to lay it out properly and make the most of what he has, but with the best will in the world there is only so much you can do with three Cs, three Ds and an E at GCSE, along with three jobs in kitchens, all of which appeared to involve a great deal of washing-up – the most recent in a fish and chip shop. Al's suggested I say he has experience in the oil industry and not mention that it's vegetable oil.

Head in hands, a black coffee in front of me, I was sitting at my desk groaning when I idly clicked on the Internet radio to hear his weekly programme. Sometimes the Portland grey clouds scud away and leave the canvas sky to a glorious cadmium-yellow sun. It turns out I was worrying about him dropping out of a construction course when he is downright great on the radio. It takes this shy, lummocky kid who is the size of a haystack all his time to meet your eye when he is talking to you, and he has a voice to melt butter. Broad Geordie, bass, mellow – what's more, he makes jokes. Revelation. Inspiration. I did a complete rewrite of yesterday's CV and I said in his application letter: 'I want to stop being the guy listening to a voice on the radio while he washes up stacks of greasy plates in a stainless-steel sink – because I want to be the voice he's listening to.'

Good deed no. 264.

Thursday, 22 September

Had Cryssie for her writing lesson, and if she didn't write the best thing she has done for me so far. Must be the weather. It was quite surreal. I had given her an exercise to write a story starting with the words 'Everything was fine till I opened the box . . .' We talked about Pandora and what might be in the box, and then I read what she had written:

> The box sat on the windowsill beside my dad's cup of cold tea. It was painted all the colours of the rainbow and on its lid, a swan swam in a glittering lake in front of a palace. It was the prettiest thing Uncle Jake had ever given me.

The box drew me towards it. As I crossed the room, my legs began to tremble. I knelt on the window seat and slid the screwdriver into the lock – it didn't take more than a minute before I heard a click. Biting my lip, I used my finger to ease up the lid and out jumped King Henry the Eighth.

Henry VIII? I didn't see that coming.

I'm not counting the writing lesson as my good deed for today, though. Daniel came up for lunch and a walk on the beach. Lunch was garlicky and the beach was sunny and empty and sad. A year has passed since his wife died, and his contemporaries have begun to sicken and to die. A couple of weeks ago he went to three funerals in five days, which seems to be pushing it. First you're invited to weddings; then to dinner parties, where talk is of schools and houses; then second weddings or silver weddings graciously announcing 'no presents necessary'; then gold weddings, when you hold each other like precious china cups full of hot china tea and waltz precariously around a church hall; then a domino spiral of funerals, one after the other after the other, all the way onwards to your own oblivion. How do we all stay sane when confronted with the inevitability of our ending, when we are destined to lose those we love the best?

Daniel, who is Jewish, said he was going home to light a Yahrzeit candle, which you light at sunset on the anniversary of the death of your loved one and keep alight for twenty-four hours to mark their passing. I told him I'd do the same in my house at the same moment in memory and friendship – that way he knows he's not alone. He won't remember as the blue-tipped match flares, as he touches it to the wick, as the candle takes the flame. Perhaps, though, he might remember hours after, as he walks to the kitchen to pour a solitary glass of red wine and gazes into the flame. Perhaps he'll think, 'Outside this glass window, across the darkness and the miles, there is family, love and friendship, and other candles burn.'

Good deed no. 265.

Not being Jewish, I hadn't entirely got round the implications of keeping a candle alight for twenty-four hours. I had the perfect candle, thick and gold and chunky, in a hurricane lantern. All well and good through the evening right up to bedtime, at which point I've turned all the lights off downstairs, I've locked the doors, I've double-checked that I've locked the doors (I get neurotic when it is just me and the kids) and I'm standing in my kitchen holding the hurricane lamp with its golden candle burning steadfastly at its glass-walled heart, my three sleeping cherubs safe in their beds upstairs, and I think, 'I am about to keep a naked flame alight all night, only for the house to burn down, and for me, and more importantly my three children, to be burnt to charcoal toast.' I ended up carrying the hurricane lamp upstairs and putting it in the ceramic bathtub for the night, while removing all bubble bath, bath scrubs and flannels from the vicinity in case a shampoo decided to commit suttee, throw itself at the flame and ignite the entire upstairs in a smooth-as-silk, diamond-bright, not-a-split-end-in-sight multicultural inferno. I didn't sleep much.

I had a full-on day for good deeds. The three-day food festival, which has kindly agreed to adopt the hospice and the Jam Jar Army as its charity, began in the local market town. (The organizer is married to the editor of the *Gazette*, who himself happens to be on the organizing committee – thank you, God.) Consequently, I was standing in the marketplace with a yellow bucket as shoppers ambled around stalls of game, and pistachio ice cream, and rye bread, and bags of spices, and jars of cookie mixture, standing there for an hour – repeat, an hour – without so much as a penny piece going into my bucket.

Momentarily hopeful, I shook my bucket in a bid to draw attention while a well-dressed, middle-aged man in a sage-green wool coat with a sage-green velvet collar and his attractive wife in a well-cut white wool coat walked by . . . and utterly ignored me. I was seriously considering tearing off the seal and placing the bucket over my head to hide my embarrassment when a nice woman dug around in her purse and then her husband dug around in his pocket for some change and I had my very first customers. Time passed very slowly. I smiled, trying to look cheerful, but I did not feel cheerful. During the next half an hour, eight people gave me money. Unless people are going to give, they do not meet your eye; instead their gaze slides over you as if you were slippery with baby oil. A young girl approached me with her purse already in her hand. She was probably around nineteen or twenty. 'I haven't got any money,' she said as she rooted around for whatever coins there were in her plastic purse, and slid them one after the other into the small slot in the bucket lid. Now this young girl without money, who was giving me what she didn't have, this girl met my eye.

Good deed no. 266.

Saturday, 24 September

My back is killing me. After I finished yesterday's stint with a bucket, I bumped into the incredibly stressed-looking organizer of the food festival and asked if she needed any help. I spent the best part of three hours hefting tables around the hall where they were to host a plush 'Dine with Novelli' dining experience with Michelin-starred celebrity chef Jean-Christophe Novelli. (Tickets £50 a head.) Once I finished hefting tables, I moved seamlessly on to arranging chairs, getting rid of surplus chairs, setting out champagne flutes, polishing wine glasses, distributing menus and titivating velvet curtains. Naturally enough, the thought never crossed my mind that I wasn't even going to the dinner. Not once.

Good deed no. 267: hospitality to friends after they had dropped off their daughter at university.

Sunday, 25 September

I received a panicky email from Karl about the website for his work-experience application: 'It says my computer has committed a security violation and that means I can't get the email address.' I sent a calming response carefully advising he print out the letter and the CV, ring the HQ to confirm the name and company address it's to go to, then send it by recorded delivery to said address (not forgetting to enclose his show-reel). If I die before they get to this stage in their lives, I sincerely hope someone goes to this much trouble for my kids.

Good deed no. 268.

Monday, 26 September

Today I went to the local middle school to help an English teacher run a lunchtime club for young journalists. He went round the table asking them to talk about their ideas for articles, and one pupil suggested a piece on the Northumberland bird club whose members bring along dead birds they've found to the monthly meetings. The dead bird society – love it.

Good deed no. 269.

Tuesday, 27 September

A couple of weeks ago, I popped into the Salvation Army shop to volunteer my services and the manager agreed to have me in for a couple of weeks. Then she rang me and said I'd have to delay it a fortnight because she was going on holiday and I needed training. So this morning I went along to the shop all excited and smiley (having had to completely floor the car after dropping the kids at school), and she said I was actually due in yesterday. I explained that I'd thought the arrangement was for today and tomorrow and Friday, and she said no, it had definitely been yesterday, and she couldn't fit me in the rest of the week (bearing in mind this is free labour I'm offering her for three whole days), but I could come back next week. Fair enough, I completely cocked up the day I was due in, but she was having this conversation with me as she was hanging jumpers, and you don't like to say, 'Look, pet, it's not that difficult to hang a jumper, is it? Exactly how much training do I need here?'

When I got back home in an extremely bad mood, I rang the hospice to check on the amount of money the Jam Jar Army had made during the food festival: £2,000 – how amazing is that? (On the upside we now stand at around £5,500, which is halfway to the target. On the downside we have one week to go till our deadline. Bollocks to the deadline.) My bucket, of course, made all the difference – all £7.03 of difference. It turns out that more than a grand of the total came courtesy of celebrity chef Novelli, who has a cookery school and suggested auctioning three places on courses – how extraordinarily kind of him.

Good deed no. 270: wrote an email to a jam manufacturer asking for matched funding for the Jam Jar Army. No reply.

Wednesday, 28 September

Good deed no. 271: picked up Lily's little one and took her to the beach.

Thursday, 29 September

Summer was lousy. Grey and miserable and windy and wet. Suddenly, though, we have balmy sunshine and blue skies and barbecues on the beach. Bliss. It was so sunny that I contemplated teaching Cryssie outside today, but it was slightly too damp first thing this morning. She has been reading *The Hobbit* and I set her the task of writing a story with the first line 'I had never met such a grumpy dwarf – thinking about it, I had never met a dwarf at all . . .' I figured she would do me an adventure story or a fairy story, but instead she wrote a piece all about how the dwarf was grumpy because he didn't have a job and he had a small family to feed, so he went to a job centre and talked about getting a job in a supermarket and then he went to a pet shop and got the job in a pet shop and cuddled the puppies and the kittens. I asked her why she had written about the dwarf getting a job, and she said she had a job working in a school library one morning a week and she had been thinking about it. The story plodded along and I was pondering on the fact she wasn't getting what I keep saying about 'showing, not telling' and the need to have paragraphs, and wondering how come she didn't write about dragons and swords. It came to me that it wasn't the story that was the problem – I was the problem. I was reading it all wrong. It wasn't a fairy story; this was a real-life story about not having enough money, about being different. It was a story about respect, the story of a massively disabled kid, someone who may look different to everyone else but who wants the same things – things like a job, a job where she can cuddle puppies and kittens and bring money home to her family.

Good deed no. 272.

Friday, 30 September

Desperate to get out of harvest festival service this evening but stymied by the fact my daughter is playing a bunch of grapes, which is apparently a 'very big part, Mummy'. My youngest son had drawn a picture of a crane driver transporting the grapes. He drew him with red hair and red eyes. 'It's Ron Weasley possessed by a demon,' he told me with some pride.

Good deed no. 273: made tea for other people's builders.

Saturday, 1 October

Bought a thriller for Merry. I only hope she isn't using them to prop up a wobbly table. I have noticed she doesn't always read them – maybe they are not to her taste at all? Perhaps I am only sending tokens of esteem, full of words – one-after-the-other-after-the-other, caught up between glossy covers. There are worse things to do.

Good deed no. 274.

Sunday, 2 October

Some days you know why you married someone. Al came out of his office looking quietly stunned, and when I asked why, he said he had got incredibly uptight with some poor chap from BT about trying and failing to log into our account. He had forgotten his password, so the system had thrown up a security question: 'What is your favourite name?' He had tried his, he had tried mine, he had tried the kids – nothing. He had tried the guinea pigs – still nothing. He had run through Manchester United and his favourite cricketers of all time – still nothing. Fuming, he had rung BT. Somewhere in Mumbai, the phone was answered by a patient, pleasant man. My irascible husband explained the problem, and there was a tapping as the chap got into the account. 'Does the word "bollocks" mean anything to you?' the patient, pleasant chap asked my husband. 'I beg your pardon?' my husband said. The nice chap from Mumbai repeated himself: 'Does the word "bollocks" mean anything to you?' 'I'm sorry?' my husband said, and as he said it a distant bell began to ring. *Bollocks?* My husband, it turns out, when asked ridiculous security questions on the Internet, answers them like Peter Cook and Dudley Moore. He had informed BT his favourite name was 'Bollocks'. I'm just glad that I took charge of naming the kids.

Good deed no. 275: watched over a small boy at rugby and brought him back to his dad afterwards. (My daughter got her first rugby trophy today for being the player of the week, and won't let anybody else touch it.)

Monday, 3 October

Spent the morning in the Salvation Army shop tagging clothes and drove straight from there to school for the Young Journalists' Group I'm helping with. I sweat virtue.

Good deed no. 276.

Tuesday, 4 October

Good deed no. 277: worked in a charity shop (steaming clothes).

Wednesday, 5 October

Caught 'Thought for the Day' with Chief Rabbi Lord Sacks on BBC Radio 4's *Today* programme. He was talking about Yom Kippur (or the Day of Atonement), the holiest day of the Jewish year. It's happening on Saturday, and is held to be the last chance to change God's judgement of one's deeds during the previous year and to set one's fate for the year ahead. Lord Sacks said: 'Too often we spend our time on things that are urgent, and neglect the things that are important: the good we do, the love we give, the difference we make to other people's lives. Yom Kippur is God's way of asking, What do you want to be remembered for? When it comes to doing good, don't leave it too late.'

Apparently at Rosh Hashanah (the Jewish New Year) the idea is that the names of the righteous and of the wicked are written in one of two books: the Book of Life and the Book of Death. Most souls, however, have the (fabulously named) ten Days of Awe between Rosh Hashanah and Yom Kippur to turn things round by repentance, prayer and good deeds before their name is sealed in one of the books. The books are a metaphor serving to remind the faithful that these days are not for easy living, but for deep reflection on the past year and hopes for the year ahead, a time when lives hang in the balance and there is the possibility of transformation.

I am nowhere on repentance and prayer, I can only hope a morning of sorting knicks-knacks at the Sally Ann shop will do.

I plumped to work in the Salvation Army shop in the local market town on the grounds that it is one of the largest providers of social, community and welfare services in the UK – that and the fact I love brass bands. I am very disappointed I don't get my own uniform. Technically the shop is part of the Salvation Army Trading Company, which boasts on its website that it has raised more than £17m over the last three years, spent on homelessness services, family tracing, elderly care and the like.

A very efficient lady called Michelle runs the shop, and last year (which was only its first year of business) it brought in £70,000. She has one paid assistant, eleven volunteers who come in regularly and ten others who come in on a more occasional basis. I've never worked in a shop before, but after tagging clothes and steaming them (at some risk to my fingers) and dusting knick-knacks, I feel I could. What struck me, though, was why would you do this? Why would you work in any charity shop - week after week - for twenty-five years in the case of the little lady I worked alongside, emptying pink plastic sacks of second-hand clothes, and not get paid for it? How good do you have to be to do that? Because it's certainly not the glamour end of retail fashion. Most of the work is done out the back in a large windowless room with stalls running along one wall piled high with sacks and sacks of clothes. You pull out a sack, you pull out the clothes in the sack, and standing at an MDF bench you tag them, hang them (making sure the hanger is the right way round), slip a plastic sizing cube onto the hanger, and hang the hanger on a lengthy clothes rail. Then you do it all over again. And again.

I asked the shop's 25-year veteran Cecily what was the worst thing she'd ever found in a bag, and she said, 'Dirty nappies, dirty knickers and dirty sheets.' When I asked the manager, she said, 'Sometimes you open a bag and fleas are jumping from it – once I opened a bag and there was a rat in there. That wasn't this shop, though.' How do you casually manage to sweep a rat up in with the bits and pieces you're giving to charity? Thank God there were no rats on my shift.

I preferred tagging to steaming. Perhaps it was my hot sweaty flush that prompted one of the other volunteers to ask: 'Do you have any grandbairns, then?' Seriously? Do I look like I have grandchildren? My youngest is five, mate. Apparently, they aren't allowed to keep knitting needles on display in the shop – they keep them in a bag out the back. If I'd known where, after the grand-bairn question I'd have stabbed myself with a pair of Number 10s, but not before I'd stabbed one of the customers.

Trailed by her husband, a bespectacled woman was walking round the rails, holding a pair of black trousers, and she asked if there was a fitting room, which there wasn't. Irritated by my response, she said why couldn't she just nip into the private staff area and try them on? Considering the huge number of bulging pink bags piled up in the corridor waiting to be taken away for ragging, I told her I thought that was unlikely, but I'd ask. Like the good shop assistant that I am, I duly trotted behind the scenes to ask my manager, whose answer was no, but very reasonably, she said the lady was welcome to buy them, take them away and return them later if they didn't fit. This I duly took back, but the woman was having none of it. She said she didn't get into town often enough, so she wouldn't bother. They cost £1.99, these trousers. Were these people short of a bob or two? Quite possibly. These are hard times and they were shopping in a charity shop. But they didn't look short of a bob or two, and she didn't talk to me as if she was short of a bob or two. Perhaps she too was a member of the 'squeezed middle', and why waste £1.99 on a pair of trousers that might not fit? Then again, how squeezed do you have to be not to think, 'If they don't fit, I'll have donated £1.99 to a good cause'?

Aside from the odd murderous impulse I made quite a good shop assistant. I steered lady shoppers to the designer labels, dug out an anorak for a man who had forgotten to bring his coat on holiday, and I even asked one tall, white-haired chap standing by the bookshelves whether he liked a good thriller. 'I certainly do,' he said, wrapping his arm around me. 'Are you offering?'

Good deed no. 278.

Thursday, 6 October

Last week, I set Cryssie the task of writing a story about 'the morning I glimpsed heaven'. She wrote a pretty realistic account of what would happen at school if she disappeared into thin air and absolutely nothing about heaven itself. What I want her to realize is that there are no limits to her imagination, which means there are no limits on what she herself can do in her imagination. In reality, she can't climb a mountain, or swim a stormy sea on the back of a dolphin, or take a gold-winged angel by the hand, but she can write about all of those things. It's a really important lesson – that the only boundaries there are on your imagination are those you yourself impose. I want her to understand that because her understanding would make this whole exercise worth doing. Maybe I shouldn't be trying to teach her how to write at all? Maybe I should be teaching her how to make believe – how to step off a cliff and fly. I really want Cryssie to fly.

Good deed no. 279.

Friday, 7 October

Living where we do at the end of a row of holiday cottages, we have taken on the role of sometime caretaker. There are definitely times I feel like a Parisian, black-clothed, bow-legged Madame Concierge who spends her time sweeping the foyer with a broom and spying on her more glamorous neighbours. Tonight, my eldest came up to the bedroom and said that Stephanie's husband wanted to watch the England match on our big TV and, if he was watching it, would it be OK if my eldest and his brother watched the first half with him? Usually that would be all right, but tonight it wasn't. It was Friday evening, I had had a long week, and I wanted to slump on the sofa in front of a roaring fire and watch classic comedy repeats and drink wine, but by the time I got down, my husband had gone round to tell him that of course it was no problem, he could watch football on our telly – it could be my good deed for the day. Bastard husband.

Good deed no. 280.

Saturday, 8 October

Cumberland and Westmorland wrestling is genuinely strange; perhaps it is the strip the wrestlers wear? White long johns, white vest and baggy velveteen pantaloons – as if they have climbed out of a black and white photograph and stepped blinking straight into a world of colour. The men stand chest to chest and rest their chin on the opponent's right shoulder. They wrap their right arm under the left of the opponent and lock their hands together around his back. They lean into each other, legs akimbo, and try to smash their opponent into the ground. Occasionally, one chap tries to unbalance the other, and the one who is trying to avoid falling is forced to wrap a leg around his opponent and hop for a while. Occasionally, one swings the other around like a fairground attraction before throwing him into the mud and falling on top of him with a loud grunting noise. I checked the rules and they say that 'the wrestlers are allowed to use every legitimate means to throw each other', which was definitely the impression I got. The first one to break their hold, to go down or to end up under their opponent loses. Bit like life.

We spent the afternoon at the Alwinton Border Shepherds' Show – the last country show of the season in the last English village before you get to Scotland. We watched the sheep judging and then we watched the terrier racing. What's not to like about terrier racing? Small dogs chase a fox's tail down the course, leaping over plastic pipes so high they occasionally turn somersaults, and all to win a rosette. We even won a second-place rosette of our own when they let the kids race and our eight-year-old stormed his way to the finish. I imagine him ancient, turning over his boy prizes in gnarled and withered hands, finding the blue silk rosette with the golden silhouette of a dog and struggling to recall the name of the dog we never had.

Good deed no. 281: helped the ladies putting away the chairs in the tea tent at a country show.

Sunday, 9 October

Good deed no. 282: donated £10 to my JustGiving page for the hospice.

Monday, 10 October

I'm completely into charity shops now, having seen the quality of what's on offer in them. In the Salvation Army shop there was a Berketex coat, an Alexon dress, M&S, Dorothy Perkins, a lovely Clarice Cliff gravy boat, and a dinky apple-shaped honeypot. So I popped into the Cancer Research charity shop, where I found a £35 Mappin & Webb covered serving dish and a £12 tweed jacket in bright yellow and green and red and blue for autumn. The only problem with the jacket is I'll stand out a mile to whoever has donated it. I'd have loved the dish – it would be like buying a family heirloom (*Oh, this old thing, yes, Great-aunt Jemima left it to me*) – but I didn't have the money. I did get the jacket, though, instead of buying a new winter coat: win-win, I get a new jacket and a cancer charity gets £12.

Good deed no. 283.

Had parents' evening for the eight-year-old and my daughter. They are at a little village school which stands abutting a field where sheep graze – even with the little ones in early years, there's only about fifty or so children at the school. Their academic reports were good, but what was even better was the fact the headteacher said my eight-year-old made a point of including younger or less able children in activities. They are training for a 'World Cup' tag rugby tournament and he's captain of the 'Ireland' team. Some of the kids won't pass the ball to a child they think will drop it. I'd have been that child, the child no one wanted to pass to, the one who fumbled and dropped the ball – any ball – and who stood there red-faced and trembling as team-mates all around groaned. The headteacher said my son had started moving the less able children down the line next to him so that he could pass the ball to them. 'Without anyone telling him,' she emphasized, and the child inside me cheered the Irish captain on.

I have been thinking a lot about children, maybe because the good deeds have brought me into contact with children which I wouldn't otherwise have had. I've known Cryssie's family for six years, but this year is the first time I have actually got to know Cryssie herself. I've ducked it before: it required too much investment of time and energy, it was easier to drink tea and talk to the grown-ups rather than sit down and concentrate on what the disabled child might have to say for herself. After all, what if you can't get away again? What if you can't catch what she is saying? What could she have to say that would interest me anyway? That was wrong. I had it wrong for six years – maybe longer. At university, Sophie used to take a disabled man swimming and to the pub afterwards. He'd be sitting in his wheelchair, his arms tight in spasm, jerking, flailing, his head turned, and he would be laughing at something my friend had said, something outrageous. I'd think, 'How does she do that? How is she so easy with him? What does she see that I can't?' But she saw past his wheelchair and past her pity.

I harry my kids to pick up after themselves and accuse them of being idle. I shout at them to stop squabbling and accuse them of being spoiled – 'spoiled rotten'. I fume when, mulish, they resent the extra homework I give them; accuse them of 'not knowing you are born, mate'. Doubtless, I have messed them up over and over again, but I know I am lucky. And I know they are lucky too – for being whole, for being healthy, for being loved. I was trawling the Net wondering whether I should abandon my own children and work in an orphanage for a couple of weeks when I stumbled across a new Barnardo's child sponsorship scheme. Barnardo's is the UK's largest children's charity. I signed up to £15 a month and was allotted a child called 'Julian' and was the immediate recipient of a message from 'Helen', Julian's support worker. (They change the names, but they are insistent these are real kids.) Apparently Julian is severely autistic, and before he went into Barnardo's he needed two full-time carers to take him to and from school and look after him at home. When he got frustrated, anxious or over-stimulated, 'he could have an outburst "out of the blue". This could be frightening – especially as Julian is quite a big lad.' According to Helen's report, Julian's communication skills have improved significantly since he moved into a Barnardo's home, and he hasn't had an outburst since last year. His parents visit him at the home. His favourite TV show is *Countdown*, he likes comics and chicken curry, his favourite sport is swimming and he enjoys *SpongeBob* and *Teletubbies*. I don't know how old he is. That's the second time today I wanted to cry.

Good deed no. 284.

THE VICTORIAN

Thomas Barnardo, born in Dublin in 1845, wanted to be a missionary and work in China. He never made it. While training in London as a doctor so that he could be all the more useful as a missionary, he was confronted daily by the poverty and squalor in which the city's children were forced to live. A year after arriving in London, he set up a voluntary Sunday and night school in the East End offering a free basic education. But free or not, an education is a luxury to a child without a home. One night a shoeless, hatless and shirtless lad called Jim Jarvis stayed late at the Ragged School, hoping the 'guv'nor' might let him spend the night by the fire, but Barnardo told him to get home to his mother and father. The lad informed him he had neither, that he lived nowhere and had no friends. The boy was ten. That night, after Barnardo fed him, the boy showed him the homeless and destitute young sleeping on London's roofs.

In 1870 Barnardo opened his first home for boys, going out into the night himself to find the destitute. By 1872, the shelter bore the sign 'No destitute child ever refused admission' after the death of an eleven-year-old called John Somers, nicknamed 'Carrots'. Carrots had never known his father, and at seven his mother turned him adrift. Promised a bed in the home in a week's time, the boy died from exposure and hunger on the streets before Barnardo could make good that promise.

Barnardo's has moved away from children's homes in recent years. The charity now works through 800 different projects with more than 190,000 vulnerable children, young people and their families every year. 'Julian' is just one of them.

Wednesday, 12 October

Karma took her time but finally came good. I signed up to do the online National Lottery last night on the grounds that if I won anything, I'd give half away to family and friends and good causes. And when I checked it this morning, I'd won – all of £5.90 in the EuroMillions draw. Which means I owe £2.95 to charity. I hope they won't spend it all at once.

Good deed no. 285: put £3 lottery winnings into a jam jar.

Still can't decide whether Cryssie's learning difficulties are an impediment to her imagination. I'd asked her to write a story about a girl whose mother was a pirate, and she came up with one solitary page. Admittedly it had a fantastic start about the girl having a magic key and ending up on a pirate ship. The only problem was that it came straight out of the Biff and Chip scheme that kids are taught to read with. I talked it through with her mum and dad when they came to pick her up, and I don't think any of us can decide the extent of Cryssie's ability to think visually because she is obviously going to say yes to the questions we ask her:

Do you see pictures in your head when you are reading? Yes.

Do you have an imagination? Yes.

Would you like me to stop asking stupid questions? Yes.

Her homework was to watch a movie with her mum and dad and talk through the story with them as it happens on screen. When she writes, I want her to 'see' the scenes she is writing in her head, but I don't know why I even want her to do that – there is nothing to say you can't write without that happening. What do I know? I'm just pretending to be a teacher.

I have been trying to volunteer with a few charities, although getting nowhere fast. I contacted one charity offering to push the disabled around the Catholic shrine of Lourdes in wheelchairs, but it required a Criminal Records Bureau check that wouldn't be through in time for their last pilgrimage of the year, so that hasn't worked. A homelessness charity is sucking its teeth, making 'I don't think so' noises because you have to make a long-term commitment. They need help in the warehouses sorting out the harvest collection of food that's come in to them from schools and churches, but apparently even that's 'problematic' because of insurance. It's sorting out tins – what can go wrong? (Unless I decided to make a massive Harvest Festival pyramid of tins, roll the undeserving poor into balls and throw them till not one can was left standing.) And I keep ringing the National Trust but I can't get through, presumably because they are too busy counting puffins or selling tea-towels. I'm not that convinced I want to get through anyway. They advertised on a website called 'Do-it' for help assisting wardens at the seasonal tern-breeding reserve, 'maintaining security of the nesting sites'. Unfortunately, a. I don't know what a tern is, and b. they require 'enthusiasm for the outdoors' and 'an element of fitness'.

Good deed no. 286.

Friday, 14 October

Good deed no. 287: pruned roses as a volunteer gardener in Alnwick Garden (a registered charity) and gave a handful of the rosebuds to Cecily, the Salvation Army veteran.

Saturday, 15 October

Good deed no. 288: went to two coffee mornings: one for League of Friends of the Hospital and one for Save the Children.

Sunday, 16 October

Good deed no. 289: sent an old mobile phone to the Salvation Army in an envelope.

Monday, 17 October

Good deed no. 290: pruned roses in Alnwick Garden.

Tuesday, 18 October

Have been trying all day to persuade people to let me do good. Why is this so hard? My initial meeting was with a refugee charity. The house is discreet, a former vicarage tucked away behind a church and down a little path with a five-barred gate, all in the middle of rows and rows of terraced houses in a northern city. It was busy even at eleven in the morning with serious-looking men of every shade and nationality making cups of tea and talking to the helpers. They all seemed to be wearing woolly jumpers and those thin blouson jackets that never keep you warm.

Admittedly, it is difficult because I'm not offering a long-term commitment, I'm saying, 'Here I am – I want to do a good deed. Go on, let me,' and I understand people who devote their entire lives to hopeless causes can be flummoxed by a wham-bam good-deed girl like myself. That said, cor blimey. The voluntary sector. You would think a good deed is as good as money in the bank. Not so.

The conversation with the director of this particular refugee charity must have lasted a good hour. If I'd been willing to fund-raise (I already have the Jam Jar Army) or set up a library of books from around the nations (shoot me now), it might have been simpler. There was a reluctance to allow me to 'befriend' a refugee because that's to do with developing a supportive relationship with someone. I can understand that, but what I can offer is a break for someone. I had in mind the fact I've a spare bedroom with its own en suite, and I live by the sea in one of the most beautiful parts of the world. Why not send a family to me for a long weekend or a week or a fortnight? Why not get some woman and her children out of some inner-city rat-hole and let them draw breath? Let her kids play with my kids. Let them eat at my table. Let's walk by the sea together. It's not much in the scheme of things, but I would have thought it would be better than nothing.

The fact I write about things is immensely complicating. 'This is just a social experiment, isn't it?' the director said disapprovingly, and I wanted to say, *Life is a social experiment, isn't it?* When I made the point any guest would be giving as well as receiving – sharing their experience of life as a refugee as well as taking the hospitality offered, she made the point that her charity gives without asking anything back. We went round and round in circles chasing down the ethics of good deeds when a book was involved, and comparing it to a student doing a thesis, who she seemed to think was somehow a much cleaner creature – forget the self-interest of a Ph.D., ignore all ambitions to work in academia or the voluntary sector. 'I'm nearly there,' she said at one point as I attempted to persuade her that I would help rather than harm. *Really?* I wanted to reply. *Because over here I'm giving up the will to live.*

She wants to make the world a better place, and it turns out that such people are very hard to deal with. We finished up by her saying she would discuss it with her staff, and put it to a client. Then I'm nearly out the door and she starts talking about the 'destitute' – those refugees who apply for asylum status and get turned down. All benefits stop; they depend on £15 a week from the charity. It used to be £10 and a bag of food, but the refugees have to go out to the coast to check in with the immigration service so said they needed the extra £5 more than the bag of food. 'Send me the destitute, then,' I said – 'I want to help.' I bet she won't.

Good deed no. 291: took a friend's daughter who has just started at university out to tea. (An unexpected perk of growing up is getting to know the children of your friends. You have your friend whom you love, and with them the child of your friend who comes free, like a teabag Sellotaped to a packet of tea.)

Wednesday, 19 October

Very good news: another approach from a Sainsbury's store, this one in Hull, saying they are interested in taking on the Jam Jar Army to raise funds through schools for Humber Rescue, the inshore lifeboat rescue service on the Humber Estuary. I am not sure what if anything happened with the Sainsbury's stores down south and in Scotland. But I have advised Patteson's (the Grimsby-based glass jar manufacturer), who sent me through the literature they are using to launch a 'Wish in a Jar' campaign in their own community to raise money for the charity When You Wish Upon a Star. The charity treats children with life-threatening or terminal illnesses to experiences like fighting Darth Vader, swimming with dolphins or meeting Simon Cowell. (I would have thought meeting Simon Cowell would finish you off, but there you go.) Their campaign, which is due to launch next year, is great. Brand-wise, it's not as light-hearted as the Jam Jar Army. Instead of a little Geordie the Jam Jar character, they have blue and turquoise stars falling into a jar and it's all very arty and professional, with a design company pulling it together rather than me and whoever is standing next to me at any one time. I feel like the Jam Jar Army had a baby and I'm jealous of it.

Sophie has made an amazingly generous offer to top us up to the £10,000 target. If I agree to take it, we have officially hit our target. My problem is – is it a cheat? And if it is a cheat, does it matter? A lady in Sophie's accounts department died of cancer very suddenly – eight weeks from diagnosis to death, with her last week spent in a hospice – and my mate maintains that she wants to give more to charity *and* that she said from the start she wanted to be supportive of what I am doing. Perhaps I am being ridiculously purist: the Jam Jar Army always was about people giving what they can afford at a time of their own choosing; and Sophie, who is a brilliant businesswoman, can afford to give, no question. Plus she is doing a belting good deed. But it was also supposed to be a grass-roots campaign with everyone giving a little, and there is a good chance a big-buck donation compromises that. Then again, I haven't solicited the money and if it was just any old businessman off the street, I would be biting his hand off. I'm still thinking it through. God, I am turning into an ethical third-sector nitwit.

Good deed no. 292: OK'd new Sainsbury's store taking up the Jam Jar Army in aid of Humber Rescue.

Thursday, 20 October

Cancelled Cryssie's writing lesson today. I am fed up chasing a halo.

I was knee-deep in empty jam jars and plastic bags of coppers in my kitchen this morning when I rang the hospice to ask them for the official Jam Jar Army running total. I estimate that with the money we have got in the kitchen which we are about to take in, we have just under £7,000. (I didn't mention the offer by Sophie because I want to talk it through with the *Gazette* editor.) When I told Angela, the nice fund-raiser from the hospice, that I thought we stood at about £7,000 currently, she said with a note of regret in her voice: 'It's not coming in as fast as you thought it would, is it?' I could have beaten the phone to death on the windowsill right then and there.

Good deed no. 293: pinged through a couple of ideas to the refugee society re political lobbying on accommodation crisis and getting in clothes for refugees (which they are short of).

Friday, 21 October

I was so annoyed yesterday at the comment about how slow the money is coming in that I ended up emailing the hospice to tell them they shouldn't be disappointed, because I wasn't (this is a lie), that the campaign was one more way of raising the hospice's profile (which is true), and to reassure them that the £10k would definitely come in, 'perhaps sooner than you think. All will be well, as they say.' I checked out my 'all will be well' assurance later, and it turns out I had corrupted it from the fourteenth-century mystic the Lady Julian of Norwich, who originally said, 'All shall be well, and all shall be well and all manner of thing shall be well.' Julian of Norwich chose life as an anchoress, living enclosed in a doorless cell attached to a church. (No one knows her real name, but the church was named after St Julian, hence 'the Lady Julian.') The cell had three windows: one into the church, one her servant could use to pass food, and one for visitors to speak and pray with her. Her book *Revelations of Divine Love* is the first to have been written in English by a woman and was written years after a series of 'revelations' or 'showings' centring on the Passion which she experienced after falling very ill. She maintained God is all about love and wishes to enfold us in rest and peace. Even my clichés are getting mystic on me.

I got a response from the nice fund-raiser at the hospice saying she was sorry she'd been 'off', and assuring me she really wasn't disappointed, it was all 'Fab', she was an impatient person and she wasn't up to speed because she had just got back from chemo. I'd be impatient if I had a life-threatening disease. It goes to prove you shouldn't sweat the small stuff, and I do sometimes. I go round and round obsessing about something which next month or next year won't even show up as a flaw in the pattern of my life's silk carpet. I am fortunate. I am not sitting outside a radiotherapy unit waiting for someone I love to come out. I am not thousands of miles away from home with £15 in my pocket to last me all week, looking up at the skies wondering whether it will rain and where I will sleep tonight. I have family who love me, I have family to love, I have friends who cradle me in a crisis and who share my joys. 'All manner of thing shall be well.' Julian of Norwich told me that.

Good deed no. 294: helped out in the bar/refreshment kiosk in the village community centre for a movie-night experiment. Tea with cups and saucers, and gin and tonics without a proper measure.

Saturday, 22 October

Did an afternoon shift at the local cottage hospital in the League of Friends shop, which is open three afternoons a week. Over the last decade the League has raised £138,171 for the hospital, not just through the shop but also through events such as coffee mornings, bag packs and donations – with £40,000 spent on a minibus, £719 on an organ for the day room, £20,000 on endoscopes and £44 on vases for wards. Better than any of that, I got to wear a tabard. I don't think I have ever worn a tabard before – it made me feel capable and sensible, like someone you could ask directions from.

There is something quietly thrilling about selling Lucozade and Fruit Pastilles, although no one was very interested in our chintzy notelet and diary sets, or the various leather goods on offer. I wanted to buy one of everything – a change purse, a comb and holder, a folding key case with small hooks, a small notebook and pen, an address book – because I loved them all. It would be like being one of the world's top athletes sponsored by Coca-Cola, except I'd have bought everything and they wouldn't say Coca-Cola, they'd say 'Friends of Alnwick Hospitals' in gilt lettering.

My companion Anne, who has macular degeneration like my mother and remains equally undaunted, wheeled the trolley of fruit gums and toiletries to the ward. I wasn't allowed, because Matron said I couldn't go up without a Criminal Records Bureau check. Presumably the authorities are worried in case I molest somebody's grandad or steal an old dear's purse. I am a middle-aged mother of three with a Samaritan complex. I am pretty confident that if you got your thrills from preying on hospitalized geriatrics, it would show in your day-to-day approach to life and an uncontrollable twitch.

While the lovely Anne was away, I sorted through second-hand books for gory crime novels for a patient, because other people dying is really what you want to read about when you are sick. And as I was sorting through the thrillers, an old lady passed by with a friend, and she was saying to the friend, 'I haven't had a visitor all week – I've seen no one.' Then Anne came back from her rounds and searched the shelves for Steradent for some chap on the wards who'd said he was desperate to clean his teeth, which made me wonder if he too was waiting for visitors who didn't come. We couldn't find any, so I rang Al to pop to Boots and bring in a tube when he picked me up. 'You want a packet of Steradent?' he said. 'For cleaning your false teeth?' 'I do,' I said. 'I only dropped you off a few hours ago. Have you actually been fitted with false teeth since then?' he said. It seemed too complicated to explain, so I just said yes, I was looking at my dentures as I spoke and I was smiling.

Good deed no. 295.

Occasionally the day slips by, it gets late and dark, the children are asleep in bed, I reach for a glass of wine and think, 'I haven't done a buggering, bollixing good deed.' I was at that point tonight when I remembered Barnardo's wants their sponsors to bond big-time with the child they are sponsoring, and as part of the bonding want you to make your own lollipop stick figure. I am hoping it goes to the child and not to their marketing department. I dug out the children's art paraphernalia and stuck foam rubber clothes on mine and gave her glittery pipe-cleaner ringlets and a leopard-skin belt. She was called Lulu Lolly. With some reluctance, I slipped her into an envelope back to Barnardo's – I wanted to keep her, but I figured that would cancel out the goodness.

Good deed no. 296.

Some days people do not want your good deeds. Usually train journeys offer great opportunities to 'good-deed it' – you help an old lady off a train, you talk to some harassed mother's toddler. Today, though, travelling from Northumberland to Leeds, I offered to share my gin and tonic with a girl sitting opposite and got turned down, and then I offered to carry an old man's case and got turned down for that too.

Good deed no. 297: put change in M&S Railway Children charity tin. (Having checked out the charity, I realize I should have gone hungry and put the money for my gin and tonic into the tin and not just the change. According to the charity, every year 100,000 youngsters under sixteen run away from home, and 30 per cent of Britain's young runaways are twelve and under. This is a problem with the whole good-deed thing – where do you start? Where do you stop?)

Tuesday, 25 October

The St James's Institute of Oncology in Leeds was built at a cost of £220m and is the largest purpose-built cancer centre in Europe. It is attached to the St James's Infirmary, where this morning I spent a couple of hours sitting around in a coffee shop. I read the paper, did the crossword puzzle, failed to do the sudoku, texted everyone I'd ever met and counted the bald people.

Good deed no. 298: took Dad for a hospital appointment.

Wednesday, 26 October

Good deed no. 299: took £537 of assorted cheques into the hospice. (Total currently stands at £7,132.)

Thursday, 27 October

Kirsty's knee and her foot are both bad after her knee replacement earlier this year and the amount of driving she is doing, having moved from Edinburgh to some remote Oxfordshire village. Since she is a Catholic, I offered to go with her to Lourdes or Medjugorje, both sites of pilgrimage, as a good deed. I wouldn't need a criminal records' check and I could push her round and sprinkle her regularly with holy water and talk loudly on her behalf when anyone stopped us to pass the time of day. There was a pause on the other end of the phone and a snort of what might have been laughter. 'That's a serious offer,' I said, all persuasive and honeyed. 'The two of us together on a road trip. Like Thelma and Louise, but holier.' 'It's fair to say you haven't grasped the idea of Lourdes,' she said, not sounding at all grateful for the offer, 'and I wouldn't want to be next to you when you're hit by a thunderbolt.'

What Kirsty doesn't understand is that I am absolutely up for a miracle. Catholics are brought up on miracles. You tend not to pray without purpose. You pray for an intention, for an intervention – you pray for a miracle. I wonder if a year of good deeds qualifies you for a miracle? Or whether they are like the lottery? All sorts of unsuitable people benefit and really deep down you think they should be disqualified. If I am entitled to a miracle, I want one for Kirsty.

Good deed no. 300: cooked a dinner party for the expats to celebrate their first anniversary in the country.

Friday, 28 October

Good deed no. 301: cooked the exact same menu as last night (halibut in Italian cacciatore-style sauce) for visiting next-door neighbours with three-year-old boy and eight-month-old baby girl, carrying it round to their house and washing up after all of us. (On the upside, they look even more exhausted than me.)

Saturday, 29 October

Good deed no. 302: sent award-winning piece of literary fiction to Merry.

Sunday, 30 October

I have spent two days shopping for my children. Yesterday was all about making sure my eldest son had all the gear he needed for an outward-bound course he is going on at school, which involves climbing up tall poles and jumping off things – why would I want to encourage such behaviour? Today, after two of them played rugby and one of them played football, the five of us went shopping in Newcastle for my little girl's birthday. Worse yet, I am in one of my periodic bouts of insomnia. Sometimes I am so tired, I could weep.

Good deed no. 303: emailed artwork and pulled together hard copy of poster and labels for Hull Sainsbury's.

Talked to the *Gazette* editor about Sophie's offer, and he actually sounded disappointed. He wants us to keep going and get it in the way we said we would. He wants us to slog away, week after week, with a Christmas target in mind, rather than take the easy way out with Sophie's nice fat cheque with lots of noughts. But because he didn't want the hospice to lose out on her donation, he said she might perhaps consider making a donation *after* we hit the target.

I was going to take it. I was going to morally compromise for the sake of an easy life. I hate people with integrity. They make the rest of us look bad.

Good deed no. 304: took the Young Journalists' Group at school. (One kid had done a great job with a piece on the local swim club, including asking an eleven-year-old swimmer why she doesn't give up when things get hard. She had told him: 'Because I've learnt that when things get tough, it's not the time to quit or give up, it's an opportunity to get stuck in and try even harder to achieve what you want to.' Ten months into my year of doing good, I am trying to bear that in mind.)

THE PHILOSOPHER

I have done more than 300 good deeds and I am still not a better person. I am bringing in the experts. Professor Robert Merrihew Adams knows a thing or two about goodness. Research professor of philosophy at the University of North Carolina, he taught at Yale, UCLA and Oxford. For nearly forty years he has been thinking about ethics, specializing most recently in character and virtue. I called him to talk through what I'm doing, and he accepted my definition of a good deed as something bringing benefit to someone else, although philosophers are more interested in the 'good deed' as the intrinsically excellent action, something which is well motivated and good in itself – even if (as sometimes happens) the deed does not actually produce benefits for another person. I prick up my ears at this – is this my cop-out on my failures? I wonder.

I told the professor that I'd noticed how good deeds factor across religions, and he agreed that all great religions have a place in their belief systems for a code of conduct which includes good deeds. 'That is because we connect spiritual happiness or peace with states of mind or characters in which there is no self-centredness or selfishness,' he said. Like Professor Dunbar, the Oxford evolutionary psychologist, he reminded me that good deeds also feature in the Darwinian system. 'Societies that don't flourish, don't survive – they have to have a moral code, a code that keeps the peace and ensures people treat each other decently.'

According to his online photo, Adams has a white beard, which seems perfect for an eminent philosopher. I imagined him tugging at it as he talked to me. He believes virtue – that is to say, good moral character – is fragmentary and frail, liable to inconsistencies and vulnerable to events. He managed not to laugh at me when I held up to view my paltry attempts at goodness. The traditional view traced back to Aristotle, he said, holds that repeating a behavioural pattern got one habituated to it, developed into a habit that would become a virtue. In Aristotle's own words: 'People acquire a particular quality by constantly acting a particular way . . . you become just by performing just actions, temperate by performing temperate actions, brave by performing brave actions.'

Adams, however, was sceptical that mere repetition could change someone in any fundamental way. 'There is probably no such thing as a pattern of behaviour making one a better person.' This man has spent nearly forty years thinking about ethics – I was expecting a bush to appear and catch light in my house any second. 'But a pattern of behaviour may well change how one feels about doing good, or how one feels about other people.' A year's good deeds, then, might make me receptive to doing more good deeds for my fellow man, for whom I would feel an increased sympathy. Or it might not.

If anyone would know whether I have a chance of becoming a better person after a year of good deeds, Adams would. After I put down the phone to him, I went back to his book *A Theory of Virtue*, published in 2006, in which he argued that 'one will probably not become wedded to virtue without discovering that in some way it "works" in one's own life.' Repetition matters less than seeing you have accomplished something good and that it is appreciated. I read on. The book argues that you can admire someone who 'strives unsuccessfully for moral improvement . . . inasmuch as the excellence of the efforts is independent, to some extent, of the success of the improvement project'. In other words, full marks for trying – but I do not want full marks for trying – in the race against myself, I want to stand on that podium with the national anthem playing and the shiny gold medal around my neck engraved with the words 'A Better Person'.

Good deed no. 305: emailed outdoors shop to highlight the brilliant service from one of their staff (knowing this risked email deluge of discount offers on crampons).

Wednesday, 2 November

Stephanie rang at 7.45 p.m. to ask me to put on her heating so the house would be warm for her mother. There were high winds, rain pelting against the windows, it was pitch dark, and I was trying to ram the kids into bed knowing I still had the kitchen to clear from tea and my daughter's birthday presents to wrap for tomorrow. Perched on the kitchen stool at the phone, I looked out into the hurly-burly night and thought, 'I am so not doing it.' Past midnight, my poor husband trailed in exhausted from a day in London to find a note lying on the kitchen table alongside the keys to Stephanie's cottage, another on the fridge (in case he pretended he hadn't seen the one on the table) and another on the front door (in case he pretended he hadn't seen the one on the fridge either), asking him to put on her heating. I pretended to be asleep when he came to bed.

Good deed no. 306: bought a poppy for Remembrance Day.

Thursday, 3 November

Cryssie came up with her most ambitious story to date. A boy went down to the sea and was swept away by a tsunami, his body washing up on the beach days later, leaving his mother grief-stricken. At a critical moment, a kangaroo appeared which looked as though it might rescue him; instead, it hopped off into the distance. Very grim. We softened the ending by the ghostly boy comforting the grieving mother by taking her hand in his, but the story was ambitious enough for me to ask her whether she wants to try something longer, which would take a lot more planning, and she is keen. She wrote the story while her brother (who has the same condition she does) was ill in hospital, and it crossed my mind she was testing out the whole idea of losing someone – the tsunami being death or our mortality. What the kangaroo represented I can't even guess at.

Good deed no. 307.

Friday, 4 November

I took my eight-year-old out to a brass band concert in Doxford Hall, a country house hotel, nearby. The concert was part of the Northumberland Music Festival – with a percentage of ticket sales being donated to Macmillan Cancer Support, the Great North Air Ambulance Service and Hospice Care North Northumberland. We created mayhem, of course, because I'd thought we could buy tickets on the door and it turned out that you couldn't.

A dapper little chap in a blazer looked genuinely shocked when I asked whether we could get a couple of tickets. 'There's a table plan,' he said, in exactly the same tone he would have used if I'd arrived at the pearly gates and he'd been saying, 'God says, "I don't think so."' Through the open oak and glass doors of the banqueting hall, the red-jacketed bandsmen were already playing 'The Standard of St George'. Fortunately, the dapper little gatekeeper was standing next to a wildly efficient, can-do colleague, who let us sit at the band's table while they were playing. Bliss – the blaze of chandeliers, a glass of cold white wine, the warm body of my son slumped against me, and golden brass filling me up. It turned out that the band was actually the Durham Miners' Association Brass Band. I doubt there are any miners in it these days, but there was a table of elderly miners towards the back of the hall. When the band struck up 'Gresford', which is known as the Miners' Hymn, these elderly men stood as one, their grey heads bent, hands clasped in solemn prayer. I asked them afterwards why they'd stood and they told me that in 1934 more than 260 miners died at Gresford, a pit in Wrexham, North-East Wales, after an explosion and fire underground – only eleven bodies were ever recovered – and I felt privileged to have seen those miners long retired pay their respects to men long since dead.

Good deed no. 308: gave the builders three pieces of chocolate birthday cake.

Saturday, 5 November

A sea of broken china is washing against the harbour walls of my skull – that is to say, I am trapped in a ferocious migraine, which I am blaming on today's birthday party horror. It was my daughter's sixth birthday party and I had bought a cake with a Tinkerbell theme, iced in pale green and mauve with edible glitter and a bas-relief Tinkerbell flying around with her friends. My mood was not improved when my eldest son, having begged to arrange the candles in the cake, stabbed Tinkerbell and managed to decapitate her, slice off her cheek and take out the entire eye. Thank God my daughter didn't see it happen. I balanced the head back on the neck and used the warmth of my index finger and spit to massage the cheek back on, but there was nothing to be done about the empty eye socket or the fact she appeared to have suffered a stroke. Less Tinkerbell, more Phantom of the Opera. Moreover, Tinkerbell then cursed the damn cake because when the time came to light the offending candles, each one of them a letter spelling out *Happy Birthday*, all but R, T and H collapsed, spluttered and went out. My little girl got to blow out three out of thirteen candles and I didn't even put the cake on the table for fear she noticed Tinkerbell's head. Instead, I held it in front of her and whisked it away again. I am not going to the next children's party.

Good deed no. 309: donated £3 to the Jam Jar Army, as per promise, after winning £6 on the EuroMillions lottery. (This is my second lottery win since making the promise; I figure the next one is the biggie.)

Sunday, 6 November

Time off for good behaviour this morning: I opted out of all childcare and spent the morning with Sophie (who had come up for my daughter's birthday) in a new café that has opened which specializes in loose tea, pan haggerty (sliced potato, onions and cheese) and girly conversation. We talked through the whole donation business. She has written a cheque for £2,500 and is happy for it to go towards the target or to supplement the £10k if we hit the target ourselves. She is very clever. Despite the recession, her company is set for its third highest sales. People are buying less, so you go get new customers. Seems like the obvious thing to do when you put it like that. I am very proud of her. She really liked my tweedy autumn jacket that I picked up from the charity shop, so I gave it to her. It fitted her slightly better than it fitted me across the shoulders, and it made it more of a fair exchange – you give me a cheque for £2,500 and I'll give you this lovely second-hand jacket which cost me twelve quid.

The gift of the jacket was going to be my good deed until we stepped outside and a small boy ran by as we were walking along the street. He must have been about two and a half or so. A car with a family in it was driving very slowly alongside him. I turned round and the driver was leaning across watching the boy, and I said, 'Is he yours?' I had this vision that the child might have refused to get in the car and was having a paddy, but the driver shook his head and said he had no idea who the kid belonged to, he had just spotted him running along the pavement. The pavement where we were standing is very narrow and on a tight bend. I scooted up the street after the boy and brought him back.

He was dressed in jeans and a jumper and a neat little blue puffa jacket, but his face was dirty and his nose running with snot. I knelt down on the pavement in front of him and said hello and asked him his name and where his mummy was, but there was no reaction whatsoever. He made as if to go and I shook my head and took his hand again, and said, 'Let's wait for Mummy, shall we?' At which point another car on the other side of the road stopped. This car had obviously seen him minutes earlier and turned around to come back and make sure he was all right. The young driver called out that he had seen the child tear out of an alleyway further down on the right, so the boy and I walked a little way and Sophie scooted off to find the alley.

An elderly couple arrived on the scene as I unzipped his jacket to see if the boy had a laminated label with his name and address on it or perhaps the words 'I'm simple'. He didn't – instead, he dug around in his pocket and came out with a toy motorbike, as if he thought it was this I was looking for.

The old man crossed the road and walked up to another corner to see if he could see anyone frantically searching for a child. I went back to kneeling and unpeeled a little bracelet my daughter had given me that morning with tiny plastic charms strung on elastic – a little piece of cake, a gingerbread man, a pink rabbit and a custard cream – and put it on the boy's wrist for him to examine. When Sophie came back, the boy having tried to make another break for it, we decided we were going to have to ring the police. At this point a black 4x4 crawled by us very slowly – presumably checking whether we were very inefficient kidnappers. At the same time, down the street, a man started pelting towards us, arriving at the bottom of the hill, breathless and white-faced. 'Mattie, Mattie,' he gasped with relief. The child took his father's hand as if nothing had happened, as if to say, 'Ah, there you are, Daddy,' as if the father hadn't just aged ten years in the ten minutes his child had been missing. It turned out the guy was Polish – as was the child – hence the complete lack of comprehension when I tried to talk to him. The father did not have the English to explain what had happened. Then again, I didn't ask. I imagine he took his eye off him for one second and he was gone. When they get home, will they wonder where he got the bracelet?

Good deed no. 310: found a lost child – my second of the year. I am keeping the third.

Monday, 7 November

Diane came over for a bacon sandwich and a cup of tea. She was smart because these days she teaches maths on a morning, which means I have hardly seen her for months. I miss her, but you do not give a friend a pattern and expect them to knit to it.

Her daughter did well at the birthday party. Despite the noise and strangeness of it all, she joined in the games, and ate the sweeties when she was tipped out of musical bumps, and even gave me a sudden hug when she was going home, which melted me. A great deal of Diane's time this year seems to have been spent on one adult or another coming to watch, assess and judge. You want anyone who watches a child to say, 'Your child is fine, your child is perfect, how proud you must be of this child.' It must be hard to watch them watching her, only for them to say, 'Your child is different, your child does not know her letters, colours, numbers, your child needs more than you can ever give.'

I told Diane how well her daughter had coped at the party and she smiled. The child is calmer, she said, because slowly they are finding the right strategies – bouncing her up and down, holding her at the point she might otherwise come apart, coming to an understanding of her sensory overload and how she might be helped to cope.

'I don't need anybody's sympathy,' she said as she gathered her things to go, 'she's glorious and we love her to bits. Some people still try to say "She's only a little girl" when she does something bizarre, and I know they mean well, but frankly, honesty helps a lot more.'

Good deed no. 311: gave Diane a bag of small Bounty and Snickers sweeties (sorted and judged wanting at the birthday party by my nut-allergic son. Turns out Diane loves them).

Tuesday, 8 November

The assistant head at Berwick Academy (formerly Berwick High School) emailed me saying they had 'some' jars to collect. *Whoop whoop* noises. I don't care how much is in them. I don't care how many there are. I do care that a few of those kids might not have eaten my jam sandwich, but went home and put money in their jars any which way. Feel like cheering. (Heard later that they sent a cheque to the hospice for £200. Cheered again.)

Good deed no. 312: signed up with an online shopping company that gives a percentage to school funds.

Wednesday, 9 November

Good deed no. 313: updated the Jam Jar Army website. (I've been sadly remiss at this, but since it boasts a grand total of two visits a day, it hasn't made it onto my priority list.)

Thursday, 10 November

Good deed no. 314: hospitality for cousin overnighting to do building work on his renovation.

Got caught up in the singathon at school in aid of Children in Need – with parents paying to sing non-stop for an hour. The very talented woman who does music with the kids was singing her heart out, strumming away on her guitar, but it didn't do it for me. My mood improved when the kids came in, but I was far too sober to enjoy 'YMCA', complete with actions, sitting in the school hall on a narrow wooden bench first thing after drop-off. 'Baa Baa Black Sheep' was my personal low point, although 'Alice the Camel Had Five Humps' ran it a close second. At one point, I craned my neck to look up at the clock above the serving hatch and fifteen minutes had passed. Fifteen. There were still forty-five minutes to go and we hadn't even reached Neil Diamond.

I have been gloomy all day, so perhaps it wasn't all down to the singathon. This coming Monday is the anniversary of my son's still-birth twelve years ago, and 11 November is the day we realized he had died in utero. That's what happens with death: it casts a shadow over what went before and what comes after. His death, his birth, Remembrance Sunday, all folded up together like a flag. All those people laying poppies for mothers' sons fallen in battle, while we wept over a Moses basket in a maternity ward. Memories and grief.

So there I was feeling sorry for myself, and I got home and the nicest thing had happened when I wasn't even looking: Karen, the caring stranger from Twitter whom I invited round for a cup of tea last summer, had sent me a box of bulbs – Tulip Ivory Floradale, pure white, with a lemon trumpet Narcissus Trena and the golden-yellow Narcissus Rapture. Other people's kindnesses can make you cry.

Good deed no. 315.

Good deed no. 316: helped another mother's child around a birthday party roller-disco (my own son needed taking for an X-ray after it).

Sunday, 13 November

Good deed no. 317: planted up a pot of narcissi and tulip bulbs for Stephanie (sharing the gift of spring around).

Monday, 14 November

I am still in one of my insomniac periods which come upon me every now and then. In the few moments I was asleep last night, I managed to dream I was dead. Seriously? I didn't even know you could dream you were dead. I thought if you dreamed you died, you actually died. I was in a tall modernistic building and sat on a brushed wire rail like you might do as a child, and tipped and fell. And as I fell, I reached to grab at the floors to save myself, only for my fingers to slip off, and to keep falling. I even got to stand to one side and look at my corpse – not many people get to do that. I now know exactly what I am going to look like when I am dead. Lunacy. If I was still in therapy, my therapist would lock me up.

Good deed no. 318: bought gifts for a ten- to fourteen-year-old boy's shoebox as part of Operation Christmas Child.

Tuesday, 15 November

On the upside, it isn't yesterday.

Good deed no. 319: encouraged a friend to finish something she started.

Wednesday, 16 November

Catastrophically low in the wake of the anniversary. I had a good deed to do in the city, but when I arrived at Newcastle railway station I had to go into a café tucked away on the far edge of the platform and sit for a while over a cappuccino I didn't want to drink and a toasted tuna sandwich it was too early in the day to eat. The part of me that was free of the emotional pall this year's anniversary has thrown over me stayed outside, looking in at me through the window and shaking her head at my self-pity. The rest of me ignored her, preferring instead to stay slumped at the slightly sticky table, watching the hands on the big round station clock go round, feeling bad because I hadn't ordered tea and because twelve years ago my son had died. I took a gulp of the now lukewarm cappuccino, almost gagging on the sweetness of the hot chocolate dusting, and rang my husband.

'I can't do this. I'm coming back home.'

There was silence on the other end of the phone.

'You haven't done your good deed, though, have you?'

There was silence on my end of the phone.

Al's voice was patient: 'You said you'd do it and you will, because you said you would and that's who you are.'

I did what I was told.

Industrial estates always make me wish I owned a white van to carry automotive parts or bargain flooring away from them – it's as if each unit is a portal to an alternative world in which I have no place. At least I had a place today, packing shoeboxes as part of Operation Christmas Child.

I stood opposite a little old lady called Enid, at a long high bench, our handbags between us, and behind each of us piles of gift-wrapped shoeboxes, one on top of the other in a mountain range of jolly Santas, snowmen and sparkling Christmas trees. We were standing because volunteers don't like to sit. Our job was checking shoeboxes bound for Belarus, which, according to a fact sheet stapled to the wall of the warehouse, has a population of 9.7m and gained its independence following the collapse of the Soviet Union, and where a significant chunk of its rural population earn less than $38 a month. According to the fact sheet, it still suffers from the impact of the 1986 nuclear disaster at Chernobyl in the neighbouring Ukraine. This year, Operation Christmas Child is planning to send 270,400 shoeboxes out to Belarus from the UK, another 8,500 from Ireland and 87,965 from Germany.

Last year, the Newcastle warehouse alone handled 22,000 boxes to a variety of countries, with another 6,000 coming to it from different collecting centres in the region.

It is heartening to see the thought and time and money and goodwill that people invest in their shoeboxes, with the stripy toothpaste and gel colouring pens and Matchbox cars for the children, the lids wrapped separately from the box. Professional mothers have it down to a fine art, packing the box with every item from the list provided, and while they are doing it, thinking, 'My children don't know they're born.' Others put in what they can afford. One box I open just has giveaways from McDonald's, perhaps given again by a child. Jack (a woman), who runs the warehouse, told me that once a box came in containing just a toilet roll and a tin of peaches, and then there was the 'dead budgie box', all beautifully wrapped in tissue and presumably meant for burial in the garden rather than a Belarusian orphan – not even orphans are that desperate. Nobody is allowed to tip out a box to inspect the contents – instead volunteers sort through or lift out the contents to make sure there are no liquids, toy guns or anything needing batteries. (The Belarus boxes are not allowed to have playing cards, for instance, and African countries do not like wild animal toys.) On the wall, volunteers are reminded not to judge another person's gift: 'We are sending out other people's Christmas gifts, not our own. If, for instance, a box does not have a hat, then that is the way it goes out. Remember, we are not judging the quality of the box by our personal opinions.' In reality, however, although there is no judgement of the giver, the shoeboxes are regularly topped up with whatever might be missing from supplies of woollen hats and gloves and sweets and toys and toiletries to make sure 'we don't pay to transport air' and that children aren't disappointed.

I'm in a groove. Aside from the occasional query about whether something is allowed or not, there is silence among us. It's like being a reader in a library or an elf in Santa's workshop. On top of each box we slip the picture-half of an old Christmas card stamped with the words 'With love from a friend at Christmas'. Enid has something even better: hand-embroidered cards. She passes me a panda she has embroidered and then crafted into a card. 'Sometimes the children keep the shoeboxes even when they're empty, and the cards as well, so I like to do something special that a child might really like to have by them.' Later still, she pulls out of a thin plastic bag exquisitely knitted white ribbed hats, some with blue and some with yellow panels; they remind me of stained glass, of treasure. She fits a bonnet in a box as if it were nothing, as if it wasn't hours of her life when she could be doing something for herself, and seals the box in the usual way with sticky white tape. Standing all the while. I want Enid as my granny. I want every child in the whole wide world to have an Enid.

This is Jack's seventeenth year with the shoeboxes: ten as a volunteer and seven as an employee. A couple of years ago, she went out to Belarus on a delivery. One child in particular hung around her. She sat with him while he opened the box. In it, the giver had sprinkled Celebration sweets. Andrei worked his way through the box, his face lighting up when he saw something from the *Cars* movie. A cuddly toy stayed under his arm as he carefully put his gifts back in the box, apart from the sweets, and put the lid back on. 'He went round all the volunteers with those sweeties,' said Jack. 'He had never been able to give anything to anyone before, and he gave all those sweets away.' She stops for a moment in the telling of the tale. 'He had a wee friend, and as Andrei came to sit back down, his friend goes into his box and gives Andrei the lollipop he'd been given.' She shakes her head again at the memory.

Good deed no. 320.

Thursday, 17 November

Cryssie arrived with her idea for a longer writing project: she wants to do something on the Vikings. We did some research on the Viking raids along the Northumberland coast and particularly on the island of Lindisfarne, and talked through some ideas. She has a character in mind called 'Goliath the Cross' who carries a sword by the name of 'Legbiter', and she wants the Vikings to have sailed out of the past in a dragon-headed ship and into the modern day in search of treasure. At the minute, she is focused on the Vikings arriving at a school she visits and getting into a row with the Christian music group over who pays for their instruments. Historically, the monks were worried enough by the Viking raids that they fled from Lindisfarne with the Lindisfarne Gospels and the body of St Cuthbert (who had died a few centuries earlier), so she could possibly tie in some of that if I can only move her out of the comfort zone of her immediate experience.

I am disappointed by one thing, though. The Operation Christmas Child publicity leaflet says the UK shoeboxes (which I was helping to pack) are an 'unconditional gift' to kids based on need, regardless of their background or religious beliefs. But it says that 'where appropriate' local partners will distribute a booklet of Bible stories along with the shoebox. (Hmm.) Moreover, the evangelical Christian organization behind OCC, which is called Samaritan's Purse, says on its website that 'needy children who received a gift-filled shoebox, without obligation, may be invited to participate in' Bible lessons. (Double hmm.) These twelve Bible lessons, called 'The Greatest Journey', include the warning that come eternity 'those who do not trust and follow Jesus will be in hell'. Luckily the children have an opportunity to sign a 'commitment certificate' that says: 'On this day I have decided to believe that Jesus is God's Son and follow Him for the rest of my life.' I am finding someone else to fill a shoebox for next year.

Good deed no. 321.

Friday, 18 November

Good deed no. 322: ate two chocolate brownies bought in aid of Children in Need (some good deeds are tougher than others).

Saturday, 19 November

I popped into a church coffee morning in the hall in the market-place rather than going to a café, only to bump into an elderly couple who worship at the same Baptist church as Cryssie and her brothers, and who act as an unofficial granny and grandad to them. The man said they had been at Cryssie's home last night for a prayer meeting and she had been full of what we were doing together, and what she planned to write.

'Thank you for doing that for her,' he said, and touched me on the arm.

'I'm getting more out of it than I ever expected,' I said, and only at that moment of hearing myself did I realize that what I said was true. Pompous, presumptuous, I expected a one-way street. I would tell her that bit I know of writing, and she would listen, and she would learn. Not true. Not true at all. She half wobbles, half walks from the car, stepping gingerly onto the paved step in the yard, not wanting to fall and break a bone. She sits down and draws the laptop to her, the muscles so paralysed in her face that sometimes I have to say, 'Say that again, Cryssie' when she speaks, and her long, slim fingers tap away at the keyboard and words appear, each one a small miracle – and I do love miracles. I have learned that you work with what you have got, no moans, no if-onlys, that life starts when you turn up for it. I have learned humility and learned respect.

Good deed no. 323: advised Karl on chasing up his application, what to say on the phone and to send his revised CV and letter to other stations.

Sunday, 20 November

Good deed no. 324: took someone else's child to rugby (the mum was away and the dad was car-less).

Monday, 21 November

Good deed no. 325: helped a little girl not fall over on the train, and helped her mum off the train with the buggy.

Tuesday, 22 November

When you get old, trips to the doctor and to hospital become part necessity and part hobby. I had to go down to Leeds for a 'Buy One, Get One Free' deal with Mum and Dad: Dad in the morning for his results on something or other, and Mum in the afternoon 'with her back'. Not that we could have gone without her back, or only if she slid along the hospital corridors on her belly like Voldemort's snake Nagini.

My dad's results were clear, so that was good. I went in with him to see the young doctor and he was busy telling the doctor that he didn't have any pain and he was feeling all-right-really-thank-you-doctor, and behind him I'm rolling my eyes and waving my hands about like Al Jolson so the doctor realizes my dad isn't fine at all – he just doesn't want to be 'a bother'. Being 'a bother' is akin in my parents' eyes to being a Nazi or a crazed psychopath with a bloodlust for curly-headed tots. It's not nice and it's not what you do.

Meanwhile, we have been waiting eight months to get my mother's back sorted out since she moved the TV in the garage with my dad. Because moving TVs when you're wracked with arthritis and osteoporosis, and you have recently climbed out of your bed after a major back operation, is what you do when you don't want to be a bother. The screaming inside my skull started when the nice Scottish doctor told us that the problem isn't a frac-tured vertebra high up the spine (as we'd thought), but lower down, around the site of the original problem. In her opinion, my 83-year-old mum might well need to have an operation to take out the two – repeat, two – shunts in her spine (which, I might add, are glued there with bone cement) and shave off some bone from the spine and slip a cage of steel rods round the spinal cord. My mother, who is remarkably game for a deaf, blind woman in constant pain, is nodding along, while I am ready to shoot myself at the sheer horror of it. 'The only problem,' my mother says, leaning on her white stick, 'is that after the last operation, I had a problem coming round. Will they have a note of that? Because I wouldn't want to be a bother.'

Good deed no. 326.

Wednesday, 23 November

I spent last night at a quirky hotel in London. It was about ten o'clock when I got in and I badly wanted a glass of wine, but the only thing you could order on room service was a glass of bubbly. According to the waitress, the owner doesn't like people drinking alcohol. Why serve anything then? Or, at the very least, let guests drink what they want but get them to sign a chit saying they are alcoholics and have a medicinal need. The hotel also appeared to be run by a battalion of young foreign women with intriguing accents and all of them dressed in black, and one of them with only one arm, the sleeve of her blouse pinned up against her collarbone. A Japanese family booked in with enormous Samsonite suitcases and the receptionist called through for a colleague, and when the skinny young thing came out, the cases weighed more than she did.

I was in London for a good deed. I arrived at the soup kitchen early this morning and then hid from the men hanging round the door waiting for entry. I am such a hypocrite. I shouldn't have hidden, I should have begun an enlightening conversation with them, or at the very least chatted about the weather. Instead, when my phone rang, I slid around the corner, and by the time I came off the phone the men had gone – even the guy sitting on the chair having his hair cut by his friend. The hostel was down from the Elephant and Castle – a tall shabby building with the Virgin Mary looking down on us. The Missionaries of Charity run a hostel for forty men who get a bed for the night, breakfast and dinner, but who leave the hostel during the day. In the late morning, their places are taken by different men hungry for a lunchtime meal.

The Missionaries of Charity are the order of nuns founded and made famous by Mother Teresa, who in 1979 received the Nobel Peace Prize for her humanitarian work among the poor. There are now 4,500 members of her order in dozens of countries across the world. I grew up on tales of Mother Teresa, who once said: 'Don't look for big things, just do small things with great love . . . The smaller the thing, the greater must be our love.'

I ring the bell, and a small nun in the familiar white habit with its blue banded veil greets me and takes me through to the kitchen where enormous pans of food steam as we wait for the signal to start serving. We bow our heads and read a prayer written on the wall, and in my head the smell of cabbage mingles with thoughts of heaven, and part of me begins to wonder if heaven itself smells of cabbage. We stand poised in the kitchen. I have lost track of time but it can be no later than elevenish when the thin sound of hymn singing stops and the volunteers form themselves into an urgent line to pass down steaming plates of stew and mashed potato, cabbage and cauliflower to the dining room. I'm at the threshold of the dining room between an Asian man without much English and a fresh-faced nun who led the kitchen prayer. I keep my head down and only when everyone is served do I go into the dining room to check who wants seconds. The plates are cleared of the stew. The mash is almost – though not quite – as popular. Like my own children would be, some of the men are less keen on the cabbage and cauliflower. There are only two women among the seventy people being fed – one black woman who asks me for rum at one point, and a large florid-faced woman who sits at the end of the table, her legs splayed. Some of the men have the faces you would expect from life on the streets, from alcohol. Occasionally, as you lean over to pass a plate, there is the smell of the street too. Many of the men are Eastern Europeans, and some of them are too young to be there. They eat fast. One clears his plate within minutes and is out the door as if he can't bear to be there, as if the food were an inconvenience to him. A few of the older or more infirm prop their crutches against the wall to eat. All of them sit and eat with jackets and coats on, and I realize that is the oddest thing, not the fact that strangers sit close by each other, nor the plastic cutlery, nor the lunch so early in the day, but the fact no one is at home, no one is staying. They eat a mix of yoghurt and caramel for dessert and drink tea, and we clear and wash up all the while, an exercise in efficiency and speed.

When the last one goes, and the last plate is dried, I sit and eat the stew. It's tasty – lightly spiced, what I guess might be turkey. Somehow it seems rude to ask.

Good deed no. 327.

Thursday, 24 November

I went from the soup kitchen for lunch to the House of Lords for dinner last night. I had rung a friend who is a working peer saying I was down, and he kindly invited me along to the Lords for dinner. The Lords does not smell of cabbage. It is fabulous – all oak and gilt and red leather and huge paintings of kings and queens and battles. It was quiet, apparently the House had risen, and every now and then as you turned a corner you bumped into the silver-haired ghost of a cabinet minister from the 1980s. We sat at a table and the waiters came up with menus and water and bread, and every time they gave my mate something they slid in the title 'my Lord': 'Bread, my Lord?', 'The menu, my Lord,' 'Your wine, my Lord.' It was very strange and ever so slightly creepy. So I waited for the latest my-Lording waiter to slip away and I said to my mate, who is a Labour politician after all, 'Tell me, that doesn't make you wince?' He buttered his bread roll and shrugged. 'That's how they do it,' he said. 'You can't do anything about it.' The conversation moved on and the first course arrived, and as the waiter slid my Parma ham and melon onto the table in front of me, he said, 'Your starter, my Lady' and then they served my friend. I waited for them to go. 'That thing I said earlier about the "my Lord" stuff making you wince, I take it back – I rather like it.'

One day you are feeding the homeless and the next day you are trying to avoid meeting their eye. I checked out of my quirky London hotel with my wheelie bag, and the homeless were everywhere – with rolled-up nylon sleeping bags, with crutches and limps, with faithful mongrels on bits of string. What is it about the homeless that inspires fear? The thought they might start shouting obscenities at you? Infect you, if you stand too close, with their addictions and misery? There were at least three *Big Issue* sellers within a couple of hundred yards of each other at Victoria and, good-deed doing or not, since I wasn't armed with a plate of cabbage, I walked on by. I had to make myself stop and dig out £2 and buy a copy. I had to make myself see another human being standing in front of me.

Good deed no. 328.

Friday, 25 November

What I had forgotten when I went along to the soup kitchen was that I might have boosted my own health – my very own 'Mother Teresa effect'. In the journal *Psychology and Health* in 1988, Dr David McClelland, a psychologist and a leading expert on motivation, described an experiment in which 132 Harvard University students were asked to watch two films – one of them a documentary about Mother Teresa working with the poor of Calcutta. Before the film, immediately after, and again an hour later (having been asked to retain the idea of loving relationships in their heads), the students' saliva was tested for immunoglobulin A (the body's first defence against cold viruses). Levels were up. The students' bodies (even if they themselves didn't like her and even though they weren't themselves benefiting) responded to the compassionate, tender care they saw on the film.

A later experiment in 1995 published in the *Journal of Advancement in Medicine* also found that encouraging subjects to feel care and compassion (without an external stimulus such as a video) had an even greater immune-efficient effect. I have got to believe then that feeling care and compassion, while engaged in caring, compassionate work with Mother Teresa's own nuns, is better than a flu jab this winter.

Good deed no. 329: filled jars with sweeties for sale at the school Xmas fair (and wanted to cry, I was so tired).

Saturday, 26 November

Good deed no. 330: sold second-hand uniform at school Xmas fair and cleared up afterwards.

Sunday, 27 November

Good deed no. 331: reassured a friend who was upset at the proposed closure of her children's school.

Monday, 28 November

Brian Burnie is a 66-year-old former businessman and hotelier who sold his £9m hotel in North Northumberland and has ploughed profits 'running into millions' into the Daft as a Brush charity, transporting north-east cancer patients to hospital in special people carriers. Consequently, Brian and his wife Shirley (who herself recovered from breast cancer) moved from their Georgian home complete with maze and spa and swimming pool into a three-bedroomed rented terraced house. As Brian said: 'You come into this world with nothing and go out with nothing – what's important is what you do in between.'

Official patient transport in an ambulance or an ambulance taxi often means an early start or long delays in getting home as other patients are picked up en route or waited for or dropped off. Daft as a Brush patients are driven by a volunteer chauffeur, picked up at a time convenient to them and brought home directly after their appointments. They are also escorted by a volunteer companion so that they aren't alone if their spouse can't come because of their own health or age, work or childcare commitments.

I travelled as a companion with a patient called Robert and his wife Jane to the Freeman hospital in Newcastle. Robert is sixty-six, tall and rangy, with a pale face and bunched-up hands thrust into the pockets of his olive-green coat as if to keep the cold away. He looks as if he would rather be walking the rolling Northumberland hills with a thumbstick and a Thermos than stuck in a car headed for the horrors of the city, and I don't blame him. Travelling down to Newcastle for the results of a bone marrow test, the former gardener is no stranger to the journey. Four years ago, he had an operation for bowel cancer; more recently, he was diagnosed with MDS – myelodysplastic syndrome – a malfunction of the bone marrow in producing the correct quantity and quality of blood cells. The disease can leave a patient chronically tired and weak due to extremely low levels of haemoglobin. It requires the transfusion of blood and platelets, there can be spontaneous bleeding and bruising, and the patient is at risk of infection. Robert is unassuming, digni- fied and uncomplaining about all of it. He was due to start his seventh round of chemotherapy today. The treatment has been can- celled so that he can get the latest results from a bone marrow biopsy. I can't believe he and Jane aren't worried in case it's bad news.

I am embarrassed to be there. I am an intruder. As I sit in the passenger seat next to Sharon the driver, who works in a café, I wonder exactly what a companion does in this situation. I could play him a favourite tune on the harpsichord – if only I had one and I could play the harpsichord. I decide that at the very least I need a lapdog to whom I could feed titbits. When we get to hos- pital, I immediately offer to fetch a cup of tea but disconcertingly Robert and Jane don't want one and within seconds they are called in to the unit so I can't force the point. Sharon, Emma (the Daft as a Brush organizer who accompanies new companions and drivers on their first outings) and I go for our own cup of tea.

We are there for three hours. Waiting. Hospitals are not so much for the sick as for those who wait – wait to see a doctor, wait for treatment, wait for the busy nurse to get around to them, wait for the drugs, wait to recover or wait to die. Perched at the end of a string of seats by a glass cabinet stacked with scarves for the bald, I sit and I wait. As I wait, I think and hope. I hope I never have to wear a scarf like that, that I never get sick, never get cancer and never die. I hope too that Robert and Jane are OK, that they aren't sitting in front of a doctor holding hands and knowing the worst. I liked Robert – he takes photographs of wildlife – the best one he has is of three badgers playing together. I liked Jane too – in her spare time she is brave. Actually, I think she is brave all of the time. Hours pass. Sharon and Emma chat to other Daft as a Brush volunteers, and they are noisy and healthy – not like the sick, and not like the families of the sick. They laugh and tell jokes. Sharon and Emma go to swap our people carrier for another one. I read *The Times*. I text. I look at the scarves and watch porters push hospital beds down the corridor. I go to the loo and look at myself in the mirror – my hair could do with a wash. I stroke my hair. I like my hair. I think about how I'd look in a scarf. This is what happens in hospitals: you sit down next to your own mortality and strike up conversation.

Finally, Robert and Jane are through. He is more relaxed. There was no conversation about results – only a blood test. He has to come back on Thursday for the bone marrow results, and we head back to the car.

Good deed no. 332.

Tuesday, 29 November

Good deed no. 333: liaised with Michael Hintze's CQS hedge fund, which has offered to have a pre-Xmas Jam Jar Army collection in the office for the homeless.

Wednesday, 30 November

Good deed no. 334: researched opportunities/advised a would-be journalist who has asked for help.

Thursday, 1 December

Good deed no. 335: taught Cryssie writing.

Friday, 2 December

THE HOLY MAN

Goodness is admirable. Perhaps the fact I felt so resolutely ordinary, so banal in my everyday interactions with people and so limited in the effect I have on the world – including on my own children maybe – influenced me in starting this project more than I thought. I wanted to change the world and I wanted to change me. To be a saint for a year. There is an irony, then, that as I have slogged my way through a year of good deeds, as chance would have it, I feel that I have less faith in God than when I went in.

Then again, faith in my fellow man has grown because not only is there a need, there are people answering that need at some cost to themselves – be it money or time or energy, and be they with or without faith. And I come back to the idea that for all the good deeds this year, my year is worth nothing set against someone like Lily, caring for a child damaged by our society, or Cryssie's parents caring for children at the mercy of their own genes, or my dad caring for my mum every day in every way. Because for some people, pain acts as a crucible for goodness and perhaps, for me, therein lies the real divine: the piece of toast spread with marmalade and placed carefully into the hands of a blind woman; the chaotic, loving family home opened to a discarded child; or the pennies dropped into a jam jar.

I met my cousin, who is a priest, in the almshouses close to Durham Cathedral. Father Ed is lionized in my extended and very

Catholic family. He is the religious equivalent of a walking, talking golden egg: a treasure and a thing of lustrous wonder. Tall and spare with trendy glasses and a beard that has started to silver, once upon a time – in a play we made our parents watch – he played Prince Charming opposite my Cinderella. Some time after, he went into the priesthood – I try not to hold myself too responsible.

On the one hand there are good deeds, on the other there are bad. In nearly thirty years as a priest, Father Ed has heard the worst of people in their confessions. 'The fact confession exists, however, is evidence of people's desire for goodness,' he said amiably, and I am intrigued by the talk of confession, secrets he has heard, sinners he has forgiven. I cocked my head and pressed my ear against the metal grille, the dusty velvet curtain of his memory. He had heard of murder, child abuse, army killing, fraud – everything but genocide. And did he forgive all? I asked. Did he wipe the chalky sins from the slate with a damp sponge of three Hail Marys and a Glory Be? Not quite. He laid on the sinner a 'proportionate penance' – not to punish, he explained, but to help the sinner towards goodness. 'When I heard confession, it confirmed for me what animals people are sexually, that if something can be done, it will be done and is being done. But . . .' He paused as he poured fresh tea into first my cup and then his own. '. . . my experience in confession affirms both the depths to which we can stoop and the heights to which we can aspire and the best that is present in each and every person – the goodness and the heroism.'

Goodness in the father of the disabled child with little time to live, confessing: 'Sometimes I give way to despair, which is a sin.' Well, who wouldn't? Father Ed said. 'But in that man's confession, what he is saying is how much he loves. You realize for that father, his good deed is holding on to the love for that child in the face of overwhelming odds, and not giving up and walking away on his family.'

For Father Ed, the good deeds are enhanced by a belief in something higher; hence the 'golden rule' shared by religions and cultures the world over: 'Do unto others as you would have them do unto you' – which comes out in Christianity as 'Love thy neighbour as thyself'. As Father Ed talked, I began to wonder whether it was possible to regard God as a metaphor rather than as an all-knowing, all-seeing, beardy guy or a white, pulsing, sci-fi source of energy. If the idea of God (across religions) brings people to goodness, and if I choose to value goodness, then surely it is possible to hold fast to a 'God' of some sort. Plus it will make my mother happy. She's never very keen when I lose my faith.

Faith is not a requirement of good deeds, though, Father Ed assured me. The doing of good deeds, however, can only be done by those who hope, or those for whom optimism is an inclination, those who believe that beyond the worst of things lies something better; and I wondered, as he told me this, whether he was doing so because he thought I needed to hear it.

Good deed no. 336: met with start-up social media company to offer advice and feedback on proposed product.

Saturday, 3 December

Good deed no. 337: sent a P. D. James thriller to Merry.

Sunday, 4 December

I may have done something stupid. I have been given the cake equivalent of a chain letter – that is to say, a bowl of yeasty gloop – and I actually asked for this so-called 'friendship cake' because I thought I could pass it on and it would be a lovely generous gift for my nearest and dearest. It is a nightmare. It turns out that it comes with all these ominous shouty instructions: 'Hello. My name is Herman. I am a sourdough cake and I am supposed to be kept on a worktop for ten days without a lid. You cannot put me in a fridge or I will die! You can cover me with a tea towel to keep me safe. If I stop bubbling, I am dead.' Talk about needy.

Every day you are supposed to stir him between two and four times. I don't get that much attention in a day. Twice, the instructions yell 'I am hungry' at you, at which point you drop whatever you are doing and feed it milk, sugar and flour. On day 9, you divide it five ways and give away four portions to friends, along with a copy of the hellish instructions. The following day, you pour in oil, eggs, baking powder, sugar, flour, salt, cinnamon and whatever else you want into the fifth Herman, bake him and eat him – providing you aren't too emotionally attached by then. The kids make eeeeurgh noises whenever I bring him out for a stir. This good deed might have been a mistake.

Good deed no. 338: fed Herman the German.

Monday, 5 December

Yesterday I spent six hours slumped over the laptop in the kitchen figuring out how to film, edit and cut DVDs of this week's forthcoming school nativity play at the behest of Lily, who had the great idea of selling parents a copy of the DVD in aid of the PTA. She asked me to find someone and I advised sending out a note round school. Foolishly, though, I told her that I would do it if they couldn't find anyone else. Since I hadn't seen any note asking for a budding Martin Scorsese, I figured I needed to step up to the mark. The only problem being that I hadn't used my video camera in two years and I hadn't edited anything since I worked at the BBC as a producer, when I used to sit next to a nice man known as an editor, bring him cups of tea and say fretful things like, 'We're running out of time.'

I had to download three different bits of software and my head went bendy in the middle figuring out how to do it – occasionally, I would string together a load of pictures only to find I had no sound, and occasionally I could get the sound but only if the pictures went to black. Halfway through, one of my children came into the kitchen and said, 'Do you think you should give up, Mummy?' and I had been about to, I had been about to say, 'Fuck the fucking nativity' and then of course I couldn't. I was trapped, just like they trapped me in this year of good deeds. I had to say, 'Mummy never gives up' and keep sitting there going utterly insane. This morning, I went into school with my video equipment to film the nativity, only to be told that the teachers didn't think the filming was happening, so thanks but no thanks.

Good deed no. 339: chased up jam jars.

Tuesday, 6 December

I trailed round in the freezing winds collecting jam jars this morning. Al has been counting into the early hours and we are up another £1,200, which takes us just over the £9,000 mark. I wanted £9k for this week's *Gazette* because I thought it would encourage us all to make that final push to the £10k mark. The editor wants a big story on 22 December, which is in two weeks. Two more weeks to raise £1,000 in tuppenny bits. Bollocks. I have drained the county of jam jars. I am not sure there is another one left to empty. Thank God Sophie gave me that cheque, because the stress would be killing me otherwise. I was getting disheartened, having had a fair few number of places with no returns. I was about to walk past the pub with the jars on the mantelpieces where the guy had boasted he didn't 'do' charity. I stood in the cold wind, my shoulders round my ears, thinking how much I didn't want to go in to see two empty jars, or possibly worse – two jars with only a risible amount of money in. I gritted my teeth. I was going to have to go in. I'd put the jars out. If anyone had found them and put anything in them, they had done that in good faith. I had to go in and extract my jars.

> I will always place the mission first.
> I will never accept defeat.
> I will never quit.
> I will never leave a fallen comrade.

As the American soldiers say.

But then the nicest thing happened. As I pushed open the door into the bar and peered round the enormous stuffed Santa Claus towards the mantelpiece, both jars were brimful of coins, and suddenly I wasn't cold any more.

Good deed no. 340.

Karl arrived with his show-reel. He has just passed his driving test, so this time he drove himself up from the village rather than arriving with his mam, which he was obviously hugely proud of. The Lovely Claire has come good and dug out a contact in radio called Joel Goldman, a journalist at Newcastle's Metro Radio, which is the big commercial station up here, with 400,000 people tuning in every week. I called him and explained that Karl had no real academic qualifications, but boy is he good on radio, and he said to send in a show-reel that he can use to persuade his station manager. Joel himself was lovely about it and apparently the station manager is one of the good guys, so fingers crossed. Today we sent off the show-reel along with a letter and his CV, and once we had done that we chased up an application he had made in September for another scheme (this one with Real Radio), found yet another scheme he could apply for, and formatted a standard letter for him to send to other local radio stations. Not counting the back and forth chasing Claire and Joel, it took more than two hours out of my day, including printing the letters out and giving him envelopes on which we wrote the addresses so all he has to do is stamp them and post them. This is in a bid to avoid the usual delay there is in the process between me asking Karl to do something and him actually getting round to doing it. I could wish that he moved faster on some of these things, that he would go knock on a few doors, but the kids who know it all aren't the kids who need the help.

Good deed no. 341.

I watched as Cryssie pecked away at the keyboard this morning. Through a disabled child, I have seen our own humanity; in her mother, glimpsed the reality of perfect love. I was only ever going to get so far in teaching her how story comes from character. Admittedly I was getting more punctuation, more paragraphing, more of those odd flashes which always make me think, 'Woh!' But had I made any real difference to her writing?

'Do you think this is helping your writing?' I asked, sipping my tea. She stopped typing. She always stops typing when you talk to her. She likes to take one thing at a time – now we were talking. When we finished talking, she would write again.

'It helps' – I sat up straighter in my chair as she enunciated the words with care – 'because I'm using different fingers on the keyboard.'

My self-esteem, which had poked a twitchy, pink velvet nose out of its burrow, poked it back in again. Cryssie has a literal approach. 'I mean, is this helping your writing process, honey, not is it helping you type faster?' Is what we are doing making any difference to who you are, how you are?

She gazed at the screen. She would like to stop talking now, like to start writing about Vikings again. There is silence and I am about to tell her not to worry, to go back to Eric the Unworthy and Goliath the Cross and his iron sword Legbiter, when she looks away from the screen again and back at me.

'I'd stopped wanting to write any more. I left my computer lying around the house. When I started coming to you I got back into writing. It makes me feel . . . good, really happy that I can concentrate and make interesting stories up.'

I smile.

Good deed no. 342.

Earlier this week, Lily rang on the way home from some training course she has gone on for parents of adopted children. She is still struggling with Ellie. Saturday was her twenty-fifth wedding anniversary, and she couldn't spend it with her husband because he was away for work and she couldn't leave the kids to be with him because Ellie couldn't have coped; they were childhood sweethearts and it was the first anniversary they hadn't been together. But when she rang, there was a different tone to her voice. She said they could get whatever psych help was available for Ellie (though she hasn't got any yet), and she could get support from the GP, and go on any number of training courses which teach adoptive parents how to cope with 'challenging behaviours', but the realization had suddenly dawned on her that there were no magic answers.

'This is as good as we get, I see that now' – there was a note of wonder in her voice – 'and I also see that it's down to me to find a way to handle how I'm feeling because the whole family mood at any time is determined by how I react to things.'

I don't have the courage Lily has. If I thought it was 'all on me', I'd blanch, desert my post and run away, away, away.

Good deed no. 343: gave some R&R to my friend's daughter at university in Newcastle, who has come up to us for the weekend. (Tried to give her a designer dress of mine that I can't fit into any more, but it was too big for her. Middle age sucks.)

The weather this week has been filthy: terrible gusting winds rattling the sash windows in their peeling frames and temperatures cold enough to freeze pig's blood. I was lying in my bed wishing I had hidden a stapler under my pillow that I could use to staple myself and my goosedown duvet to the mattress, when the force of nature that is my eight-year-old hurtled into the bedroom yelling, 'It's snooooowing!' True enough, when we pulled back the curtains, the fields between us and the sea were smeared over with a thick layer of white icing, and the cold which had been a steadfast enemy turned into a sudden friend.

Good deed no. 344: met a friend's niece to advise her on getting into journalism. (I should open a recruitment agency. 'Young, bright, baffled? Join Old Fart Talks Bollocks. Let Us Help You to the Future that's Behind Us.')

Sunday, 11 December

I divided Herman into five, baked the fifth part complete with grated Cox's apple, chewy hazelnuts and dark chocolate and ate him with a degree of caution. He was yummy – better yet, he didn't kill me.

As I packed the car with my own kids and my friend's daughter and pots of slop, it crossed my mind that my friends were not necessarily going to be delighted to find me on their doorstep with a bowl of gloop and an innocent smile. I slammed the boot before the gloop crawled out and insisted on driving.

The Lovely Claire was my first target, on the grounds that she is one of nature's enthusiasts. Pans for the Sunday lunch steamed and bubbled on the Aga as I explained that the gloop was a thank you for helping with Karl's work experience, and beaming, she said, 'I'll cook him right now,' and I said, 'Noooooooooo' and explained she couldn't cook him for another ten days. 'I'll put him in the fridge then,' she said, and moved towards the fridge, and I said, 'Noooooooooo' and leapt to barricade the path. Her smile faltered. Her blue-grey parrot, Sybil, sitting on the back of a dining-room chair, eyed me scornfully. Sybil is as mean as Claire is good and kind, and has been known to bite ears, fingers, backs and arms. Claire wonders why I never stay long.

My second target was Diane. Diane is an altogether tougher mark than the Lovely Claire. Fortunately, she was out on a healthy forced march down to the ponies through the freezing cold with children and dogs, so I left the gloop on the side along with the instructions as a nice surprise when she came back home. She can thank me later.

I honestly thought Lily was out as well, which was why I didn't knock on the door. Instead I did a rapid three-point turn in her gravelled yard, parked up with my nose pointing back towards the narrow bridge we had come in over, left the car running and was scrawling a note of explanation when she appeared in a beige velveteen leisure suit studded with diamanté bits. I cursed under my breath and clambered out of the car. The Ratmobile's boot is broken at the moment; not only do you have to slam it shut as if you were closing the gates of Hell against legion slathering, leathery-winged demons, but the spring mechanism is gone, which means you have to heave then fling it wide open while remembering to keep one hand on it at all times, otherwise it is liable to fall and chop you clean in two. I handed Lily the gloop. 'This is a friendship cake,' I said. She held the bowl away from her as if she didn't trust it or me. I handed her the 'Don't kill me' instructions and she scanned them. 'I've got to stir him and add ingredients over ten days, then pass him on?' she said. 'Do you not think my life is effing complicated enough?' I brought the fourth pot back home.

Good deed no. 345.

Monday, 12 December

Diane told my husband she is only doing Herman for me, and did I realize she would have to be giving away pots of gloop virtually on Christmas Eve? I am not convinced Herman has been altogether a success. Lily rang to tell me that her rooster Lucky Lazarus got luckier: she fed him Herman the German, and did I know that, courtesy of the yeast, when chickens poop enormous bubbles, they look very surprised indeed?

Good deed no. 346: emailed my friend's niece re her next step onto a journalism course.

Tuesday, 13 December

Good deed no. 347: chased up Karl's work experience with Metro Radio.

Wednesday, 14 December

Ages ago, I wrote a letter to Father David Myers, the head of the Rosminian order, which Father Kit had been a member of. Then I carried the letter around in my handbag till November wondering whether there was any point posting it, thinking, 'Who cares what I think?' and 'Why would they listen anyway?' The letter said:

> I'm pretty sure you will have had a lot of these letters. Letters of confusion and pain – nothing like the pain of those poor abused boys who are now men, but pain nonetheless. When news broke of Father Kit's past (alongside his fellow priests) we were still celebrating as a family the First Communion of my eight-year-old son. We had been too busy that morning to read the papers, so friends rang to ask if we had seen the news. I have to say, Father Myers, that the sense of betrayal runs so deep that if I had read the reports earlier that day, my eight-year-old might well never have taken his First Communion.
>
> We Catholics out here in the real world take all sorts of flak for being Catholic, you know. Intelligent friends think we should know better. We have carried on regardless and tried to ignore the anachronisms and illogicalities. The abuse, however, is something else again. Speaking as a mother of three children – baptizing them, having them do their First Communions, teaching them day in and day out that they are Catholic – I can assure you that if you lose the mothers, the game is up and you lose everything.
>
> Perhaps you are wondering why I am bothering to tell you this. I'm supposed to be doing a good deed a day this year. My good deed

today is to ask you to bankrupt the Rosminian order, sell every last pot and crucifix and oaken bench and pay those victims of abuse every penny. It wouldn't be enough but it might just be a start.

Eventually I thought, 'What the hell' and posted it, and today I got a reply. Father Myers told me that 'there are many issues, in my opinion, that are even more important than money like healing and reconciliation in this sad saga.' That would be a no to my polite request for them to provide a shedload of money then. Nice reply, though, plenty of reassurance to me as a mother, that is to say 'our hope for the future and . . . the ones who provide the next generation with the wonderful vision of the gospel of love'. Oh and an offer of a meeting to discuss the issues in depth. I hereby declare myself an official, and almost faithless, Catholic mother – hear me roar. I have done nearly a year of good deeds now, and if they had made me a better person, perhaps I'd have been able to forgive Father Kit. I wasn't his victim and it isn't for me to forgive him the abuse. But I am trying to forgive him for his betrayal, for the hurt I feel that he wasn't who I thought he was, and it is hard. I am trying to remember the man who gave food to the homeless, and the man who offered consolation when my son died. I am trying.

Good deed no. 348: picked up the last jars from coastal village shops and the community centre.

Thursday, 15 December

I dropped the kids at school and went straight round to Lily's smallholding to pluck a turkey. Usually, if you ask her for a coffee, she comes up with some lame excuse or other along the lines of 'I have to clean out the pigsties/de-bollock a lamb/put the geese in before the foxes gobble them up.' It would be simpler just to say no. This year, she has reared half a dozen turkeys – her first ever – and was up half the night dreading plucking them.

As I walked into the barn, Slade's 'Merry Christmas Everybody' was on as if Lily was hoping that Christmas being here might distract us from the massive black-feathered birds hanging by their yellowing feet from the rafters. My bird had had its wattled throat cut and had been eviscerated, which required at least George Michael's 'Last Christmas I Was an Egg and the Very Next Year You Ate My Leg'. They were freshly butchered, which meant they were warm, which I swear to God made me feel like some sunken-eyed heavy about to torture the good guy for information. Apparently, it is best to pluck them warm because the feather follicles are open, but it took until I had plucked a hole as big and smooth as the palm of my hand before I could see it as something to eat and not as Jack Bauer. It would have helped if we had known what we were doing, since there must be a skill to it (a skill like buy a turkey from a butcher, Lily). Allegedly, you can blowtorch the feathers off, and most of the turkeys we eat are plucked by machine, but we were hand-plucking without much of a plucking clue. By the end, I had plucked the whole thing – the wings being the most difficult, and the only casualties a couple of bits on the breast where the skin tore.

I asked how things were going with Ellie.

'Ever since I realized this was down to me, somehow I've got more capacity to understand – more tolerance maybe,' she said. Some time before, as Lily had parked up at the supermarket, Ellie opened her door, climbed out and, before Lily could reach for her, ran out in front of a car, which only just managed to avoid her. Shaking, her almost-broken heart thunderous in her chest, Lily had gathered her fragile, fly-away daughter up into her arms and held her in a never-let-you-go kind of way. 'A while ago if you'd asked me, I'd have said I loved her but I wasn't "in love" with her as you are with your natural children' – she went back to her plucking, a few torn scraps of skin exposing the raw breast – 'but that's not true any more. I feel exactly for her what I feel for my son. I'm "in love" with her.

'None of this is her fault. She is trying her very best and I am too. Sometimes my best isn't enough, but I wouldn't change her for the world. She's my daughter and I'm proud of her – how far she's come. I know we've further to go, but I love the very bones of her. A while ago, I'd have said she was killing us. Now I'd kill for her, and I'd kill anyone who tried to take her from me.'

I used my right index finger to rub the corner of my right eye where a feather must have got in, and we went back to plucking in a companionable silence – give or take a Christmas classic. 'Have you noticed,' I said, reaching for the gently swinging carcass, 'that a plucked turkey's warm neck feels quite like a penis when you take it in your hand?'

Good deed no. 349.

Friday, 16 December

Maybe we need each other more when the economy tanks. When bills go up and jobs disappear, when winter comes. Perhaps then we know we can make the biggest difference. Maybe we need each other more too when trust slips away in our politicians, our bankers and our priests. In the hungry years then, that's when we need the fellowship and the kindnesses we can do, one for the other. A London initiative called the Kindness Offensive, set up in 2008, has given out more than £3.5m of goods and is aimed at demonstrating that 'kindness is more than just a nice ideal, it's actually a viable way of existing in the real world'; while an Art on the Underground project on the Tube, the creation of Young British Artist Michael Landy, celebrates simple human kindness. In Acts of Kindness, passengers and Underground staff were invited to submit their stories of kindness, which Landy put up on posters around the Central Line stations and trains. In an interview, the artist explained: 'I want to find out what makes us human, and what connects us, beyond material things. For me the answer is compassion and kindness.' He defines kindness as 'a gesture of trust between two people' which goes beyond the self to acknowledge someone else's needs and feelings. Among the stories of lost and found again property, struggling mothers who are helped with buggies, commuters who are helped with suitcases, there is compassion, comfort, community and a celebration of life:

> 'I was in the pit of a severe depression, sitting on the Tube, staring at my knees, trying not to cry. I could just see the man opposite me, folding a piece of paper. The train stopped and in my lap the man placed the piece of paper, which he had folded into a beautiful little white horse. He smiled and left the train. A light appeared in the pit.'

Good deed no. 350: took a day trip to London to visit my Irish aunty in the run-up to Christmas.

Saturday, 17 December

Good deed no. 351: checked on a sick friend.

Sunday, 18 December

Good deed no. 352: held a door open for a heavily loaded woman (who didn't say thank you or even notice; I resisted letting it close on her heels).

Monday, 19 December

Good deed no. 353: organized a thank you in the paper for the designers and IT and bank staff involved in the Jam Jar Army.

Tuesday, 20 December

We all needed a rest, so we'd driven up to Kielder Water's Winter Wonderland on Sunday and have been staying in a log cabin for a couple of days. The kids met Santa, rode a carousel and went snow tubing. The last activity before we were due to set off for home was ice skating. Only, my daughter fell on the ice and, when she stood up again, couldn't move her neck.

We headed back to the car and she cried as we put her in her seat, big fat tears falling one after the other, and we dosed her with Calpol and she was still crying because of the pain. My husband carried her over to reception to have her looked over by their First Aid person, and the next thing we know the First Aider is holding her head immobile in a cradle of his two hands for forty-five minutes while we wait for an ambulance. The road ambulance arrives with two paramedics and the air ambulance choppers down with two paramedics, and suddenly they are medevacking her out of Santa's Winter Wonderland by helicopter on the grounds it is an hour and a half bumpy journey by road, it is a neck injury, she is six and nobody is taking any chances.

I never want to see anyone strapped like that again. They strapped her body and her neck and her head and then strapped her neck and her head again and the only things she could move were her eyes and her hands. I went with her in the helicopter and my husband drove the boys. I am sitting in the helicopter thinking, 'If I vomit in sheer terror, they will throw me out and I won't be able to be with her, so I can't vomit.' At one point the paramedic asked, 'When was she born?' and I couldn't even tell him.

It took twelve minutes to airlift us out of Kielder and down the snow-smeared country to Newcastle, where we landed on the roof of the hospital to be met by four firemen who wheeled her off the roof, down the zigzag slopes and into Resus. Resus as in 'Resuscitation', as in 'Otherwise you die'. Twelve minutes and I aged ten years. The doctor said it was soft tissue damage, that she had probably pulled or torn muscles, but there was no bone damage to the neck. He recommended ibuprofen and hot compresses and baths. *And for me?* I felt like saying, holding out my trembling hands. *What do you recommend for me?*

Good deed no. 354: dropped change into a charity collecting tin at the Royal Victoria Infirmary coffee shop after the air ambulance out of Kielder.

Wednesday, 21 December

Good deed no. 355: got Karl an offer of work experience next year alongside a presenter at Metro Radio. Very impressed by Metro's public-spirited willingness to support a local youngster.

Thursday, 22 December

Official declaration in the *Gazette* that we have made our grand total for the Jam Jar Army: £12,868 and 69 pence. Headline 'You've done it!', which Al had money on them running. The total represents a shedload of work, but it means more because I didn't raise it – everyone raised it. I reckon around 2,000 to 3,000 people must have given. Sure, I had the idea, but the *Gazette* ran with it and the hospice ran with it and schools and old people's homes and shops and pubs, Martin who has a van selling coffees at the railway station, and Sharon who saw it in the paper and started handing out jam jars and collecting them every week, and Josie the school cook who quietly left her jars of copper and silver without any expectation of thanks. Norma in the post office who handed them out to her regulars, and Mary in her café with a jar on every table and special Jam Jar Army scones, and a couple of thousand people I have never met giving what money they could.

I did assemblies and a couple of interviews. I got the stickers and the posters organized and handed out jars myself, and Sophie's contribution came because it was my baby, but at a certain point people were giving because they chose to, because they wanted to, because it was something they could do for each other. I went into a retirement home at one point asking them to put up a poster and take a couple of jars, but the residents were already doing it. That was a good day. A letter from the hospice says: 'This is probably a record for us for this sort of community fund-raising effort . . . Community effort it certainly was and apart from the obvious financial benefits, it did help foster a community spirit.' Even better, though, the *Gazette* editor plans to keep it going. He is asking readers to nominate the next charity we can collect for. Which is great. I am just hoping he doesn't want me involved.

Good deed no. 356.

Friday, 23 December

Good deed no. 357: gave a dozen jars of jam to the Northumberland Gazette *editor and his reporters as a thank you for running the Jam Jar Army appeal, and wine to the local heroes in the village Barclays bank who took in all the counted change and never blinked at the number of tuppenny bags. (Have realized we've eaten everything I put aside for the expats' Christmas hamper – maybe next year?)*

Saturday, 24 December

After the excitement of the air ambulance on Tuesday, I figured we should be safe enough from harm going round to Diane's farmhouse this morning for a Christmas Eve coffee and a piece of her very own Herman the German – only for my youngest son to go climbing on hay bales and plummet like the White Rabbit twenty-four feet down a hole in the middle of the bales to the floor of the barn. What is it with my children?

The massive cylindrical bales were stacked three high, virtually up to the roof of the barn, in a cluster of four stacks. They had been pushed together, leaving a hole in the middle between the stacks, and when my youngest son's foot slipped as he tried to climb to the very top, he plummeted into the darkness. My eldest ran to the farmhouse for help, and the farmer kicked away one of the bales before he and my husband let down a rope and pulled my son up – uninjured, aside from a grazed nose, but very shaken up. And all the while, I am reading books to Diane's daughter who couldn't be persuaded to leave the kitchen.

The lucky, those who haven't suffered loss, don't know how

brave we are to let our children cross a road – even holding tight to our hand, even looking first, right and left, and right again. How we must screw our courage up to let them travel in a car that might smash, bash and crash; to walk along a slippy, slidey dune all ready to smother them; to sleep in a bed when the wind blows hard against the house and trees wait to hammer down through our slated roof and crush what is within. To eat food that isn't tasted. Nobody is more neurotic than we are about possible harm to children. When you lose a child, that is how you get, how you are left. Scared all the time that something might happen. That lightning disaster might strike again, and take that which is best in your life – that thing you love the most. If I lost another child, my heart and soul would shrivel. Even if I was walking and talking, if I was standing right in front of you, you'd be wrong if you thought that was me. That would be a stranger, because inside that skin-and-bone impostor, I'd have died, you see.

Good deed no. 358: read books with Diane's daughter.

Sunday, 25 December

My inclination is always to consider festivities a battlefield, with resources deployed so that targets can be taken and losses kept to a minimum. Life is not a war, though. Hosting a celebration is a gift I can give to the people I love. That said, today had its challenges. My eldest decided to make an early start – 2.30 a.m. early, to be precise. At 4 a.m. the excitement got too much once again and he wandered into our bedroom with the glad tidings it was Christmas morn, and wandered straight back out with tidings of his own. Groaning, I got up to find he had woken his brother who was reading in bed under the multicoloured fairy lights, which were promptly turned off in no uncertain terms with ne'er a 'Merry Christmas, my lovie'. When I marched downstairs, an avenging spirit of Christmas Yet to Come, my eldest was lying on the sofa, hiding under a duvet – presumably on the grounds he had covered his bed with the contents of his stocking. Apparently, he couldn't sleep after I had put him back to bed the first time (having fuelled himself with a potent combination of chocolate coins and novelty penguins). Oh, and at 6 a.m. he came back in to tell us that he had been reading his book since we'd put him back to bed. Ah, the joys of Christmastide.

Good deed no. 359: provided a neighbour with Nurofen Gel after he dropped the grate on his finger (also laid on Christmas for nine people, including parents and expats).

Monday, 26 December

Went for a beach walk with my best gay boyfriend and the children. My little girl got a plastic habitat for insects for Christmas, so at considerable risk to his Australian workboots, my boyfriend dared the roil and broil of the sea to fill the habitat with saltwater and sand and we threw in a couple of rocks and twists of seaweed and two limpets. It turns out that limpets can live till they are teenagers if they are undisturbed; consequently, I feel really guilty that my six-year-old has a pet limpet. Plus it means I have taken on a couple of teenagers lying around in a plastic condo doing sweet Fanny Adams and refusing to speak to me.

Good deed no. 360: sent flowers home with my best gay boyfriend for his eighty-year-old mother. (Technically this was re-gifting because the flowers came from someone thanking me for an earlier good deed.)

Tuesday, 27 December

Good deed no. 361: opened a door for a little girl who was pushing when she should have been pulling ('Story of my life, pet,' I should have said).

If Jesus had never been born, chocolate manufacturers would have been forced to invent him, wrap him and sell him to small children with black and rotten teeth. My own children have eaten themselves stupid with chocolate over Christmas, but I decided enough was enough after a purple-faced, tear-splattered spat between the eldest and youngest over the exact and legal ownership of a Mars Bar: was it the rightful owner of the selection box it came from, or the person who found it lying around and built a settlement on it? My husband was physically holding them apart as a neighbour walked in with three more selection boxes. She was dutifully thanked and told to keep them for her own kids, but I notice they are still on my kitchen side.

I have called in all the chocolate the children have left and piled it into a black bin alongside a huge tub of Quality Street. The contents include:

 four bags of Buttons
 three Crunchies
 three and a half Caramel bars
 four Flakes
 three slim bars of Dairy Milk
 four Fudges
 one Twix
 one bag of Milky Bar buttons
 twelve fun-sized bags of Maltesers
 fifteen fun-sized and two full-sized Milky Ways
 one Mars Bar
 one half-eaten tube of Smarties
 three lollipops
 two chocolate Santa lollipops
 six small chocolate novelty penguins
 ten small chocolate Santas
 two Chocolate Oranges
 forty-nine large chocolate coins
 one sugar mouse (minus an ear)

There is nothing for it but to eat them myself. One day, they'll thank me.

Good deed no. 362: made a welfare call to Aunty Effie.

Thursday, 29 December

Usually, I start going insane round about now. This year, however, my parents have gone home unusually early, the expats are on holiday in South Africa, I have told the Yorkshire cousins who usually come up that we aren't taking visitors, and refused all invitations from friends to pop round for tea, drinks, parties, and another for Diane's annual beach-walk. Tra la.

We did go down to the sales, where I tasked myself to be extraordinarily nice to everyone I came across, as a good deed. I stood back at escalators, so much so that I caused a traffic jam at one point when some bastard also stood back and we had a war of wills as to who would give way first. I stood back in doorways for other shoppers to walk right through and smiled as they did it. I engaged with shop assistants, and some of them were rather stretched by the time it got to about fourish. One assistant was abrupt with me about how long it would take to deliver a canteen of cutlery, but I was soooooooooooo nice to her that she softened completely (it turned out she had worked three eleven-hour days on the trot with another two to go, and they don't even get paid overtime). Another shopper and I even did that classic thing of both taking hold of a sparkly bargain at the exact same moment and, bearing in mind my good-deedery, I withdrew my hand as if it was aflame. 'You take it. I was only admiring it,' I gushed. When we were en route up another escalator to be utterly sweet to someone else, I leaned against my husband and said, 'Don't you think this is such a good deed? I'm being so nice, aren't I?' and he sighed and said, 'I just hope someone doesn't hit you,' which was not in the spirit of the thing at all.

Good deed no. 363.

Friday, 30 December

Made my husband and little girl go down to the beach and free the limpets. Or at least the limpet that survived. I bet he tells the other limpets that when they came for him there were bright lights and probes, and none of the other limpets believe him.

Good deed no. 364: cleared a disgusting dead mouse (complete with trap) from next-door neighbour's house. The mouse had leaked gore onto their kitchen's linoleum, which meant I had to mop it, which led to me giving the whole downstairs of the cottage a quick wipe, dust and mop-through and taking a seat cover away to wash, in case they come up for the new year.

Saturday, 31 December

Took more than two hours doing the last application for an internship for Karl. I doubt the lad has any idea of the time this has involved. I have advised him, written an impressive CV and two applications for formal internship programmes for him, along with letters to send to local stations asking for work experience (letters he still hasn't sent), researched radio on the Net, dug out a college course and then talked to the college about him, as well as getting him a day's work experience at LBC in London and the prospect of a few days at Metro Radio in Newcastle. Anyway, it is done now. I have pointed him in the right direction and given him a hefty shove. How fabulous to be eighteen and have it all to do again. Then again, how fabulous not to be eighteen and have it all there to do again.

It was ten to midnight when I finally finished Karl's application and before I could stagger in from the study to Al. He was making a fire in the lounge, an open bottle of champagne on the coffee table by the sofa. The fire caught and my husband stood up to kiss my cheek. Groaning, I threw myself onto the sofa. 'Congratulations,' he said formally, handing me a glass of champagne, his hands still grubby from the ash, 'for completing your 365 good deeds. I'm proud of you.' On the television, in London, Big Ben struck midnight and the first chime rang out across the city, across the crowds lining the banks of the River Thames waiting for the old year to end and the new year to begin. I have no idea what this coming year will bring. I took a sip of my champagne. One thing I do know about tomorrow, though: tomorrow, I'm not doing another bloody, bollixing good deed all bleeding day.

Good deed no. 365.

Epilogue

So I spent a year doing good deeds and time afterwards thinking about what I had done and why, reading, and talking to people who know more than I do (which frankly isn't hard). Everywhere I look, there is goodness in action – good deeds. Integral to faith is the requirement to do good for our fellow man, and in science there is an explanation of how good deeds reward us as individuals and as a species. Is this why we are here – to do good for our fellow man? God's design or evolution? Either which way, you don't choose a good deed; apparently, it chooses you.

And after a year of such good deeds, the question of whether I am a better person remains. I encouraged young people as they stumbled their way into adulthood, supported a disabled teenager in her desire to write, and helped a friend stay sane while she attempted to salvage a future for a child who deserves a chance. In between, I packed shoeboxes with toys, steamed and tagged second-hand clothes, fed the needy and bought a stranger Steradent. I found not one but two lost children, reported a car crash, paid for someone's parking and raised money for charity – encouraging others to do the same. I disposed of dead mice and reburied the ashes of a neighbour with honour. I tried to comfort the bereaved, listened to the lonely and the sad, offered hospitality, and gave away flowers and ice cream and books, and Herman the German. None of those things of course in itself makes me a better person.

After this year of doing good, my faith in the divine is less, but my faith in man is more. And that's OK – with everyone but God, probably. Then again, I keep coming back to that truth 'Love thy neighbour' – without thought of reward, reciprocity, or any hope they will love us back. Because sometimes we don't get loved back.

Perhaps the power of religion lies in the fact that it addresses a fundamental human truth we need to hear. Not that in certain death there is the possibility of resurrection, but that in loving our neighbour we become truly ourselves. Maybe we can't be good; perhaps, though, we can do good, and perhaps we have to. After all, we have each other to keep us warm, to keep us fed and clothed – whether any God watches over us or not.

We are the product of our upbringing, of parents who visit the sick and who drive the elderly to church, and I'm glad of that. But did I change the world? Maybe not. Maybe I just changed the way I see my particular world – then again, it's my world I live in. When I started the year, there was a risk I would get fed up of doing good – but I discovered the reward there is in goodness, and I don't mean eternal sunshine, but cards and flowers, the pleasure at getting someone a chance, at levelling the playing field just a little. The compliment and boost to your own self-esteem when someone believes your opinion counts, even for no other reason than because you are old and they are young. As too does the affection if you cultivate, rather than ignore, a relationship with someone you might otherwise have dismissed. The thanks, time and time again, for whatever tiny thing you have done to make things better, for the privilege of being able to help, and it is a privilege. Often you do good and you feel good, and I don't care if it is our own biology and evolution that make it so. And am I happier after a year of doing good? To my surprise, I am.

My year of good deeds ended up being about more than day after day of opening doors and collecting pennies and tipping dead mice into black bin-bags. My resolution became a quest. My very particular, tiny, nothing-to-write-home-about practical deeds edged me towards some fundamental truth about how, in doing things for each other, we give meaning to ourselves.

Was my year of doing good self-serving and self-indulgent? Yep. Did I fall short? How shall I list the ways? Did my good deeds fail? Sometimes. Oftentimes. Did I say the wrong thing as well as the right thing, do ill as well as good; should I have done more?

You betcha, you betcha, you bet. The little old lady I hardly visited; a friend I never seemed to have the time for; impatience I showed to those who move slower than I do or who refused my help or who wouldn't get involved – as was their absolute right; the fact I didn't get Karl a job, that I didn't say to my parents, 'Come live with me right this moment.' But to my surprise I have discovered that some among us live good lives, the best of lives, and I rejoice in them and for them. Because when I looked closer, my friends were more than my friends. They were the most admirable of people. Ordinary lives made extraordinary in how they are lived.

No, I am not a better person. I am as flawed as I ever was. I am someone who did 365 good deeds, is all. Maybe more than 365, as I appear to have acquired a habit – despite myself. To date the Jam Jar Army has raised more than £20,000 for charity, including nearly £6,000 (and counting) for a local youth theatre; £800 for the Humber inshore rescue service through Sainsbury's in Hull; £400 for London's homeless, collected by CQS; and £240 collected by Derwentside Mind. Cryssie's writing lessons went on, while the other day a woman dropped her leather glove at the railway station and, all unknowing, chatting to her pal, trit-trotted up the concrete slope of the ironwork bridge and over the tracks. Standing on the concourse, my eyes narrowed as I eyed the offending glove. I wanted to leave the station. I fought the urge to pick it up. I willed my fellow travellers to spot the glove and carry it across the bridge to the woman. No one did. Cursing, I broke off from the call I was making on my mobile, picked up the glove and crossed the bridge.

There are as many meanings to life as there are people in this world. Our life's work is to give meaning to our own lives. But it is true to say that in kindness, respect and in generosity to each other, a certain beauty is lent to our own lives, some kind of joy. In those things, there is meaning. In doing good there is meaning. In loving the right person, in the right way, at the right time, there is meaning. In loving at all, there is meaning. In losing those whom we love, there is meaning. In failure, there is meaning. Life, after all, is in the detail. Life is in the good we do each other.

As for my New Year's resolution this year? Something simpler.

To get younger?

To get thinner?

To grow taller?

I can do that.

Top Tips for Doing Good Deeds

1. Pick up the phone and call someone who you suspect may need to talk. Illness, isolation, grief. We can't make everything better; then again, who says we can't try?
2. A kind word costs nothing.
3. Warning: a good deed can take time. But in these recessionary days, sometimes time is all we have to give each other.
4. Treat yourself. Good deeds are often rewarded with thanks, flowers and smiles. Even if they aren't, they are often a reward in themselves. Don't let the usual good-deed doers keep that sense of satisfaction all to themselves.
5. If you yourself are in need of a pick-me-up, do something for someone else. 'This really works,' as the adverts used to say.
6. You don't need to be a millionaire philanthropist (if you are reading this and you are a millionaire philanthropist, write a cheque, mate); you can, however, start collecting coppers and silver in a jam jar, and when it's full, take it in to a charity. Pennies make pounds. Pennies make a difference. You make a difference.
7. Pick up a piece of litter.
8. Support the young in their ambitions. You have more wisdom than they do: don't waste it. Use it on their behalf. After all, what goes around comes around: those who are helped will help others in their turn.
9. Use your particular skills and talents. No one says a good deed is a big deed – it is OK to think small. You don't have to commit to working a day a week in a charity shop, but try to use what talents you have to help someone else.

10. Grab an opportunity. If you think you could do a good turn, you are probably right.
11. Bear in mind that occasionally the good deed might not work out, despite your best intentions, and you might fail. That's OK. Next time, you'll succeed, and remember sometimes it is less about the outcome and more about the effort.
12. Appreciate someone for what they do for you or what they do for someone else. Notice them. Thank them. They're worth it.
13. It's never too late.

Doing Good by Numbers

Good deed	Number of times accomplished
Working on the Jam Jar Army	44
Giving a gift	29
Showing kindness to a stranger	28
Mentoring the young	27
Supporting a good cause	25
Doing a favour for a neighbour	22
Using contacts/professional skills for someone else	19
Bereavement support	17
Charitable giving	16
Consoling/assisting/giving a treat to a child (who is not mine)	16
Helping out another parent	15
Hospitality and care	15
Teaching a disabled teenager to write	15
Helping newcomers settle	12
Supporting friends with parenting challenges	9
Volunteering	9
Supporting the sick	8
Listening	7
Visiting/phoning/kindness to the elderly	7
Going the extra mile for parents	6
Showing kindness to a friend	5
Picking up litter	4

Charities Featured in This Book

Alnwick Garden Trust: http://www.alnwickgarden.com/
Barnardo's: http://www.barnardos.org.uk/
Berwick CAB: http://www.citizensadvice.org.uk/
Daft as a Brush: http://www.daftasabrush.org.uk/
Derwentside Mind: http://www.derwentsidemind.co.uk/
Humber Rescue: http://www.humber-rescue.org.uk/
League of Friends of the Alnwick Hospitals
Macular Disease Society: http://www.maculardisease.org/
Mark Wright Project: http://themarkwrightproject.org.uk/
Missionaries of Charity of Mother Teresa of Calcutta Trust
North Northumberland Hospice: http://www.hospicecare-nn.
   org.uk/
RNLI: http://www.rnli.org.uk/
Salvation Army: http://www.salvationarmy.org.uk/

Bibliography

Adams, Robert Merrihew, *A Theory of Virtue* (Oxford: Oxford University Press, 2006).

Aristotle, *The Nichomachean Ethics*, translated by David Ross, with an introduction by Lesley Brown (Oxford: Oxford University Press, 2009).

Barnardo, Mrs, and James Marchant, *Memoirs of the Late Dr Barnardo* (London: Hodder and Stoughton, 1908).

Brawer, Dr Naftali, *A Brief Guide to Judaism* (London: Robinson, 2008).

Dawkins, Richard, *The Selfish Gene* (Oxford: Oxford University Press, 2006).

Dunbar, Robin, Louise Barrett and John Lycett, *Evolutionary Psychology* (Oxford: Oneworld, 2011).

Flint, Thomas P., and Michael C. Rea (eds), *The Oxford Handbook of Philosophical Theology* (Oxford: Oxford University Press, 2011).

Grayling, A. C., *What is Good?* (London: Phoenix, 2007).

Jacobson, Simon, *Toward a Meaningful Life: The Wisdom of the Rebbe Menachem Mendel Schneerson* (New York: HarperCollins, 2004).

Kolodiejchuk, Brian (ed.), *Mother Teresa: Come Be My Light* (New York: Rider, 2008).

Lewis, C. S., *The Screwtape Letters* (London: HarperCollins Publishers, 2002).

London Gazette, number 58182, 15 December 2006, supplement no. 1.

Luks, Allan, and Peggy Payne, *The Healing Power of Doing Good* (Lincoln, NE: iUniverse, Inc., 2001).

MacIntyre, Alasdair, *After Virtue* (London: Bristol Classic Press, 2011).

Nesbitt, Eleanor, *Sikhism: A Very Short Introduction* (Oxford: Oxford University Press, 2005).

Panza, Christopher, and Adam Potthast, *Ethics for Dummies* (Indianapolis: Wiley, 2010).

Post, Stephen, *The Hidden Gifts of Helping* (San Francisco: Jossey-Bass, 2011).

Post, Stephen, and Jill Neimark, *Why Good Things Happen to Good People* (New York: Broadway Books, 2007).

Robinson, David, and Chris Garratt, *Introducing Ethics* (London: Icon Books, 2008).

Tutu, Desmond, and Mpho Tutu, *Made for Goodness* (New York: Rider, 2010).

Acknowledgements

As ever, my friendship and thanks to the extraordinarily talented Venetia Butterfield of Viking, who refuses to let me overwrite even though I beg her, and the dynamic and talented team at Penguin. I am deeply grateful to Caroline Pretty, my copy-editor, who makes everything seem better than it is, and to Kirsty Howarth for bearing with me.

Thanks as well to my agent Patrick Walsh, who is always in my corner, and his clever, energetic colleagues at Conville and Walsh.

I am grateful to all those already mentioned in the book who were generous enough to share their expertise, advice and time and whose reputations in their respective fields go before them. I owe a particular debt of thanks to my sometime theological advisers Father Ed Hone, Dr Robert Song (Durham University) and Rabbi Dr Naftali Brawer (Spiritual Capital Foundation); as well as to my brother-in-law Dr Rob McCall and Dr Malcolm Bates, who tried their best to keep me right on the science. Any mistakes are mine and not those of my expert advisers. A special hat-tip to my first readers, Sophie Atkinson, John Woodman, Father Ed and Malcolm, for their friendship and insights; to Abigail Bosanko for her wisdom; and to Sue Brooks and Andrew Macdonald for everything.

During this year I was privileged to meet many good-deed doers, some of whom feature in this book and some of whom don't. Credit must go to the team at HospiceCare North Northumberland; Paul Larkin and his staff at the *Northumberland Gazette*; Julie Harris; and Michael Hintze, Michael Rummel and Sarah Hands at CQS. I am particularly aware of the trust placed in me by some of my favourite people, who have been brave enough to share their personal stories of good-deed doing (and of difficult times) – you know who you are (or maybe not, now I have changed the names). To all my good-deed enablers, my beloved friends and family, and to those who bore patiently with my obsession with jam jars (most of all my husband and children), I salute you.

JUDITH O'REILLY

WIFE IN THE NORTH

Maybe hormones ate her brain.

How else did Judith's husband persuade her to give up her career and move from her beloved London to Northumberland with two toddlers in tow?

Pregnant with number three, Judith is about to discover that there are one or two things about life in the country that no one told her about: that she'd be making friends with people who believed in the four horsemen of the apocalypse; that running out of petrol could be a near-death experience; and that the closest thing to an ethnic minority would be a redhead.

Judith tries to do that simple thing that women do: make hers a happy family.
A family that might live happily ever after. Possibly even up North . . .

'Funny, poignant and beautifully written' Lisa Jewell

'Genuinely funny and genuinely moving' Jane Fallon, author of
Getting Rid of Matthew

'I howled with laughter, tears of recognition at every page' Jenny Colgan

He just wanted a decent book to read ...

Not too much to ask, is it? It was in 1935 when Allen Lane, Managing Director of Bodley Head Publishers, stood on a platform at Exeter railway station looking for something good to read on his journey back to London. His choice was limited to popular magazines and poor-quality paperbacks – the same choice faced every day by the vast majority of readers, few of whom could afford hardbacks. Lane's disappointment and subsequent anger at the range of books generally available led him to found a company – and change the world.

'We believed in the existence in this country of a vast reading public for intelligent books at a low price, and staked everything on it'
Sir Allen Lane, 1902–1970, founder of Penguin Books

The quality paperback had arrived – and not just in bookshops. Lane was adamant that his Penguins should appear in chain stores and tobacconists, and should cost no more than a packet of cigarettes.

Reading habits (and cigarette prices) have changed since 1935, but Penguin still believes in publishing the best books for everybody to enjoy. We still believe that good design costs no more than bad design, and we still believe that quality books published passionately and responsibly make the world a better place.

So wherever you see the little bird – whether it's on a piece of prize-winning literary fiction or a celebrity autobiography, political tour de force or historical masterpiece, a serial-killer thriller, reference book, world classic or a piece of pure escapism – you can bet that it represents the very best that the genre has to offer.

Whatever you like to read – trust Penguin.